Cultural Encounters in the Romance of Medieval England

Cultural encounter necessarily defines and shapes the romances of medieval England: the fluidity and openness that characterise the romance genre allow it to flourish with particular strength in a world distinguished by its different cultural layers. The essays in this collection consider both the early insular tradition and later Middle English traditions – classical, Anglo-Saxon and Continental, and the intersection of lay and clerical, as well as the meeting of genres themselves, in particular romance and chronicle. Romance, history and politics are shown to intersect within individual works, while romances also oppose the past and present, savage and civilised, real and ideal, and reflect on the particular cultural dynamics of gender and politics; equally, different cultures meet in the rewriting of material from French to English, from clerical to secular, from medieval to Renaissance. Romance is shown to be a highly self-conscious mode, as English romanciers play with and reshape its conventions and expectations, and its intersection with reality, in a variety of ways.

Studies in Medieval Romance

ISSN 1479–9308

Series Editors
Roger Dalrymple
Corinne Saunders

This series aims to provide a forum for critical studies of the medieval romance, a genre that plays a crucial role in literary history, reflects medieval secular concerns, and raises complex questions regarding medieval reading and writing, social structures, human relationships, and the psyche. The scope of the series extends from the early Middle Ages into the Renaissance period, and although its main focus is on English literature, comparative studies are welcomed.

Proposals or queries should be sent in the first instance to one of the addresses given below; all submissions will receive prompt and informed consideration.

Dr Corinne Saunders, Department of English, University of Durham, Hallgarth House, 77 Hallgarth Street, Durham, DH1 3AY

Boydell & Brewer Limited, PO Box 9, Woodbridge, Suffolk

Already published

Cultural Encounters in the Romance of Medieval England

Edited by
CORINNE SAUNDERS

D. S. BREWER

First published 2005
D. S. Brewer, Cambridge

ISBN 1 84384 032 4

D. S. Brewer is an imprint of Boydell & Brewer Ltd
PO Box 9, Woodbridge, Suffolk IP12 3DF, UK
and of Boydell & Brewer Inc.
668 Mt Hope Avenue, Rochester, NY 14620, USA
website: www.boydellandbrewer.com

A catalogue record of this publication is available
from the British Library

Library of Congress Cataloging-in-Publication data
Cultural encounters in the romance of Medieval England / edited by
Corinne Saunders.
     p. cm. – (Studies in medieval romance, ISSN 1479–9308)
  Includes bibliographical references and index.
  ISBN 1–84384–032–4 (Hardback : alk. paper)
  1. Romances, English – History and criticism. 2. Politics and literature –
Great Britain – History – To 1500. 3. Literature and society – England –
History – To 1500. 4. England – Civilization – 1066–1485. 5. Literary
form – History – To 1500. I. Saunders, Corinne J., 1963– II. Series.
  PR321.C85 2005
  821'.03309358 – dc22   2004018212

This publication is printed on acid-free paper

Printed in Great Britain at
the University Press, Cambridge

Contents

Preface

The essays in this volume are all based on papers presented at the Eighth Biennial Conference on Romance in Medieval England, held at University College, Durham in April 2002. The focus of the Romance in Medieval England conferences is insular romance, generally non-Arthurian, in any language. Essays in this collection consider both Middle English and Anglo-Norman romances, as well as Latin sources and analogues, and intellectual contexts from a diverse range of discourses. The theme of the book emerged naturally from the conference, at which a recurrent subject was the encounter of different cultures – national, intellectual and literary – and the ways such cultural encounter shaped and informed the romances of medieval England.

Numerous debts were incurred both in the organisation of the Conference and in the editing of this volume. I am grateful to the British Academy for the generous provision of a Conference Grant, and to the Arts and Humanities Research Board for a Research Leave Award, which allowed me to complete this book. Emmanuel College, Cambridge provided me with the pleasantest of settings in which to work on the volume. I should also like to thank my colleagues in the Department of English and the Centre for Medieval and Renaissance Studies at the University of Durham, the fellows and staff of University College, Durham, my postgraduate assistants, Richard Brewster and Michael Huxtable, and all those who attended the Conference. Caroline Palmer and the staff of Boydell & Brewer have given invaluable assistance and support; Roger Dalrymple has been an excellent fellow editor of the Studies in Medieval Romance Series. David Fuller, as ever, has offered unfailing interest, advice and encouragement. Most of all, however, I should like to thank the authors of these essays for their generous, stimulating contributions and their unstinting good humour.

Notes on Contributors

Elizabeth Archibald is Reader in Medieval Studies at the University of Bristol. She is the author of *Apollonius of Tyre: Medieval and Renaissance Themes and Variations* (1991) and *Incest and the Medieval Imagination* (2001), and the co-editor of *A Companion to Malory* (1996), and has published widely on medieval romance.

Nancy Mason Bradbury teaches in the English department at Smith College in Northampton, Massachusetts. Her work on medieval English romance includes the book *Writing Aloud* (1998) and a second article on *Athelston* (*Medium Ævum*, 2004).

Derek Brewer is Emeritus Professor of English at the University of Cambridge and formerly Master of Emmanuel College, Cambridge (1977–90). He has published extensively on medieval English literature.

Neil Cartlidge is a Lecturer in English at University College Dublin. He is the author of two books, *Medieval Marriage: Literary Approaches 1100–1300* (1997) and *The Owl and the Nightingale: Text and Translation* (2001).

Helen Cooper is Professor of Medieval and Renaissance English at the University of Cambridge. Her many publications include *The English Romance in Time: Transforming Motifs from Geoffrey of Monmouth to the Death of Shakespeare* (2004).

Roger Dalrymple currently teaches for the Department of Continuing Education at University of Oxford. His publications include *Language and Piety in Middle English Romance* (2000) and *Middle English Literature: A Guide to Criticism* (2004).

Tony Davenport is Emeritus Professor of Medieval Literature in the University of London and Fellow of the English Association. His most recent book is *Medieval Narrative: An Introduction* (2004).

Ivana Djordjević obtained her doctorate from McGill University and is currently based at Robinson College, Cambridge, where her postdoctoral research on Anglo-Norman romances is funded by the Social Sciences and Humanities Research Council of Canada.

Rosalind Field is Reader in Medieval Literature at Royal Holloway University of London. Her main research interests are in medieval romance, Middle English and Anglo-Norman, and Chaucer.

Phillipa Hardman is a Senior Lecturer in English at the University of Reading. She has edited *The Heege Manuscript: A Facsimile of NLS MS Adv. 19.3.1* (2000) and *The Matter of Identity in Medieval Romance* (2002), has written articles on late medieval English literature and its manuscript context, and is at present working on the Middle English Charlemagne romances.

Robert Rouse has lectured in medieval literature at the Universities of Durham and Nottingham. He is the author of the study, *The Idea of Anglo-Saxon England in Middle English Romance* (2005).

Corinne Saunders is Reader in the Department of English Studies at the University of Durham. Her publications include *The Forest of Medieval Romance* (1993), *Rape and Ravishment in the Literature of Medieval England* (2001), *Chaucer* (Blackwell Guides to Criticism, 2001) and *A Companion to Romance: From Classical to Contemporary* (2004). She is English editor of the journal *Medium Ævum*.

Judith Weiss is a fellow of Robinson College, Cambridge. Her interests lie mainly in the field of Anglo-Norman romance and historiography: a parallel text and translation of Wace's *Roman de Brut* appeared in 1999. At present she is translating *Boeve de Haumtone* and *Gui de Warewic* for the series 'French of England' (Medieval and Renaissance Texts and Studies, Arizona).

1

Introduction

CORINNE SAUNDERS

Cultural encounter necessarily defines and shapes the romances of medieval England. The convergence of cultures within post-Conquest Britain – Anglo-Saxon, Norman and French – was reflected not only in linguistic and social intersections but also in the intersection of different intellectual and literary traditions. Alongside these cultures, the powerful institution of the Church and the spheres of learning associated with it brought continued access to Latin literature, and to the clerical discourses of theology and philosophy. It was not coincidental that this period of marked cultural change, from the Norman Conquest to the fifteenth century, saw changes on all levels and in all manifestations of society. The dynamism of the period was especially evident in the growth of the arts.

The energy of insular romance is precisely rooted in the many kinds of cultural encounter that occurred within medieval England. The genre of romance is notoriously difficult to define, partly because it is fluid and receptive: that fluidity and openness allowed romance to flourish with particular strength in a world distinguished by its different cultural layers, which sometimes co-existed uneasily, but more generally enriched the social and imaginative lives of those who experienced them. Through cultural encounter of diverse kinds, romance too became 'something rich and strange'.

Cultural encounter is evident in the early insular tradition, which brings together English and Norman cultures to shape distinctive Anglo-Norman treatments of romance, while later romances written in English very frequently translate and modify Anglo-Norman and French sources. In a different way, cultural encounter occurs in the convergence of different intellectual traditions within romance: classical, Anglo-Saxon and continental materials meet and may become the matter of story, while clerical discourse may also play an influential role. Similarly, genres themselves coincide: romance and chronicle, for instance, enjoy a dynamic relationship, so that chronicles may draw on romance models as well as influencing romance. Romance, history and politics intersect within individual works. The form of romances too reflects cultural encounter: the English alliterative and tail-rhyme traditions engage with and modify French forms. Romance is a highly self-conscious mode, and English romanciers play with and reshape the conventions and expectations of the genre, and its intersection with reality, in a variety of ways.

The consideration of romance in terms of cultural encounter demonstrates that the classic opposition in romance criticism, between views of romance as mimetic or non-mimetic, as situated within the world of fantasy or reality, is much too simple. To view romance as the product of cultural encounter is to recognise that romances find their individual power through engagement with precise historical moments, yet also are rooted in human universals, in conventions that find their force in their sustained relevance and repetition over time. Northrop Frye's notion of romance as a generic plot or *mythos* is compelling: for him, romance is largely non-historical, treating 'implicit mythical patterns in a world more closely associated with human experience', and hence playing on archetypes, large patterns, conventions and repetition of motifs.[1] Frye's analysis captures persuasively just how the conventions of the genre may function, and it opened the way for stimulating work on Jungian archetypes and for other psychoanalytical approaches to romance, as well as illuminating links between romance and folktale.[2] Yet similarly persuasive are those analyses that place romance firmly back within its historical period: thus Erich Auerbach argued famously that the function of romance was primarily social, that it emerged from and shaped the values of the new, chivalric class of twelfth-century France.[3] Susan Crane persuasively places English medieval romance as growing out of and reflecting the conservative social concerns of the barony.[4] Both the mimetic and the non-mimetic approaches developed in the second half of the twentieth century have variously influenced the analyses in this volume. In the notion of cultural encounter, so peculiarly relevant to medieval England, the duality of historicity and timelessness is shown to fuel romance.

The process of cultural encounter at work can best be seen by example. The early Middle English romance *Sir Orfeo* offers a sophisticated instance of cultural integration: classical, Celtic, and specifically English strands interweave, and reflect a heightened awareness of diverse literary traditions. Found in the celebrated Auchinleck manuscript and two other, fifteenth-century, manuscripts, and usually dated c.1300–1325,[5] *Sir Orfeo* transforms

---

[1] See Northrop Frye, *Anatomy of Criticism: Four Essays* (Princeton, 1957), pp. 186–206 (157). See also Frye, *The Secular Scripture: A Study of the Structure of Romance* (Cambridge, MA, 1976).

[2] See, for example, Anne Wilson, *Traditional Romance and Tale: How Stories Mean* (Cambridge, 1976) and Derek Brewer, *Symbolic Stories: Traditional Narratives of the Family Drama in English Literature* (London, 1980).

[3] See Erich Auerbach, *Mimesis: The Representation of Reality in Western Literature*, trans. Willard R. Trask (Princeton, 1953, originally published in German, Berne, 1946), chapter 6 ('The Knight Sets Forth'), pp. 123–42.

[4] See Susan Crane, *Insular Romance: Politics, Faith and Culture in Anglo-Norman and Middle English Literature* (Berkeley, 1986).

[5] A. J. Bliss surmises that the poem was written in the second half of the thirteenth century, *Sir Orfeo* (Oxford, 1966), p. xxi. Apart from Bliss's scholarly edition, considerations of the literary history and contexts of *Sir Orfeo* include J. Burke Severs, 'The Antecedents of *Sir Orfeo*', *Studies in Medieval Literature in Honor of Albert Croll Baugh*, ed. MacEdward Leach (Philadelphia, 1961),

the story of Orpheus and Eurydice into an explicitly medieval romance with a happy ending. It is a critical commonplace to attribute the rewriting of the tale to 'the influences of Celtic tradition'.[6] That the poem was perceived as a Breton *lai* is clearly suggested by the fact that both fifteenth-century manuscript versions begin with the twenty-four line prologue of *Lai le Freine* (also contained in the Auchinleck manuscript), which describes the genre of the Breton *lai*. It is fairly certain that a 'Celtic' or Breton telling of the Orpheus story already existed: the Old French *Floire et Blancheflor*, *Le Lai de l'Espine* and the prose *Lancelot* all refer to a *lai d'Orphey*. The replacement of the classical underworld with a Celtic otherworld of faery resonates through and shapes the narrative of *Sir Orfeo*. Yet the view that the poet simply offers a Celtic retelling of a familiar story is a reductive one, for it fails to take account of the complex intersection of traditions in the romance, and the ways that this creates a sophisticated, highly nuanced text. *Sir Orfeo* retains aspects of the classical myth, in particular the emphasis on the powers of music and of love, and intertwines these with a set of Celtic motifs relating to the faery, to offer a detailed, haunting vision of the connection of human and otherworld. Both Celtic and classical aspects, however, are presented from a specifically Christian and English perspective. The romance plays with English dynastic history and Christian chivalric ideals: Orfeo is a model of English kingship and emblem of chivalry, whose court is situated in Winchester. At the heart of the work is an exploration of the nature of social order, right rule and associated moral values, especially that of *trouthe* in its various senses.

There is some evidence for a unique English vernacular treatment of the Orpheus story, and it is this on which *Sir Orfeo* seems ultimately to draw, perhaps through an earlier, now lost, English *lai*. The classical story of Orpheus would have been known in the Middle Ages through Ovid's *Metamorphoses* and Virgil's *Georgics*.[7] Boethius' brief retelling of the story in his *Consolation of Philosophy* provided the basis for the widely known medieval moralised versions of the story: for Boethius, the story represents the danger of looking back to old sins and losing good. There seems, however, to have been an alternative English version of the story, perhaps the invention of Alfred in whose translation of Boethius' *Consolation of Philosophy* it first appears. Alfred develops Boethius' metre significantly: he recounts in detail

pp. 187–207; Constance Davies, 'Classical Threads in *Orfeo*', *Modern Language Review* 56 (1961), pp. 161–6; Patrizia Grimaldi, 'Sir Orfeo as Celtic Folk-Hero, Christian Pilgrim, and Medieval King', *Allegory, Myth, and Symbol*, ed. Morton W. Bloomfield, Harvard English Studies 9 (Cambridge, MA, 1981), pp. 147–61; Jeff Rider, 'Receiving Orpheus in the Middle Ages: Allegorization, Remythification and *Sir Orfeo*', *Papers on Language and Literature: A Journal for Scholars and Critics of Language and Literature* 24 (1988), pp. 343–66; and Roy Michael Liuzza, '*Sir Orfeo*: Sources, Traditions, and the Poetics of Performance', *Journal of Medieval and Renaissance Studies* 21 (1991), pp. 269–84.

6   Stephen H. A. Shepherd, ed., *Middle English Romances*, A Norton Critical Edition (London, 1995), p. 345.

7   Ovid, *Metamorphoses*, X, ll. 1–85; XI, ll. 1–66; Virgil, *Georgics*, IV, ll. 453–527; retold in Boethius, *The Consolation of Philosophy*, III, metrum 12.

the ability of Orpheus to charm the wild beasts, and remarks, though without explanation, that Eurydice died and was taken to hell, whereas Boethius simply begins with Orpheus' sad song. Particularly striking with regard to the Middle English *Sir Orfeo* is Alfred's depiction of Orpheus' choice to seek exile in the wilderness before his voyage to hell:

> Ða sceolde se hearpere weorðan swa sarig þæt he ne meahte ongemong oðrum monnum bion, ac teah to wuda, *ond* sæt on ðæm muntum ægðer ge dæges ge nihtes; weop *ond* hearpode ðæt ða wudas bifeodon. . . .[8]

> . . . then the harpman became so sad that he could not live in the midst of other men, but was off to the forest, and sate upon the hills both day and night, weeping, and playing on his harp so that the woods trembled. . . . [9]

This detail is unique. In the *Georgics*, by contrast, we are told only that Orpheus' journey is undertaken as he sings of 'love's anguish' ('aegrum . . . amorem'), and his great lament and his harping in the wilderness occur after his voyage to the Underworld, as he roams across the northern ice.[10] Similarly, in the *Metamorphoses*, Ovid states that when Orpheus has 'mourned her to the full in the upper world' ('quam satis ad superas . . . deflevit'), he attempts the caverns of the Underworld; it is after he has lost Eurydice once again that we hear of his anguish and deprivation:

> . . . septem tamen ille diebus
> squalidus in ripa Cereris sine mundere sedit;
> cura dolorque animi lacrimaeque alimenta fuere.

> Seven days he sat there on the bank in filthy rage and with no taste of food. Care, anguish of soul, and tears were his nourishment.[11]

In the *Metamorphoses*, Orpheus' songs form the context of the Maenads' furious tearing of his limbs.

The poet of the Middle English romance makes striking use of the Anglo-Saxon tradition of Orpheus' exile in the wilderness. In *Sir Orfeo*, the pattern of the abduction of Orfeo's queen, Heurodis, is repeated in Orfeo's flight:

> '. . . now ichave my queen y-lore,
> The fairest levedy that ever was bore,
> Never eft I nill no woman see.
> Into wilderness ichill te

8 *King Alfred's Old English Version of Boethius' 'De Consolatione Philosophiae'*, ed. Walter John Sedgefield (Oxford, 1899) XXXV, vii, p. 102.
9 *King Alfred's Version of the Consolations of Boethius*, tans. Walter John Sedgefield (Oxford, 1900) XXXV, p. 116.
10 Virgil, *Georgics* in *Virgil: I – Eclogues, Georgics, Aeneid I–VI*, trans. H. Rushton Fairclough, rev. edn, Loeb Classical Library (Cambridge, MA, 1978) IV, l. 464.
11 Ovid, *Metamorphoses*, trans. Frank Justus Miller, vol. 2, Loeb Classical Library (Cambridge, MA; London, 1958) X, ll. 11–12, 73–5.

And live ther ever-more
With wilde bestes in holtes hore.'[12] (185–90)

The poet plays on a complex set of literary motifs. Orfeo lives out the disappearance of his queen, taking on the physical characteristics of the Wild Man, the legendary inhabitant of the wilderness, his body 'oway dwine . . . and al to-chine' (237–8) and his hair 'black and rowe' (241), grown down to his waist. He also follows the literary convention of the flight into the forest of the lover maddened by grief or loss: the wilderness becomes the appropriate locus for the expression of the extremity of Orfeo's grief.

The episode draws too on the Christian eremitic tradition: Orfeo rejects society, material comfort and status to follow a solitary life of abstinence. The poet describes in poignant detail the change, 'When he that hadde been king with croun / Went so poverlich out of toun!' (211–12): his wealth and lands are replaced with the hard heath, the winter weather, the poverty and dangers of the forest where 'ever he liveth in gret malais' (216). As in hagiographic tradition, the wilderness takes on a redemptive quality for the ascetic. Although the narrative does play on the conventional romance notion of the hero as elect, chosen to experience adventure, Orfeo's journey is not a chivalric quest. He does not seek Heurodis, but chances to see her 'on a day' (279), to find his way into the otherworld, and, ultimately, to regain her. He appears as the object of grace: as he lives out his life of withdrawal, fate is favourable to him. At the same time, the forest functions according to romance conventions: like the orchard, it is a transitional place, a world where faery and human can meet, and whence Orfeo will enter the otherworld to win back his queen. In the remarkable and eerie portrayal of the land of Faery, the poet returns, it seems, to Celtic folk tradition, once again weaving together different motifs: the magical tree, the faery abduction, the wild hunt, the world of the Un-dead with its figures caught in the throes of violent death, yet accompanying the faery hunt that catches 'no best'.

The poet of *Sir Orfeo*, then, takes the English tradition of Orpheus' exile and lament at the death of Eurydice as the focal point of his poem, and shifts it into the form of the Breton *lai*, so that death is replaced by faery abduction, the shadows of Avernus by the enigmatic otherworld of Celtic romance. In portraying Orfeo's decision to resign his throne and seek exile in the forest, the poet employs both romance and hagiographic conventions of exile, with their respective thematic associations of loss in love and penitential quest for grace. In addition, the narrative incorporates material probably drawn from Book VI of Virgil's *Aeneid*, the account of Aeneas' voyage to Avernus, to describe Orfeo's journey to the otherworld. Classical sources, a specific emphasis on English history, and the English vernacular tradition of Orfeo's

---

[12] *Sir Orfeo, Middle English Verse Romances*, ed. Donald B. Sands, Exeter Medieval English Texts and Studies (1966; Exeter, 1986), pp. 185–200, ll. 185–90. All subsequent references to *Sir Orfeo* will be from this edition and cited by line number.

exile, are interwoven with archetypal Celtic motifs – the faery taking, the faery hunt, the passage to the otherworld, the otherworldly landscape – and with more general literary conventions. Cultural encounter shapes classical legend into a Breton *lai* of faery, but also into a Christian romance of chivalry and *trouthe* and an example of English kingship, within a particularised Anglo-Saxon tradition of exile.

To begin to understand the nature of romance in medieval England is to imagine this kind of complex process of cultural encounter as occurring with regard to all aspects of romance: language, sources and story matter, literary form, conventions, motifs and thematic emphases. The first essay in this volume, that of Ivana Djordjević, raises the technical question of translation: what happens when texts are adapted to languages and audiences? Djordjević points out the special situation of Anglo-Norman and Middle English as co-existent cultures, and the more contrastive cultural encounters evident in later rewritings of early texts. She offers the intriguing example of the portrayal of Beves's mother in the Anglo-Norman and Middle English romances, *Boeuve de Hamtoune* and *Sir Beves of Hamtoun*. The translation of the Middle English seems particularly faithful, yet the shift from one socio-historical context to another results in the heightening of conventionality in character portrayal, and in a differently nuanced portrayal of marriage. *Beves* also provides a reminder of the longevity of romance, undergoing a series of narrative transformations yet remaining in circulation well into the Renaissance period and beyond.

The following four essays address in different ways the idea of kingship and right rule. The essays explore how historical or romance models are adapted to contemporary insular understandings, in the context of lesser-known texts from the twelfth and thirteenth centuries. These works often engage self-consciously with the idea of the past, and with issues of national identity. Thus Tony Davenport considers how the story of a great Anglo-Saxon king and lawgiver, Ine, is interpreted and drawn into the romance mode. In the progression from the *Anglo-Saxon Chronicle* through the chronicles of William of Malmesbury, Gaimar and Henry of Huntingdon to those of Langtoft and Robert Mannyng, we see the gradual development of the skeletal narrative into a 'male Cinderella' story and one of romantic love, drawing on familiar romance motifs. History moves towards romance, even as romance is often found to have historical origins.

Rosalind Field explores another kind of historical mythologising in her consideration of the exile-and-return motif and its contexts in a range of late twelfth- and early thirteenth-century Anglo-Norman romances, including *Horn*, *Havelec*, *Gui* and *Boeuve*. She demonstrates that the motif is more than a simple building-block of folk tale, arguing that in England the story of the rightful heir and his return from exile, and the contingent notion of good rule, had characteristic and compelling political resonances for the period after the Norman Conquest. The power of the myth is clear in its survival until the

Renaissance and beyond, as Field's title, 'the king over the water', with its reference to the Stuarts, suggests.

Whereas these two essays consider the figure of the ideal ruler, engaging both with romance and religious models, Judith Weiss examines the motif of the ineffectual monarch, which develops into a powerful literary *topos* in several twelfth- and thirteenth-century Anglo-Norman romances – *Ipomedon*, *Robert le Diable* and *Octavian*. Weiss demonstrates the potential for social critique in romance: failed rule and abuse of secular power are contrasted with spiritual and national responsibility. As in Field's essay, the intertextuality of romance is illuminated, and we are made aware of the ways familiar conventions and motif may be invested with acute social and political meaning.

Robert Rouse explores the treatment of law in three Middle English romances: *Havelok the Dane*, *Horn Childe and Maiden Rimnild* and *Beves of Hamtoun*. Rouse probes further the issue of the relation of medieval England to its past, suggesting the desire to define English identity through the notion of a set of inherited laws. Rouse's essay examines images of the king as lawgiver, and the contrasts drawn in romances between the laws of the English and those of other societies – including Danish and Welsh laws. English legal practice is specifically presented as rooted in the 'good old law' of the Anglo-Saxons, and forms another crucial aspect of right rule.

The next group of essays deals with the transformation of story matters and motifs as romances are rewritten across cultures and languages; these essays mainly focus on later, Middle English romance. Phillipa Hardman extends the notion of insular romance to consider how French romances could be adapted into English for a fourteenth-century audience. She offers a unique defence of the little-valued romance of *Sir Tristrem* or *Tristrem and Ysoude*, as she suggests it should more appropriately be named. Hardman shows the work to be written for a particular, English audience, familiar with the *Tristan* legend and with French romances. The narrative is rewritten to emphasise the themes of truth and fidelity, but also to highlight emotion and drama, and with new emphases on marriage and education, which are particularly suited to the romance's manuscript context.

In a different type of analysis of narrative transformations, Elizabeth Archibald takes a specific, resonant but little explored motif, that of baths and bathing, to explore its distinctive English treatment. She draws attention to the opposed views of historians on the prominence of bathing in medieval society and literature, and to the high cultural status of bathing, both as a ceremonial ritual and as an hygienic and medicinal practice. In romance, however, and particularly in English romance, by contrast to French, bathing is a relatively rare motif, though a potentially fruitful one. Archibald probes this disparity to illuminate the gap between romance and reality, and to show that cultural contexts are not always directly reflected in literary emphases.

Derek Brewer, in an essay based on his provocative and wide-ranging plenary lecture for the Romance in Medieval England Conference, offers a searching analysis of and retrospective on perhaps the most prominent romance motif of all, that of 'fin'amor'. Brewer takes as his starting point his own review of C. Stephen Jaeger's study, *Ennobling Love: In Search of a Lost Sensibility* (1999), to revisit and develop questions of sexuality, male friendship and 'courtly love'. While Jaeger persuasively connects earlier homosocial to later heterosexual love, to focus on adultery, frustration and tragedy in medieval literary treatments of love, Brewer shows through a wide survey of Middle English romances that the discourse of love is larger, more various and sometimes more naturalistic than Jaeger's thesis may suggest, and that marriage can play a prominent and positive role.

Two further essays on fourteenth-century Middle English romance treat the intersection of different discourses, clerical or political, with the world of romance, and the ensuing opposition of gender stereotypes and assumptions. Neil Cartlidge examines the encounter between theological and romance discourses, between male clerics and female subjects and readers, in the Breton *lai* of *Sir Gowther*. Cartlidge draws on a wide range of theological, legal and literary texts in Latin and English to explore the romance's self-conscious engagement with the possibility that fiction can be damaging or threatening, in that it speaks the unspeakable – here, the situation of rape by the devil. The narrator is in a sense infected by the shame associated with demonic rape, yet also drawn into consideration of an issue that attracted much clerical debate, and raised controversial questions regarding gender and sexuality.

Nancy Mason Bradbury also addresses the topic of gender in a specific romance, the lesser-known Middle English work of *Athelston*. Bradbury offers a new reading of a romance that seems unequivocally to deny women's agency, in its symbolic incident of the kick delivered by the king to his pregnant queen. Yet Bradbury's analysis shows that in fact the women in *Athelston* are allowed both political wisdom and social agency. The essay looks particularly at secular, patriarchal ideas of space, power and common profit, and how these intersect with the portrayal of women subjects, revealing the tension surrounding gender issues in actuality and for medieval writers. Again the issues of right law and social justice are central.

Finally, two essays consider the rewriting of romance in later periods. Roger Dalrymple offers a striking defence of a little-known Middle English composite romance, *Torrent of Portyngale*, which dates from c.1400 and was popular enough to be twice printed in the sixteenth century. Dalrymple shows how motifs may accrue to shape a work that is in some ways conventional but in others highly individual. The essay focuses on cultural encounters between human and other – dragon, giant or Saracen – and sets these, and in particular the encounters of the hero with no fewer than five giants, within the literary and cultural contexts on which they depend for their significance.

In the essay that concludes this volume, Helen Cooper considers the legendary romancier, Thomas of Erceldoune. Cooper teases out the complex transformations of the narrative and prophecies of Thomas from the middle of the fifteenth century to the Renaissance. The legend of Thomas finds its way into ballad, romance and prophecy, and it is in the latter genre, including the discreet prophecy of Spenser's *Faerie Queene*, that the potential political impact of romance becomes most evident. The special fluidity and intensity of this romance matter allows for its constant rewriting to fit new social and political actualities. Cultural encounter shapes the legend of Thomas of Erceldoune, like so many aspects of romance, into something at once strange and eerily familiar. In this essay, as throughout the volume, romance figures as an enduring mode of infinite potential, which can both reach beyond the mundane to the marvellous and the ideal, and yet remain firmly rooted within the familiar and the historical moment.

2

Original and Translation: Bevis's Mother in Anglo-Norman and Middle English

IVANA DJORDJEVIĆ

Translation is the paradigmatic cultural encounter. Translators mediate between cultures separated by geographical distance and articulated in different languages. When they change their source texts, we assume that they do so in order to adapt them to their target audience and its cultural expectations. Middle English translations of Anglo-Norman romances deviate from this straightforward model, however. The cultural distance their translators had to negotiate is not defined in spatial terms, and because of the unique linguistic situation in post-Conquest England it is not primarily defined in linguistic terms either. It is the passage of time that accounts for the most important cultural misunderstandings in this process of translation, and it is from this perspective that I shall look at *Sir Beves of Hampton* as the translation of *Boeve de Haumtone*.[1] In what follows I want to trace the way the author/translator of *Beves* uses common translation strategies to make sense of the cultural gaps that result from the temporal separation between original and translation. By analysing the portrayal of the hero's mother I intend to show how the translator, misreading the cultural connotations of the Anglo-Norman text, rewrites some important thematic strands in it precisely when he is trying hard to be faithful to his original.

Although many Middle English romances are translations of earlier Anglo-Norman or continental French texts, the implications of this uncontroversial fact are still insufficiently taken into account by literary scholars. This is the result of a couple of widely held but largely unexamined assumptions about what translation is and what translators do. First, translation is thought of as a process of textual recasting that implies maximum equivalence between the original and the derived text; it follows that a textual relationship of imperfect equivalence is either a translation gone wrong or not a translation at all. And second, the translator's work is believed to consist in transmitting

---

[1] The Anglo-Norman text will be quoted from *Der anglonormannische Boeve de Haumtone*, ed. Albert Stimming, Biblioteca Normannica 7 (Halle, 1899), and the Middle English from *The Romance of Sir Beues of Hamtoun*, ed. Eugen Kölbing, EETS ES 46, 48, 65 (London, 1885–94; repr. 1973). A much more satisfactory, but not easily accessible, edition is Jennifer Fellows, '*Sir Beves of Hampton*: Study and Edition', 5 vols (unpub. Ph.D. diss., Univ. of Cambridge, 1980).

the textual intentions of the original author to a target audience. These wide-spread presuppositions have favoured some analytical approaches and explanatory models while precluding others. If we think of translation as the search for the Holy Grail of equivalence we shall be inclined to disregard the translational relationship between the French and English texts in the romance corpus because it is not as close as our definition of translation requires; in this case we are likely to exaggerate the differences between them. If, on the other hand, we are looking at a Middle English text to which the label 'translation' has already been attached we shall collapse it and its original together and treat them as if they were identical; in this case their differences will be left unexamined.

The notion of the translator as simple mediator between original author and target audience has likewise been a methodological impediment. The translator is credited with a preternatural communion with the author of the original text, whose intentions are entirely transparent to him, but at the same time he is presumed to have immediate access to the expectations of his audience. The translator is not a perfect machine, however, or a kind of disembodied translational agency, and his omniscience is a fallacy. His work is subject to important limitations occasioned by factors outside his control and to the equally important operation of translational automatisms.

In the case of the Middle English romance, the translator's presumed audience, commonly defined in terms of its social status, level of sophistication and literary tastes, could not serve as an explanatory nostrum even if we knew more about it than we do. The translator may have made some changes in order to please his readers – if he knew who the readers were going to be, which could have been the case occasionally, but by no means always. Many changes he made were conditioned by other factors: his initial choice of prosodic form; the grammatical, lexical, semantic and pragmatic resources of his language; the quality of his exemplar or exemplars (more than one may have been available); the structure of the contemporary literary system and the extent of his familiarity with it; his motivation and the practical circumstances under which he worked; his literary ambitions and talents; the very fact that he was a translator, thought like a translator and therefore approached the work of textual transfer in ways that seem to be peculiar to translators everywhere and in all ages;[2] and his familiarity with the topical issues of an earlier time. In my analysis of the opening section of the Middle English romance *Sir Beves*

---

[2] Translation scholars now recognise that certain kinds of textual manipulations occur so regularly in translation that they have been described as 'translation universals' or even 'laws of translation'. In what is not a conscious strategy so much as a professional reflex, translators automatically expand condensed passages, insert modifiers, qualifiers, or conjunctions to achieve greater clarity, add extra information, disambiguate whatever is ambiguous and insert additional background information in order to fill in cultural gaps. The textual effects of this mental habit, known as explicitation, have often been noticed in Middle English romances but, to my knowledge, scholars have never sought to explain them by reference to the automatisms inherent in the process of translation. Other important translation universals include simplification (implicitation) and repertorisation, which I shall describe below.

of Hampton and its Anglo-Norman original, *Boeve de Haumtone*, I shall focus more closely on the last two constraints.

The first few hundred lines of *Beves* are usually described as a very close translation.[3] Even the different redactions of this narrative with a famously tangled textual tradition show unexpected uniformity at this point. And yet a careful comparison between the Anglo-Norman and Middle English texts demonstrates that the translator, who is not omniscient but puzzled, as all translators are, has changed a great deal. I describe the translator as puzzled because puzzlement is unavoidable in any encounter with a text produced by someone else and therefore in need of interpretation. With no access to the author's intentions (contrary to popular misconceptions), the translator carries out his interpretive work by trying out a number of hermeneutic circles to see which will fit the text best: which general assumption about the meaning of the text – or a section of it – will yield the most plausible solutions for the translation of small textual details, and which micro-textual translational choices will in turn produce a coherent macro-textual whole. This is tricky work and the potential for slippage is considerable. A translator who has partly misread the whole will produce numerous shifts in minor textual details. They may be so small that if looked at in isolation they can easily be taken for examples of a high degree of fidelity in translation, yet their accumulation will produce significant difference even at higher textual levels.

In the opening sections of *Beves*, significant difference was produced by the translator's misreading of the hero's mother and her troubled marriage. Writing about *Beves*, Jennifer Fellows remarked that Bevis's mother, the countess of Southampton, 'is seen most explicitly as a threat to patriarchal values' and that her treatment 'seems to be part and parcel of a more general male-centred, anti-feminist ethos in the romance'. At the same time, she noticed 'a certain lack of sureness in the poet's handling of the episodes that concern her'.[4] The generalised misogyny and the 'lack of sureness' were not in *Boeve*; both are the result of the translator's interventions.

The character of Bevis's mother has at least two functions in the Anglo-Norman romance. As an element of the plot, the countess plays a limited but significant role: she sets in motion the conventional exile-and-return pattern and later provides the hero with a suitable focus for revenge.

---

3   Critics agree that the first part of *Boeve*, the hero's 'enfances', is translated with remarkable faithfulness. According to Judith Martin [Weiss], in the first 555 lines of *Beves* the author 'borrows more words from *Boeve* than in any other section of his poem, and diverges very little from events or even details in the Anglo-Norman' ('Studies in Some Early English Romances' (unpub. Ph.D. diss., Univ. of Cambridge, 1967), p. 114). Albert C. Baugh says of the early part of *Beves* that, compared with *Boeve*, '[t]he incidents and the sequence of incidents are, almost without exception, the same throughout, the English reproducing many small and quite casual details' ('Convention and Individuality in the Middle English Romance', *Medieval Literature and Folklore Studies: Essays in Honor of Francis Lee Utley*, ed. Jerome Mandel and Bruce A. Rosenberg (New Brunswick, NJ, 1970), pp. 123–46 (p. 126)).
4   'Mothers in Middle English Romance', *Women and Literature in Britain 1150–1500*, ed. Carol M. Meale (Cambridge, 1993), pp. 41–60 (pp. 52, 54, 53).

She is not ideally suited to her plot function, however. Exile-and-return tales tend to rely on a conventional usurper figure, typically an outsider, to get the plot going. (The stories of Horn and Havelok are good examples.) The evil mother is quite an oddity.[5] What is such an uncommon character type doing in a story whose author is not exactly renowned for the originality of his narrative motifs? Why complicate a simple plot device by having the mother engineer the father's murder, then marry the murderer, and finally sell her own son into slavery, but only after a failed attempt to have him killed too? This is unnecessarily distracting unless the mother has thematic functions as well as a purely narrative one.[6]

We first meet the hero's mother as the wife of the hero's father. The introductory narrative sequence, which I shall analyse in greater detail below, is not the story of an unnatural mother but of a treacherous wife, one of the partners in a dysfunctional marriage. She is important for the plot as the hero's mother, but it is as a wife that she acquires thematic significance. Like Riwalin and Blanscheflur in Gottfried's *Tristan*, Bevis's parents provide a mirror image, playfully ironic in Gottfried but grim in *Beves*, of the hero's principal erotic relationship.[7] In the narrative economy of *Boeve* the marriage of the hero's parents is set up as a negative example for the hero to avoid and the character of his mother functions as a foil to that of Josiane, his *amie* and future wife.[8]

Let us look at the early history of this disastrous marriage, up to the point where the countess decides to dispose of her husband. To facilitate comparison, I shall quote in full the relevant section of both texts:[9]

3

Seignurs, iceo quens Guioun dount vus chaunt	Lordinges, þis, of whan y telle,
estoit bon chavaler, pruz e combataunt;	Neuer man of flesch ne felle
	15 Nas so strong,

---

[5] Unlike the evil stepmother and the evil mother-in-law, both of whom are stock characters in many kinds of medieval narrative. In a number of metrical romances the plot is set off by the machinations of such a figure, who typically makes an attempt on the life and/or honour of the hero or heroine. Mothers do occasionally serve the same narrative purpose but their motivation is different. Fresne's mother in Marie's *lai* and its English derivatives is thoughtless, but not evil – unlike the mothers-in-law in *Emaré* or *Octavian*, for example.

[6] The countess's importance is partly obscured by the fact that she alone of all the main characters remains nameless in all the texts, English as well as Anglo-Norman, as if she were indeed no more than a peg on which to hang a plot function.

[7] The classic analysis of how the story of Riwalin and Blanscheflur provides a contrast to the complexities of 'Tristan-love' is W. T. H. Jackson's in *The Anatomy of Love* (New York, 1971), pp. 65–70.

[8] Constraints of space prevent me from analysing the parallels in greater detail. My main concern here is to demonstrate how, by his unwitting rewriting of the countess, the translator who produced the Middle English text blurred the parallelism and thus reduced the thematic complexity of the Anglo-Norman narrative.

[9] Since Middle English texts of *Beves* do not differ significantly at this point, I quote from the Auchinleck MS (Edinburgh, National Library of Scotland, MS Advocates 19.2.1), the only one that can be followed without significant distortion in Kölbing's edition. I have laid out the two texts in a way that emphasises the correspondences between them.

And so he was in ech striue,

15 mes de une chose lui alout home blamaunt,   And euer he leuede wiþ outen wiue,

k'ainz ne vout femme prendre en tot son vivaunt,   Al to late and long.

dunt pus se repenti par le men ascient.

Whan he was fallen in to elde,

20 Þat he ne miȝte him self welde,

He wolde a wif take;

Sone þar after, ich vnderstonde,

Him hadde be leuer þan al þis londe,

Hadde he hire for-sake.

4

Mes quant il fu veuz home e out long tens vescu, 25 An elde a wif he tok an honde,

donk prist il femme que de haute gent fu,   Þe Kinges douȝter of Scotlonde,

20 file au roi de Escoce cele dame fu.   So faire and briȝt.

Guioun la prist a femme, lui chevaler membru.   Allas, þat he hire euer ches!

Puis avint cel jour que mult iré en fu,   For hire loue his lif a les,

ke il perdi le chef par desus le bu.   30 Wiþ mechel vnriȝt.

5

La dame si estoit bele e afeité.

Þis maide ichaue of y-told,

Faire maide ȝhe was & bold

And fre y-boren;

25 Le emperur de Alemaine la out avant amé   Of Almayne þat emperur

35 Hire hadde loued paramur

Wel þar be-foren.

e a son pere la out sovent demaundé,   Ofte to hire fader a sente

And he him selue þeder wente,

For hire sake;

40 Ofte gernede hire to wiue:

mes lui roi de Escoce li avoit devée   Þe King for no þing aliue

Nolde hire him take.

Si la dona Guioun ov la chere membré.   Siþe a ȝaf hire to sire Gii,

A stalword erl and hardi

45 Of Souþhamtoun.

Pus en perdi le chef (allas, quele destiné!)   Man, whan he falleþ in to elde,

30 pur la amour de la dame que il out esposé.   Feble a wexeþ and vnbelde

Þourȝ riȝt resoun.

6

Seignurs, icele dame dunt jeo vus ai dist

estoit bele dame saunz nule contredist,

mes mult fu felunesse, ne out le quer parfist;

mult ama son seignour Guioun petit,

35 einz le hai sur tuz e le teneit en despit.

Jhesu la confounde, ke tot le mound fit!

7

Ele out de son seignur un emfaunt avenaunt,   So longe þai ȝede to gedres te bedde,

50 A knaue child be-twene hem þai hedde,

15

l'em le apele Boefs, ke mult esteit sachaunt;

bien out passé dis aunz, le unzime est entraunt.

40 Un jour se purpense la dame malement
ke estoit bele femme, jovene e avenaunt,

e son seigneur fu veuz homme e alout declinaunt;

ne le lerrai, ceo dist ele, pur nul homme vivaunt
ke ele ne lui face tuer a dol e a torment.

8

45 La dame se purpense par graunt felunie.
Ele apele un messager, ne demora mie. [. . .]

Beues a het.
Faire child he was & bolde,
He nas boute seue winter olde,
Whan his fader was ded.

55 Þe leuedi hire mis-be-þouȝte
And meche aȝen þe riȝt ȝhe wrouȝte
In hire tour:
'Me lord is olde & may nouȝt werche,
Al dai him is leuer at cherche
60 Þan in me bour.

'Hadde ich itaken a ȝong kniȝt,
Þat ner nouȝt brused in werre & fiȝt,
Also he is,
A wolde me louen dai and niȝt,
65 Cleppen and kissen wiþ al is miȝt,
And make me blis.

I nel hit lete for no þinge,
Þat ich nel him to deþe bringe
Wiþ sum braide!'
70 Anon riȝt þat leuedi fer
To consaile clepede hir masager
And to him saide [. . .]

Apart from some omissions and additions, the Middle English text carefully matches the Anglo-Norman. Indeed, the omissions and additions are all attributable to the translator's desire to remain close to his original, and easily explained as instances of explicitation and simplification. In the opening sections of *Beves* the translator combined these universal translation strategies with an effort to mirror the versification of the Anglo-Norman poem by matching his own tail-rhyme stanzas to the *laisses* of the Anglo-Norman poem.[10] Thus, for example, he expanded *laisse* 4 to two stanzas, probably in order to accommodate the content of the *laisse* to his shorter prosodic form. Or, in another recurring pattern, in which one line of the French text is expanded to a triplet in the English, he split *laisse* 5 into three units (ll. 24–5, 26–7, 28–30), each of which became a separate stanza in translation. Explicitation often takes the form of substituting direct discourse for reported speech or thought in the original, and this is what the English translator/poet did in rendering *laisse* 7, into which, taking his cue from the presence of free indirect discourse in *Boeve* 43–4, he inserted a stanza-and-a-half of direct speech, allowing the countess to lament her situation, which was described briefly and matter-of-factly in *Boeve* 41–2. In a contrary but complementary

---

10 On the influence of the *laisses* of *Boeve* on the tail-rhyme section of *Beves* see Ivana Djordjević, 'Versification and Translation in *Sir Beves of Hampton*'. Forthcoming in *Medium Ævum*.

translational impulse, the poet suppressed *laisse* 6, no doubt considering the information in it superfluous.[11] (The countess's resentment of her husband would presently become obvious anyway, both through her actions and through her speech in ll. 58–69.)

The above passage therefore seems to present us with as faithful a piece of translation as we can expect from a thirteenth- or fourteenth-century practitioner of the art. There are some changes, but they are all innocuous and in no way affect the narrative substance. This impression, however, may be deceptive. Fidelity is no doubt what the translator aspired to here – but it is not quite what he achieved. Let me summarise the matrimonial drama narrated in *Boeve* and highlight the way that significant details of it are changed in *Beves*.

As the Anglo-Norman story opens we meet the earl of Southampton, a man who refuses to marry although this exposes him to censure. At last he gives in to pressure, as we find out from ll. 15–16, which refer implicitly to the motif of the ruler urged by his retainers to marry. We are told that the earl is at this point an old man, but there appears to be no direct link between his age and his belated acceptance of marriage. Indeed, lest we should think that old age has weakened him we are reminded in line 21 that despite his age Gui is still a strong and capable man. We learn too that the lady whom he eventually marries, and who had been unsuccessfully sought in marriage by the German emperor (25–7), is high-born (19–20) and beautiful (24, 32) but that she is also evil and disloyal, feeling nothing but hatred and contempt for her husband (33–5). The first reference to the disparity in age between the spouses does not occur until they have been married for more than ten years (41–2). At this point the juxtaposition of references to the countess's youth and attractiveness on the one hand and her husband's physical decline on the other adds a hint of sexual dissatisfaction to the lady's long-standing animosity towards her husband. In brief, this is the story of a man whose first mistake is to have refused to marry and who then made an even worse mistake by marrying a woman who did not want him. The narrator draws our attention to the injudiciousness of both the earl's initial resistance to marriage (15–17) and his eventual choice of bride (22–3).

What does the Middle English translator do with this? First, there is no pressure on Guy to marry in *Beves*. The fact of his wifelessness is stated neutrally and, positioned as it is within the stanza, almost as an afterthought (17–18). When he does decide to marry, his decision is directly linked to the ravages of old age (19–21). The connection between old age and the earl's marriage is reinforced at the beginning of the next stanza (25), and the earl's decline is strikingly underscored yet again in the proverbial-sounding addition

---

11 Explicitation and simplification are considered complementary because the purpose of both is to smooth the flow of information in the text. The former achieves this by adding textual material felt to be lacking and the latter by deleting material felt to be unnecessary. In this section of *Beves*, in which prosodic matching is an important concern of the translator, omitting a supposedly repetitive *laisse* would have been a good opportunity to make up for some of the explicitating amplifications.

in 46–8. In spite of the superficial similarities between the two texts, their implications are quite different. *Boeve* implies that a sensible man should not refuse to marry. If he does, the people around him are right to consider such wilfulness blameworthy (15) and he himself will come to repent of his obstinacy (17). *Beves* implies that a sensible man should not marry. If he does, it is presumably because old age has clouded his judgement and he no longer knows what is good for him.[12] In the space of just a few stanzas and by means of minor changes, the Middle English translator has introduced an element of misogamy that was not present in the original. From the idea that marriage is bad when it is untimely (and when it involves the wrong choice of partner) we have moved to the notion that marriage is bad by definition.

We could argue that the translator's shift towards misogamy here is deliberate and that his introduction of a particular ideological position is meant either to reflect his own prejudices or to flatter those of his intended audience. I am reluctant to accuse him of intentional distortion, however, since there is a more innocent explanation of his changes in terms of another 'translation universal' – repertorisation. Also known as the 'law of growing standardization', this general tendency is defined as 'the conversion of source-text textemes into target-language or target-culture repertoremes'.[13] Rendered from translation studies jargon into plain English, this means that the special (and specific) textual relations created in the source text are often replaced by conventional relations in the target text. When translators need to find an equivalent for a textual or cultural convention in the original text, they usually reach for ready-made solutions from the repertoire of conventional items available in their own language or, more broadly, literature or culture. In *Boeve*, however, a number of motifs that would appear as mere conventions to later readers or rewriters were in fact grounded in the original poem's socio-historical, as opposed to purely literary, context.

One such motif is that of a ruler or nobleman whose vassals urge him to marry. The motif is a common one, especially in twelfth-century French and Anglo-Norman narratives. We find it in Chrétien's *Cligés* (2592–621), several of Marie de France's *lais*,[14] the Anglo-Norman *Amis e Amillyoun* (169–80) and, most famously, versions of the Tristan story. More than a mere literary device, this motif reflects powerful contemporary anxieties. Failure to marry and produce heirs could and did lead to dynastic crises with serious repercussions not only for individual aristocratic families but for all those who depended on them or, in the case of royalty, for the realm itself.[15] When the

---

[12] In *Beves*, Guy's marriage does not come in response to outside pressure or prompting: it is an old man's whim. The link between age and the decision to marry is obvious, but the translator does not clarify its nature. Does Guy, who can no longer 'himself welde', need a wife to take care of him? Or is his sudden desire for a wife a symptom of his growing decrepitude rather than a proposed palliative?

[13] Gideon Toury, *Descriptive Translation Studies and Beyond* (Amsterdam, 1995), p. 267.

[14] *Guigemar* 645–56, *Equitan* 197–201 and *Le Fresne* 313–44.

[15] Like *Boeve*, most of the works just cited date from the second half of the twelfth century, when England was still recovering from the mid-century shock of anarchy – a direct consequence of the

same motif occurs in English, it is nearly always in translations, all of them produced at least a hundred years after the original texts. By then the connotations of the original historical context were irretrievably lost and the motif, detached from a concrete historical setting, had become no more than a conventional literary device. Middle English translators retain it when it is crucial to the plot, as it is in *Lai le Freine*,[16] but when its significance is not obvious they make short shrift of it.[17]

In *Boeve*, the significance of the motif is not obvious and the motif is implied rather than explicitly stated: instead of describing the fears of the earl's vassals and relating their negotiations with their lord, the author invokes the entire situation in a casual reference (15–16), confident that his audience, used to encountering the motif everywhere and acutely aware of its topicality, will know what he is talking about. The Middle English translator, however, could not recognise the motif because he did not possess the same frame of reference. The consequences of his unintentional misreading of this twelfth-century commonplace have important repercussions. Oblivious to the signifi-

---

situation created by the death, in 1120, of Henry I's sole legitimate male heir. The fifty-seven-year-old king, by then a widower, hastily remarried, but the hoped-for heirs never came. (After his death, his second wife did have children by a new husband, William d'Aubigny, for whom *Boeve de Haumtone* is thought to have been written.) The importance of dynastic concerns for twelfth-century French narrative, continental as well as insular, has been stressed repeatedly in the past couple of decades. R. Howard Bloch's study *Etymologies and Genealogies* (Chicago, 1983) has been particularly influential in this respect (Chapter 5 deals specifically with 'The Economics of Romance'). On succession crises among the nobility of comital rank, to which the probable patrons of *Boeve* belonged, see, for example, RaGena C. DeAragon, 'Dowager Countesses, 1069–1230', *Anglo-Norman Studies* 17 (1994), pp. 87–100 (p. 92).

16 Even here, the thirty-two lines of Marie's text are reduced to only sixteen in the English poem (311–26). It is true that *Freine* is shorter overall than its original, but only by about a hundred lines or one-fifth of Marie's *lai*. The passage in question is disproportionately cut in spite of its importance for the plot.

17 The example of what happens to the Anglo-Norman *Amis* in translation is especially relevant to my argument. When Amiloun returns to his own lands,

    Sa gent [. . .]
    A femme prendre li consaillerent.
    Par lor conseil se mariat:
    Une gentile femme esposat
    Qe fille d'un conte estoit,
    E pere e mere perdu avoit;
    Pur heritage la moyté
    Li fuit escheu del counté.
    De beauté avoit le pris
    Sour touz les dames du pays.
    Bien furent entre eux couplés
    De parage e de beautez. (169–80)

Instead of the concrete details that make it clear not only that Amiloun was advised to marry (though he himself might have been otherwise inclined) but also why his bride was a particularly good match (as the orphaned daughter of an earl who inherited half of her father's property – and happened to be pretty too, though this is not essential), the Middle English translator gives us a tail-rhyme cliché: Amiloun 'spoused a leuedy briȝt in bour/ & brouȝt her hom wiþ gret honour/ & miche solempnete' (Auchinleck text, 334–46). The Anglo-Norman text is quoted from *Amys e Amillyoun*, ed. Hideka Fukui, ANTS Plain Texts Series 7 (London, 1990) and the Middle English from *Amis and Amiloun*, ed. MacEdward Leach, EETS OS 203 (London, 1937; repr. 1960).

cance of *Boeve* 15–16, he read the characters of Bevis's parents in the light of his own misinterpretation of the initial narrative situation. The hero's father is no longer a man who marries reluctantly and only after protracted nagging from his dependants but an old man who suddenly decides that he wants a wife. He has become a *senex amans*, a literary stereotype more at home in the fabliau than in the romance. The translator underscores this interpretation of the character by insisting on the earl's advanced age and its effects, and isolates the disparity in age between Bevis's parents as the main cause of their marital catastrophe.

The romance and the fabliau are both conventional genres, inhabited by conventional character types. In the hands of a skilled artist a conventional type can be brought to vivid life but it still triggers an automatic response in the audience – a reflex inculcated by many previous encounters with similar characters in similar situations. Whether a *senex amans* is as likeable as the gullible carpenter in 'The Miller's Tale' or as unsavoury as Januarie in 'The Merchant's Tale', he is always a figure in which pathos and comedy exist in awkward tension. The tension enriches the experience of hearing a fabliau, as the audience hesitates briefly between pity and laughter and finally decides not to take the duped husband's tribulations too seriously. But when a fabliau cliché migrates to romance, the 'intergeneric textuality' results in 'a two-way dialogue, with a *remise en question* of both genres and the audience's expectations of them'.[18] Although the portrayal of Guy as a fabliau stereotype invites the audience to laugh at his self-deception, this would be a wholly inappropriate reaction. Guy's fate is not to be made a fool of while his wife is entertaining a lover in his own bed or in a pear tree but to be killed defending (as he believes) his wife and son. The Middle English Guy will regain some of his eroded dignity in the scene of his heroic death but his stature has been undermined by the generic connotations imported into *Beves*.[19]

---

[18] Karen Pratt, 'Introduction', *Shifts and Transpositions in Medieval Narrative* (Cambridge, 1994), p. xvi. Pratt is talking about the 'intergenre' created by the incursion of an epic hero into a romance situation but the implications are the same no matter which two genres are involved. In romance, for example, the old man who suddenly decides to marry is hardly ever a benign figure (Garcy in *Le Bone Florence* is an especially repulsive specimen). His desire for a wife usually has far more serious consequences than probable cuckoldry. Cf. Corinne Saunders's suggestion that 'The Merchant's Tale' is 'one of the more disturbing narratives' in the *Canterbury Tales*, '[p]erhaps because of its combination of *fabliau* and romance elements' (*Rape and Ravishment in the Literature of Medieval England* (Cambridge, 2001), p. 295). More recently, Saunders has drawn attention to the way that the marriage of Bevis's parents 'echoes the uneasy relation' of January and May or of Florence and Sir Garcy ('Desire, Will and Intention in *Sir Beves of Hamtoun*', *The Matter of Identity in Medieval Romance*, ed. Phillipa Hardman (Cambridge, 2002), pp. 29–42 (p. 39)). She does not refer, however, to the Anglo-Norman antecedent of the Middle English narrative.

[19] The Middle English translator's attempts to salvage the earl's reputation as a fighter in this scene result in some inadvertent absurdities. In *Boeve*, the earl, accompanied by no more than three knights, is attacked by a force of seven hundred. Although he defends himself 'par graunt hardement' (174), he is soon wounded in ten places and his companions are killed. If circumstances had been different, the narrator comments, '[b]ien se fust eschapé' (176), but the only choice left to Gui now is to kneel before his attacker and beg for mercy. His plea is rejected and he

If the character of Bevis's father is pushed towards a particular literary stereotype, the same is true of his bride, who is herself read in terms of a popular cliché. She becomes a *malmariée*, logical partner of the fabliau's *senex amans*. And just as the *senex amans* threatens to pull the romance too far in the direction of fabliau, the *malmariée* brings with her the generic baggage of both the fabliau and a subgenre of the lyric – the *chanson de malmariée*. In the fabliau she is a comic figure whose machinations we observe with some disapproval, yet we cannot help but be on her side as she openly expresses her sexual needs and sets out to find an appropriately aged lover. In the *chanson* she is a figure of pathos, the ill-treated wife of an old and often obsessively jealous husband. When she pours out her misery in confessional verse we sympathise even more readily. We are not meant to sympathise with Bevis's mother, however. When the author of *Boeve* exclaims, 'Jhesu la confounde, ke tot le mound fit!' (36) we are supposed to agree – and we do. So did the Middle English translator, who could not have intended to soften the portrait of the 'felunesse' (33), yet did just that. He did this by allowing the lady to express her feelings in her own words and at some length (58–69), in what amounts to a miniature *chanson de malmariée*. Although much of what she says does not show her in a particularly good light, and her determination to 'bringe [. . .] to deþ' her husband (68) is downright repugnant, it is hard not to feel at least a flicker of understanding for her wistful evocation of a young knight who would love her 'dai and niȝt,/ Cleppen and kissen wiþ al is miȝt' (64–5).[20] This moment of sympathy has nothing to do with a reader's or listener's personal opinion of January–May marriages: like the impulse to laugh at Guy's predicament, it is a habit of mind that comes from familiarity with a popular genre and its conventions.[21]

The *malmariée* is an ambiguous figure not only because of the uneasy tension between comedy and pathos inherent in the character type but because

is decapitated without further ado. In *Beves*, on the other hand, the old earl performs much better. Outnumbered by enemy troops (in different manuscripts their numbers range from two hundred to ten thousand), he not only holds his own but manages to strike off anything between forty and three hundred heads (again depending on the manuscript) without sustaining any injuries himself. If he had not been at such a disadvantage he would have done better than just to get away with his life, as in *Boeve*. Indeed, '[a]l þe meistre hadde ben his' (251). The piling up of hyperbole does momentarily transform Guy into a near-mythical figure, but the effect is shattered soon afterwards when, although unharmed, he begs for clemency as urgently as his seriously wounded counterpart in *Boeve*.

20 Jennifer Fellows has noted that the translator's use of direct speech here creates an imbalance 'by the deflection of attention away from the wronged Guy and by the suggestion of a degree of sympathy for his young wife' (*'Sir Beves of Hampton'*, vol. 1, p. 63). It should also be noted that while the wish for the old husband's death is frequently expressed in the *chanson de malmariée* it seldom comes true. In no lyric that I am aware of does the unhappy wife take the initiative and make arrangements for her husband's assassination.

21 The automatic response provoked by the *chanson de malmariée* is skilfully used to elicit sympathy for the wronged heroine in several romances and similar narratives including, for example, the lengthy lament in Marie de France's *Yonec* 67–104. On the special propensity of this lyric genre for infiltrating other genres see Pierre Bec, *La lyrique française au moyen âge*, vol. 1 (Paris, 1977), p. 80.

her frank acknowledgment of sexual desire, found in some of the more senti-
mental *chansons* as well as some of the more licentious fabliaux, complicates
the way that she functions and is perceived in both genres. Just as our disapproval of the fabliau wife's shenanigans is mitigated by appreciation of her
sexual needs as expressed in the *chansons*, our sympathy with the plight of the
malmariée of the lyrics is tempered by our awareness that 'what she proposes
to do is exactly what the *fabliau* wife does'.[22]

The outspoken sexuality that this literary type carries with it in its
intergeneric migrations becomes the dominant trait in the portrayal of the
mother in *Beves*. This is facilitated by the removal of *laisse* 6 of *Boeve*, in
which we are told specifically that the young countess was 'felunesse' and
disloyal, a woman who hated her husband and had nothing but scorn for him.
No reasons are explicitly given for her animosity (although the narrative situation makes them obvious enough), but it is clear that her feelings and actions
are those of an individual who finds herself in a specific set of circumstances.
The Middle English translator may have suppressed the *laisse* because it
seemed to him redundant, but in so doing he deprived the countess of her
individuality and opened the door to a reading of the character as a typical
representative of womanhood, her excessive and destructive libidinousness
perfectly understandable in terms of the commonplaces of medieval (and
post-medieval, for that matter) misogyny. This instance of repertorisation by
reference to ubiquitous cultural stereotypes distorts the representation of the
countess, but also of her marriage with Guy. Thus in the Middle English
romance the marriage is plagued by two main problems, both derived from
literary and cultural convention. First, the partners are ill-matched in age. And
second, marriage is a bad thing by definition. The discourses of misogyny and
misogamy, always closely related, come together in the countess's lament as a
malmariée, in which female antagonism to piety and martial prowess (a
literary and cultural commonplace) is explained by the fact that they both
interfere with sexual gratification (the former by making men less available
and the latter by affecting their performance).[23]

The author of *Boeve* portrayed the marriage differently. Sexual frustration,
expressed so forcefully and directly in *Beves* 58, is indeed discreetly hinted at
in the paratactic hiatus between lines 41 and 42 of the Anglo-Norman text but
it is introduced as a new element in the narrative at this point. By then Bevis's

---

22 John F. Plummer, 'The Woman's Song in Middle English and Its European Backgrounds', *Vox
Feminae*, ed. John F. Plummer (Kalamazoo, 1981), pp. 139–54 (p. 148). Plummer believes that the
speaker in a *chanson de malmariée* is always an object of satiric humour. Cf. Anne Klinck, who
reminds us that most female-voiced poems were written by men and that the 'mode of woman's
song [. . .] reflects male desires and fantasies about women' ('The Oldest Folk Poetry?', *From
Arabye to Engelond*, ed. Christa Canitz and Gernot Wieland (Ottawa, 1999), pp. 229–52 (p. 229)).

23 *Beves* 59–60, 61–2. The idea that a life spent in the wars makes a man an unsuitable lover is not
always put in the woman's mouth. In *Le Bone Florence* the narrator, very disapproving of Garcy,
describes him in terms very similar to *Beves* 62. Garcy is not fit to be a lover '[f]or he was bresyd
and all tobrokyn,/ Ferre trauelde in harnes and of warre wrokyn' (103–4; quoted from *Le Bone
Florence de Rome*, ed. Carol Falvo Heffernan (Manchester, 1976)).

parents have been married for eleven years, and while the countess may have been ill-disposed toward her husband from the very start there is no suggestion that she had cause to complain of his sexual inadequacy.[24]

The main reason for marital failure in *Boeve* is not an excess of sexuality in the countess but a lack of loyalty. Two reasons are suggested for it. The first, explicitly stated in line 33, is that Gui's bride was not exactly a pleasant person. The second, which emerges from the narrative itself, is that she has been forced into a marriage she did not want. We have not yet been told how she had reacted to the emperor's wooing, but subsequent events will show that he would have been her choice. If the countess in *Boeve* is a *malmariée*, she is so to the extent that she was married against her will; the disparity in age between her and her husband is not the most important consideration in this account. Rather, age is an underlying factor chiefly in that young women are likely to be *given* in marriage (often, indeed, to older men) against their will. As a matter of fact, the Anglo-Norman narrator's only explicit comment on the unwisdom of January–May marriages is formulated as a criticism not of either partner in such a union but of those who allow it to happen. As he launches into the description of Gui's murder, the narrator says: 'Ore oiez, ke *il fest graunt pecché/ que doune* jofne femme a viel homme barbé' (120–1; italics added).[25] If such an alliance results in disaster, a considerable part of the blame belongs to those who denied one of the partners her freedom of choice.[26]

The issue of consent in marriage and what happens when it is withheld is either prominent or at least touched upon in a number of twelfth-century narratives.[27] *Boeve* is one of them. It shares with some other texts the device

---

24 The Anglo-Norman author sprinkles the text with proleptic comments on the dire consequences of Gui's marriage (*Boeve* 22–3, 29–30) but he does not say, as the translator does, that the earl had reason to rue his decision soon after the wedding (*Beves* 22–3). Since the 'sone þar-after' of line 22 is present in most manuscripts of *Beves*, it is unlikely to be just a scribal whim. Furthermore, the Anglo-Norman Gui had less reason to be disappointed since his marriage was a concession to the dynastic concerns of his retainers rather than a caprice attributable to senility. It is indicative that when his bride is mentioned the first thing we learn from the Anglo-Norman narrator is that she came 'de haute gent', being 'file au roi de Escoce' (19–20), which confirms her eligibility in the context of the twelfth-century feudal marriage economy. The translator recasts the information by repertorising it as a formulaic element of popular romance. His 'Kinges douȝter of Scotlonde' makes a suitable bride because she is '[s]o faire and briȝt' (26–7), not because of her lineage. The author of *Boeve* does not refer to the bride's beauty and charm until the following *laisse*.

25 The lines are omitted by the translator, which is surprising in view of his fondness for moralising commentary.

26 The attitude is backed by contemporary canonists. In a frequently quoted passage, Gratian concluded that if a forced union results in fornication the sin will redound upon the person who enforced the marriage. Trying to answer the question of whether a daughter may be given in marriage against her will, the eminent canonist cited an earlier decision by Urban II: 'Quorum enim unum corpus est, unus debet esse et animus, ne forte, cum virgo fuerit alicui invita copulata, contra Domini Apostolique preceptum aut reatum discidii, aut crimen fornicationis incurrat. *Cuius videlicet peccati malum in eum redundere constat, qui eam coniunxit invitam.*' The quotation is from John T. Noonan's account of Gratian's position in 'Power to Choose', *Viator* 4 (1973), pp. 419–34 (p. 419; italics added).

27 In *Marriage Fictions in Old French Secular Narratives, 1170–1250* (London, 2002) Keith

23

of juxtaposing two different marriages, one based on coercion and the other on free choice, and invites the audience to compare them. In the Anglo-Norman *Amis*, for example, Amiloun is betrayed by his wife, to whom he was married on the advice of his men and with practical considerations in mind (see above, n. 17). Amis's wife Florie, on the other hand, has wooed her man with as much zeal and ingenuity as Bevis's *amie* Josiane. Her loyalty knows no bounds and does not stop at the sacrifice of her own children, when Amis requests it. The parallels between the two women have indeed been remarked upon by critics. M. D. Legge has drawn attention to 'the contrast between the behaviour of the wife who has married a man she loves "par amurs" and that of the wife who has made a *mariage de convenance*', and Judith Weiss has noted that 'the two unions are carefully contrasted: though Florie begins by wooing her future husband in a way which seems to confirm all male prejudice against women, the resulting marriage is far better than one contracted in an orthodox manner'.[28] A similar parallelism in *Boeve* has gone unnoticed, probably because the two marriages are not staged for us simultaneously and therefore do not obviously invite comparison. In *Amis*, the action constantly goes back and forth between the two friends and their wives. In *Boeve*, on the other hand, by the time Josiane has decided that she wants the hero and is taking steps to get him the countess has been off the stage for a while and will not reappear until the scene of her come-uppance, much later.[29]

In *Boeve*, as I suggested above, the marriage of the hero's parents is the negative of the hero's own marriage. Bevis's mother, whose disloyalty to her husband stems from the fact that he was imposed on her although she preferred another suitor, is the antithesis of the hero's wife Josiane, whose unflinching loyalty follows naturally from her free choice of partner. The contrast between the two women, and between the two marriages, is blurred in the Middle English romance because the translator was unaware of this thematic aspect of his original. Marriage, after all, is not the central concern of *Boeve*, which is not *about* consent and coercion in marriage. The *Boeve* author's main purpose was no doubt to entertain, which he did by relating his hero's adventures, but he spiced up his narrative by weaving into it numerous references to matters of current interest and topics of ongoing debate. In these *clins d'oeil* to his audience he showed off his familiarity with the issues

---

Nickolaus provides a good survey of twelfth-century marriage reforms and the debates on marital consent. He also analyses the reflections of these issues in contemporary narratives, including the *romans d'antiquité*, versions of the Tristan story, Chrétien's *Cligés*, as well as *L'Escoufle*, *Partonopeus de Blois*, *Girart de Roussillon* and *Flamenca*, but leaves out the Anglo-Norman romances.

28 M. D. Legge, *Anglo-Norman Literature and Its Background* (Oxford, 1963), p. 118; Judith Weiss, 'The Wooing Woman in Anglo-Norman Romance', *Romance in Medieval England*, ed. Maldwyn Mills, Jennifer Fellows and Carol Meale (Cambridge, 1991), pp. 149–61 (p. 159).

29 Howard Bloch calls this kind of phenomenon 'narrative attrition'. He notes that 'matrimonial romances' are often quite long 'and the clarity with which they focus in places upon issues like marriage choice and inheritance is more than undermined by a general loss of narrative coherence' (*Etymologies and Genealogies*, p. 195).

involved, acknowledged the importance of these issues for his listeners' self-representation as a social group, and may even have attempted to influence, in a modest way, his listeners' thinking on the subjects alluded to. Because the audience was very familiar with the issues at stake it could be relied upon to catch topical allusions even when they were introduced with a very light touch.[30] Working a hundred years later, the Middle English translator could have no access to the socio-historical context in which such allusions were made and inevitably missed them, especially since they were so easily mistaken for cultural and literary stereotypes that he was familiar with. The pros and cons of marriage by coercion could be assimilated to the argument against marriage in general, just as the treachery that resulted from denying one woman her choice of marriage partner could be read in terms of the treacherousness of all women.

I have argued that the Middle English translator's misogamy was a consequence of repertorisation, not necessarily a reflection of his own or his audience's personal prejudices. Nor do I think that, being more misogynous than most of his contemporaries, he went out of his way to blacken women in his translation. He was, however, as misogynous as the average person in his time and, faced with the apparent absence of motivation in his original, automatically resorted to the one-size-fits-all explanations that the discourse of misogyny offered, thinking that they were already present in the text he was translating. This is not to say that the author of the original was *not* a misogynist, but that the misogyny in his text is more nuanced. It is triggered by specific circumstances and at times minimised, or even entirely switched off, by the author's individualisation of his female characters. In the translation, misogyny is more sweeping and unreflecting, the knee-jerk anti-feminism of pervasive cultural stereotypes. Jennifer Fellows describes this trait of the Middle English text as 'gratuitous misogyny'.[31] Compared to it, the misogyny of the Anglo-Norman *Boeve* could be described as functional or situational.

Rather than try to interpret the translator's changes as an effort to please his hypothetical audience, I believe it would be more accurate to describe them as a natural consequence of what I referred to above as the translator's puzzlement. By this I do not mean the sense of panic that a translator feels when, looking at the text before him, he realises that he does not understand half the words but, on the contrary, the deceptive reassurance he derives from a text that appears utterly transparent. Translators are most puzzled when they are not even aware that they are puzzled. As anyone who has ever translated knows, the competent translator's greatest fear is not of failing to solve a translational problem but of failing to see that there is a problem at all. This typically happens at the lexical level, when the translator does not recognise

---

30 The subject of marriage would have been of particular interest to the probable patrons of *Boeve*. The upwardly mobile d'Aubigny (Albini) family owed much of their wealth and remarkable social success in the twelfth century to advantageous marriages.
31 'Mothers in Middle English Romance', p. 53.

so-called false friends and assumes that a familiar-looking word means one thing when it means something entirely different.[32] But false friends occur at other textual levels too, and a translator may fail to recognise a variety of literary, cultural, historical and other references, either because they are not available in his own culture at all or, on the contrary, because, as in the case of lexical false friends, something deceptively similar *is* available and the translator wrongly assumes that it is really the same thing.

The analogy between lexical and cultural false friends is not perfect. Lexical false friends are easy to identify and explain, but the analysis of cultural false friends forces us to look at extratextual structures of far greater complexity than the lexical systems of two languages. In examining these extratextual structures we have to bear in mind that translation is second-degree literature. A translation is a metatext and its primary frame of reference consists of other texts: the original, of course, but also the literary system as a whole. This can create problems in the translation of topical allusions. The dominant model of this process in translation studies has the translator setting out to update the socio-historical or socio-cultural references in his original for the benefit of his intended audience. He finds his reference points in the socio-historical context he shares with his readers, and substitutes the realia known to them for the realia of a less familiar world.[33] The assumption is that the omniscient translator always recognises these textual elements for what they are. This, however, is not the case. The ignorant or indolent translator may indeed fail to see the obvious, but many topical allusions are not obvious at all. More importantly, the textualisation that an element of the historical context undergoes when it is written into a literary work makes it easy for even a conscientious translator to mistake it for an entirely textual element – a discursive commonplace or convention. When a text has been severed from the original context of its production, it is the logic of literary models rather than historical reality that will be applied in its elucidation, and this is what happens when *Boeve* becomes *Beves*. This happens, too, in other Middle English narratives that derive from French originals, whether continental or insular. If we are to gain a fuller understanding of these texts, we should do well to redirect our attention from the conjectural expectations of their elusive audiences to their authors, translators of whose work we have tangible evidence in the texts that we study.

---

[32] Examples would include translating the French 'eventuellement' as 'eventually' or 'délai' as 'delay'.

[33] He may, of course, decide that there is not much to be gained from such a substitution and choose not to change the original, trusting his readers to make the necessary interpretive moves, or he may even leave out the topical allusion altogether.

3

Chronicle and Romance:
The Story of Ine and Æthelburgh

TONY DAVENPORT

Although 'Matter of England Romances' has proved a useful sub-heading for classifying romances according to subject matter, the actual matter of England referred to in the various versions of the stories of Horn and Havelok, in the ancestral romances of Guy and Bevis, and in *Athelston* and *Gamelyn* does not have a very certain identity. In *King Horn* not only have Viking enemies been transformed into Saracens and the geography of Horn's journeys blurred by fictional place names, but the narrative patterns of exile and return, the hero's winning two princesses in different realms and his having to rescue the heroine from two rival suitors have absorbed any references to Denmark or Norway and distorted those to Ireland; the history has to be hypothesised and recovered.[1] The version of the story in *Horn Childe and Maiden Rimnild* is superficially more exact, set in Yorkshire, Ireland and Wales rather than Suddene and Westernesse, and with a number of local references, but it is all no more than window dressing. Though the origins of *Havelok the Dane* in the tenth-century uniting of Denmark and England under Canute are more clearly identifiable, here too the popular appeal of the hero recovering a lost kingdom and winning a destined bride who is true heir to the English throne has rubbed away the hero's original identity and the relationship of the action to historical fact: the tale seems to have been read as history but its appearance in Gaimar's *Estoire des Engleis* gives the story 'undeserved authenticity', as Barron puts it.[2] Even more obviously in *Athelston*, loose reference to the pre-Conquest history of the reign of Athelstan (924–32) and of the life of St Edmund has been fused with allusion to the post-Conquest confrontation between Becket and Henry II within folklore motifs of sworn brotherhood and trial by ordeal; the recoverable history is a matter of disjointed pieces rather than a coherent sequence. Similar queries arise from the stories of Guy and Bevis. Rosalind Field points out some of the problems

1   As, for example, for the Anglo-Norman version of the story by Judith Weiss, 'Thomas and the Earl: Literary and Historical Contexts for the *Romance of Horn*', *Tradition and Transformation in Medieval Romance*, ed. Rosalind Field (Cambridge, 1999), pp. 1–13.
2   W. R. J. Barron, *English Medieval Romance* (London, 1987), p. 69.

associated with the idea of the 'Matter of England', particularly the wide temporal and geographical range it has to cover, the lack of central, recurrent figures and of a common environment, style or theme, and is surely right to suggest that 'the Matter of England grouping is perhaps more problematic than has been admitted or realised'.[3] If the group of romances were larger and not limited to English texts, perhaps the relationship between early history and later romance would be clearer. R. M. Wilson argued that, while 'only those [Matter of England] romances of which earlier French versions are extant have been written down in English', many more romances of English history, known now only from casual references, probably once existed.[4] Whether or not this is so, I find it instructive to reverse the usual process of seeking the historical origins of romance adventures and to move forwards from the history towards romance, as one can do with the story of the Wessex king Ine and his queen: no post-Conquest English romance was written on the topic, as far as I know, but the processes by which Anglo-Saxon history was, by the twelfth century, turned into romance may be observed.

Ine is one of the more memorable of the West Saxon kings before Alfred, known as a significant leader and commemorated by a simple slab saying 'Ina' in the floor of Wells Cathedral, because he ruled for nearly forty years and continued the extension of the West Saxon kingdom that his predecessor Cædwalla had pursued.[5] His main claim to fame is his codification of the West Saxon laws and the later incorporation of the laws of Ine into the laws of Alfred. Among the interesting things that Alfred's laws convey is that Ine's father Cenred was still alive when Ine was king: kingship was presumably not simply a matter of descent from father to son; it could have been elective, not hereditary, or a period of multiple kingship. As David Dumville puts it: 'Bede's evidence hints strongly that in the seventh century the "King of the West Saxons" was no more than an overlord of a number of petty kings.'[6] However, the laws also seem to indicate that Ine was accepted as king as far east as London and Surrey (Erkenwald is referred to by Ine as 'my bishop'), while in the other direction it was probably in Ine's time that the Saxons completed the conquest of Devon.

The record of Ine's reign in the *Anglo-Saxon Chronicle* is fragmentary.[7] It begins with the annal for 688:

---

3   Rosalind Field, '*Waldef* and the Matter of/with England', *Medieval Insular Romance: Translation and Innovation*, ed. Judith Weiss, Jennifer Fellows and Morgan Dickson (Cambridge, 2000), pp. 25–39 (p. 30).

4   R. M. Wilson, *Early Middle English Literature*, 2nd edn (London, 1951), pp. 216–18 and *The Lost Literature of Medieval England* (London, 1952), pp. 123ff.

5   Stenton calls Ine 'the most important king of Wessex between Ceawlin and Egbert': F. M. Stenton, *Anglo-Saxon England*, 2nd edn (Oxford, 1947), p. 70 (hereafter referred to as Stenton).

6   David Dumville, 'The West Saxon genealogical regnal list and the chronology of early Wessex', *Peritia* 4 (1985), pp. 21–66.

7   '... most of the annals of which it consists stand in isolation and refer to persons and events otherwise unknown', Stenton, p. 70.

688. Here Ine succeeded to the kingdom of Wessex and held [it] 37 years; (and he built the minster at Glastonbury *[marginal note, made c.1001–12]*). And the same year Cædwalla went to Rome and received baptism from the pope, and the pope called him Peter, and 7 days later he passed away. This was Ine Cenred's offspring, Cenred Ceolwald's offspring; Ceolwald was the brother of Cynegils, and they were the sons of Cuthwine Ceawlin's offspring, Ceawlin Cynric's offspring, Cynric Cerdic's offspring . . .[8]

The record here of Ine's accession, the length of his reign, and his genealogy may give the reader a confident feel that the basic facts are established but there are several uncertainties even about these. First, there is no explanation of *why* Ine succeeded Cædwalla: if the two were at all related, the relation seems to be no nearer than through their great-great grandfather.[9] One modern historian comes up with the ingenious hypothesis that they were step-brothers through an unknown British mother.[10] Second, since the date of Ine's death is later given as 728, the arithmetic doesn't work. Third, for all the apparent exactness of the genealogy, it doesn't correspond to later Anglian genealogies[11] – this one has probably lost a couple of generations, and been tweaked to create an 'authorised' version of West Saxon succession. As Barbara Yorke says:

> It cannot be proved that the *Chronicle*'s claim that all those who ruled in Wessex were members of the same royal house and descended from a common ancestor is correct.[12]

The subsequent annals provide tantalising scraps:

> 694. Here the inhabitants of Kent came to terms with Ine and granted him 30,000 *[i.e. sceattas = a king's wergild of 7,500 shillings]* because they had burned Mul earlier *[brother of Cædwalla]* . . .

> 709. Here Aldhelm passed away: he was bishop to the west of the wood. And in the early days of Daniel, the land of Wessex was divided into two dioceses – and earlier it had been one; Daniel held one, Aldhelm the other . . .

> 710. Here . . . Ine and Nunna, his relative, fought against Geraint, king of the Welsh . . .

> 718. Here Ingeld, Ine's brother, passed away; and their sisters were Cwenburh and Cuthburh; and that Cuthburh founded 'the life' *[i.e. the monastic life of the community]* at Wimborne; and she had been given to Aldfrith, king of Northumbria, and they separated during their lifetime.

---

8 *The Anglo-Saxon Chronicles* (the Winchester Manuscript), rev. edn, ed. and trans. Michael Swanton (London, 2000), p. 40.
9 See the genealogy of West Saxon rulers in Barbara Yorke, *Kings and Kingdoms of Early Anglo-Saxon England* (London, 1990), p. 134.
10 T. Dayrell Reed, *The Rise of Wessex* (London, 1947), pp. 255–7.
11 Under the year 855 the genealogy of Æthelwulf shows an adapted version of these.
12 Yorke, *Kings and Kingdoms*, p. 143. See also Dumville, as cited in n. 6 above, and 'The West Saxon genealogical regnal list: manuscripts and texts', *Anglia* 104 (1986), pp. 1–32.

721. Here Daniel travelled to Rome. And the same year Ine killed Cynewulf.

722. Here Queen Æthelburh threw down Taunton, which Ine built earlier
. . . and Ine fought against the South Saxons . . .

728. Here Ine travelled to Rome and there gave up his life; and Æthelheard
succeeded to the kingdom of Wessex and held it 14 years.[13]

In these bits and pieces one can recognise several different areas of information. First is the evidence of Ine's widespread military activity: in 694
forcing a huge amount of blood-money from Kent; in 710 fighting the Britons,
probably in Cornwall; in 722 fighting the South Saxons. These all support the
idea of Ine as extending West Saxon power and boundaries. Then there is the
evidence relating to religious foundations in Ine's time (even if one ignores
the interpolated bit about Glastonbury, which belongs to early eleventh-
century romanticising); in 709 a new diocese based on Sherborne with
Aldhelm as bishop is created, leaving Daniel at Winchester; in 718 his sister
founds the combined monastery and convent at Wimborne. A third area of
interest is the family information: the names of Ine and Ingeld contrast with
those of the sisters, Cwenburh and Cuthburh, and suggest the idea of
step-relationship, while the marriage of Cuthburh to the king of Northumbria
might be associated with the story of Ine's own taking a wife from the north;
one would like to know more about the implications of the news of her separation. In 722 Queen Æthelburgh enters the cast-list, playing what sounds like a
significant part in affairs – but what does it mean? Stenton, not much given to
wry asides, calls it a 'by no means luminous statement'.[14] Finally, in 728 Ine
follows the example of Cædwalla by ending his reign in a pilgrimage to
Rome, and is succeeded by yet another unexplained branch of the family,
though the similarity of name to Æthelburgh may indicate that Æthelheard
was of the queen's kin.

Here then is a skeleton narrative – a sort of post-modern piece of disjointed
and not fully reliable life-writing with most of the cultural indicators left out.
Bede, though he was writing a historical narrative rather than annals and
though, when he completed his *History of the English Church and People* in
731, he was writing of a contemporary, does not have much more to say about
Ine: Wessex is a good distance from Northumbria and he is more knowledge-
able about, and interested in, Ine's bishops, Aldhelm and Daniel (who was one
of Bede's informants), than in political events. However, Bede does state that
Ine was 'of the blood royal', whatever that means, and reports that Ine is no
longer king and that he abdicated in order 'to visit the shrines of the blessed
apostles' and to end his life 'in the vicinity of holy places'.[15] Modern histo-

---

[13] Extracts from *The Anglo-Saxon Chronicles* (the Winchester Manuscript), trans. Swanton, pp.
40–2.

[14] Stenton, p. 70.

[15] Bede, *A History of the English Church and People*, Book V, Chapter 7, trans. Leo Sherley-Price
(Harmondsworth, 1955).

rians have varied in their interpretations of this sketchy record: some have celebrated Ine as the unifier of a greater Wessex with a span from Land's End to Dover, while others have remained cautiously non-committal in the face of the obscurities, confusions and gaps.

The post-Conquest chronicle treatment of Anglo-Saxon history in Latin and in Anglo-Norman also varies, though not in the same way. For Geoffrey of Monmouth (and Wace) Ine, appearing as Yni, comes at the end of the 'History of the Kings of Britain', and so at the separation point between British and English history.[16] Cædwalla, Ine's predecessor as king of Wessex, here has been translated into Cadwallader, son of Cadwallo and nephew of Penda, the last British king ruling over all Britain, driven into exile in Brittany by a period of plague and famine followed by the invasion of the Angles. For Geoffrey this is the place for lamentation for the end of British power: all that is left for Cadwallader's son Yvor and his sister's son Yni, since Cadwallader (on his return from Brittany) is told by an angelic voice that the British will never regain Britain until Merlin's prophecies are fulfilled, is the role of dispossessed Britons, now to be called Welsh and to enter into a history of perpetual strife and failure, in contrast to the wiser Saxons, who, by keeping peace among themselves, by building cities and castles, have stabilised the country under their leader Adelstan, seen as the founding king of a new dynasty. The conversion of these seventh-century Wessex kings, who were themselves engaged in extending Saxon control over British territory, into the remnants of a British royal family is an indicator of the incompleteness and insecurity of the historical records available to Geoffrey, unless one takes it as evidence of his 'love of lying', a preference for his own post-Conquest historical myth of the decline of the once-powerful British nation. Wace follows Geoffrey but refers to Ine as one of Athelstan's ancestors (attributing the original institution of the tax called Peter's Pence to Ine) and so has him present both in a Celtic and a Saxon identity.

Gaimar in Anglo-Norman and Henry of Huntingdon in Latin use the *Anglo-Saxon Chronicle* as their main source. Neither adds much to what the *Chronicle* tells them, though Henry in the *Historia Anglorum*, written 1125–55, produces a joined-up version of the early chronicle, expanding by means of fluent narrative padding: he sees Ine as one of the 'good' kings, but knows no more than the Anglo-Saxon annalist tells him. There is a different story from further west in Wiltshire, where William of Malmesbury, writing about 1125, is openly critical of the inadequacies of the *Anglo-Saxon Chronicle*, and, taking Bede as his model, seeks out archive material and tries to make an intelligent account of the episode as with the rest of early history.

---

16 Wace emphasises the idea of separation at this point by inventing a passage on language: the Saxon settlers keep their own customs and translate the place names of their new country into their own language, but 'Among the Welsh the correct way of speaking the British language is still preserved': Wace's *Roman de Brut: A History of the British*, ed. and trans. Judith Weiss (Exeter, 1999), p. 371.

But, of course, he has his own agenda in which an interest in religious obser-
vances plays a leading part, together with religious foundations, especially the
history of his own monastic house at Malmesbury, which leads him to focus
on Aldhelm, one of its founders; he carefully argues away a tradition that
Aldhelm was Ine's nephew. However, William shows in his Chapter 35
greater knowledge of Ine than the *Anglo-Saxon Chronicle*.

> I.35. On [Cædwalla's] departure for Rome, the kingdom received a fresh
> start from Ine, the great-nephew of Cynegils through his brother Cuthbald,[17]
> who was called to the throne more for his acquired prowess and energy than
> for any blood link with the royal line. A paragon of valour, the image of
> wisdom, and in religion without peer – these were the arts by which he ruled
> his life, and won favour at home and respect abroad . . .
> [*Account of his wresting blood-money for Mul from the men of Kent
> follows.*] But let this account of his military successes here find its end; for
> the rest, his stature in things of God is clear from the laws he published to
> improve the standard of behaviour, in which a living image of his own high
> character can to this day be seen reflected . . . [*Ine is then credited with the
> establishment of the monastery at Glastonbury and the convent at
> Wimborne, though William is more interested in praising Aldhelm.*][18]

Here William both places Ine in a family tree and indicates that the succession
is doubtful; trying to sound judicious he ends up being contradictory. Was Ine
'of the blood royal', as Bede says, or was he not? It is on the basis of his laws
and the foundation of religious houses that William praises Ine highly as a
model. In the chapter that follows he introduces the figure of Æthelburgh:

> I.36. Ine also had a wife, Æthelburh, a woman of royal lineage and character,
> who frequently dropped in her husband's ear the plea that they should bid
> farewell to the world, even late in life. He put her off from one day to
> another, and she eventually made a plan to overcome him by guile . . .[19]

From this he develops a lengthy dramatic scene in which he can exemplify the
theme of kings and queens coming to realise the vanity of the world and
deciding to leave secular pomp behind; I shall return to this later.

Later histories such as Langtoft's and Robert Mannyng's Chronicle in the
early fourteenth century have different glamourised versions of Ine's story:
Mannyng has Ine on the throne for sixty-three years and sees him as an
English king driving the Britons into Wales and Ireland. However, outright
romanticisation of the past is identifiable at an earlier date in the unlikely form
of a Latin ecclesiastical history.[20] In a Register of the Priory of Bath

---

17 This looks like a conflation of Cutha/Cuthwine (thought to be the great-grandfather of Cædwalla
  and of Ine), and Cynebald, Cutha's son.
18 Extracts from the *Gesta Regum Anglorum* of William of Malmesbury, vol. 1, ed. and trans.
  R. A. B. Mynors, R. M. Thomson and M .Winterbottom (Oxford, 1998), pp. 49–51.
19 Ibid., p. 53.
20 Noted by Antonia Gransden in her magisterial survey of historical sources, *Historical Writing in*

(preserved in the Lincoln's Inn Library and identified as Hale MS 185), which contains copies of all documents relating to transactions of the Abbey from about 1200 until 1360, with a few earlier ones, there are (according to the Victorian antiquarian the Rev. Joseph Hunter[21]) 870 separate items (grants of land, individual professions of those entering the Abbey, and so on) among which is a late twelfth-century history of the bishopric of Somerset to the time of Bishop Reginald in 1174. The anonymous cleric who wrote it, possibly a canon of Wells, has like William an agenda of his own lying behind his version of the story of Ine: in this case concern with west-country ecclesiastical affairs.[22]

In the introduction to what it is fair to call a romance extravaganza[23] the writer expresses his 'earnest desire' to know how 'the Pontifical Seat was transferred to Wells from some other place, & how in the process of time it was removed to Bath'. And so, he says he has consulted:

... the writings of the annalists, and the narratives of the ancient fathers ... the facts which I thence collected I have thrown here into one narrative ...[24]

He then moves to the church in Somerset and to Bishop Daniel:

This Daniel, as we are told, was the last who sat in the episcopal seat at Congresbury. He it was who transferred that seat to Wells.[25]

And so the story follows: I have divided it into two episodes.[26]

England c.550 to c.1307 (London, 1974), p. 273. The story had earlier been noted and retold by Edward A. Freeman, in the course of a general review of Ine's career and the uncertainties in the historical records: 'King Ine' in *Proceedings of the Somersetshire Archaeological and Natural History Society* 18, pt 2 (1872), pp. 1–59.

21 Joseph Hunter, *A Catalogue of the MSS in the Library of the Honourable Society of Lincoln's Inn*, (London, 1838), p. 151; Hunter describes this Bath Cartulary as 'a depository of many of the transactions of the bishops of the diocese'. It is a bound volume, which was, according to N. R. Ker, rebound in Oxford in the early sixteenth century but which preserves the original paper binding within (N. R. Ker, *Medieval MSS in British Libraries*, vol. 1, London (Oxford, 1969), pp. 124–40).

22 This text, found on pages formerly numbered 189ff. in Hale MS 185 but later renumbered as 96r ff., was printed in *Ecclesiastical Documents*, ed. and trans. Joseph Hunter, Camden Society, OS 8 (London, 1840) as *A Brief History of the Bishopric of Somerset from its Foundations to the Year 1174*. I have edited Hunter's translation and supplied a translation of a sentence that he omitted, as indicated below.

23 Freeman calls it 'a very wild legend', 'King Ine', p. 17.

24 One must be aware, since there is no surviving evidence for any of what follows, particularly the shifting of the see, that the writer may be either credulous or untruthful.

25 Hunter argued that Kingsbury (the present-day village of Kingsbury Episcopi between Somerton and Yeovil) was a more likely place for the earlier episcopal seat than Congresbury, though the information in the *Anglo-Saxon Chronicle* leads one to expect reference to the division between Winchester and Sherborne.

26 See appendix for the Latin text.

Tony Davenport

First Episode: The Quest for a King

There was a time when two kings reigned in England, one beyond the
Humber, the other this side of it.[27] It happened that the king this side of the
Humber, the number of his days being accomplished, went the way of all
flesh, leaving no heir. As a result, in the realm he had ruled over justice
ceased and injustice grew, so that no room was left for peace and law.[28] The
unjust man condemned the just, the strong oppressed the peace-loving, and
the more power a man had, the more he inflicted injuries on his nearest
neighbour. What could be worse? The lack of an heir to the kingdom was the
source of wretched desolation. When the bishops and the leading men of the
realm saw this, they gathered in London to consult the Lord there, seeking a
king for themselves. The reply they received was that they should seek a man
who was called Ine, and make him king. When the chiefs of the kingdom
heard this, immediately they sent many messengers in all directions to
search for this man Ine and bring him back with them. After seeking for a
long time without finding anyone of that name, some of them who had been
searching in the western provinces, that is Cornwall and Devon, were
making their way, weary at heart, back towards London. As they were
following their road through the region and had come to a certain village
called Somerton, they saw a farmworker in the field with his plough who
was crying out in a loud voice, and he was calling for 'Ine', asking him to
come with his father's oxen – the father was the husbandman's partner.
When they heard this, the messengers interrogated the ploughman, asking
what he was calling. He replied that he had called for Ine, the son of his
colleague, to come with his father's ox-team. As soon as the messengers saw
Ine, and had taken in that he was a handsome young man, tall in stature,
robust in strength, they rejoiced with great joy: 'This,' they said, 'is the one
we are looking for!'

When they expressed their wish to take him away with them, they were
not allowed to do so by the young man's father, nor by the neighbours,
without the precaution of their giving a pledge and security that no harm
should befall Ine in their hands. When this had been done, they brought him
to London to the chiefs and leading men of the kingdom. When they saw Ine,
this young man so very handsome, and, judging by his appearance, very
vigorous, they made him their king, committing the kingdom to him and all
that pertained to it, and he was immediately consecrated by the bishops.

This story of Ine's becoming King of Wessex is presumably a west-country
tradition accounting for that gap of uncertainty in Ine's succeeding Cædwalla.
Whatever the real explanation it now appears as a rags-to-riches folktale of a
humble peasant achieving the throne. It can be identified as a 'male-
Cinderella' story, with resemblances to the romance of Havelok in its hero

---

27 Obviously this is a confusion of seventh- and tenth- or eleventh-century history.
28 The period of famine, plague and anarchy described by Geoffrey of Monmouth and Wace may lie
behind this.

34

who 'passes effortlessly from one social level to another'.[29] He shows the qualities of a leader by physical prowess, though here there is no magic flame or kingmark, but simply his having the right name, with the bonus of being handsome and vigorous. The emphasis on finding a man with the right name is suggestive, since Ine is conspicuously outside the pattern in the Wessex genealogy (Cenred, Cuthwine, Ceawlin, Cerdic, etc.). As Freeman said: 'the story that a king was a churl's son could have been spread abroad only about a king whose accession had something about it that was strange and unexpected, and who stood far away from the most obvious line of succession'.[30]

Even more striking is the second half of the tale, the story of Ine and Æthelburgh's courtship and marriage.

Second Episode: Courtship and Marriage

Even while these events were coming to pass there came a messenger who told the King that the king beyond the Humber had just died and left as his heir his only daughter, Æthelburgh by name. On hearing this the King had royal emissaries despatched to propose to Æthelburgh that they should marry and that a single monarchy be made of their two kingdoms. However, when Æthelburgh received the proposal, she scorned it and held in contempt the idea of marriage with the King, because he was said to be the son of a peasant. When he was given this reply, King Ine, believing that he would have a better chance of success, took on the embassy himself. Disguising himself as the king's messenger, he came to Æthelburgh, and conveyed to her the words and the proposal which she had heard earlier. But she nonetheless rejected the proposal as before, for the reason that a peasant had begotten the King. When Ine heard this, thinking carefully what he should do in order to gain ground by some means or other, he decided to remain with her for some days, even months, taking up the role of a servant attending upon her.

Now it came about that Æthelburgh gave orders for a banquet to be given for the highest ranking and the most important people in her kingdom. On the day of the feast Ine was assigned by his mistress the office of placing the dishes on the table at the banquet. When he was carrying out this task, clad for the occasion in royal garments and handsome in appearance far beyond all the others present, the lady, more and more often letting her gaze rest on him, became heated by desire for him, and at the end of the evening she ordered a bed to be prepared for him in her own bed-chamber. And so Ine, after lying down close to her, and then relinquishing his own bed and making straight for the lady, came to knowledge of her – with no resistance or even a word of objection from her.[31] When in the silence of this irregular night things so happened in the greatest secrecy between them,[32] Ine opened

---

29 Barron, *English Medieval Romance*, p. 85.
30 Freeman, 'King Ine', p. 20.
31 This sentence is absent from Hunter's translation: were church history and sex less compatible in 1840 than in 1174?
32 The meaning is not quite clear here. The Latin text reads: 'Cumque in *[this is the end of a line]*

35

afresh his suit to Æthelburgh, but he could by no means gain a hearing, until finally he disclosed to her who he was, and revealed the fact that he himself was the King. At this, regarding him with ardent wonder, Æthelburgh was amazed and willingly yielded to his pleas.

Once this was settled the King departed, and when he was back in his own kingdom, immediately sent messengers for her in greatest pomp and splendour. When she arrived at the town which at that time was called [T]iderton but now Wells, they were married with due solemnity. The service of marriage was joyfully performed by Bishop Daniel, and he, by the mediation of the Queen, obtained the gift of the town to himself so that he might transfer the episcopal seat there. Accordingly Daniel without delay moved the bishop's chair from Congresbury to Wells.[33]

This is possibly a story accounting for Ine's marrying from outside Wessex (the north, as his sister did, or Kent as Æthelburgh's name might suggest?), but the surprising appearance of this Hollywood scene in an ecclesiastical justification document has rather the effect of a re-telling of the story of *Lady Chatterley's Lover* in a Ministry of Agriculture pamphlet on the rearing of pheasants. Again there are resemblances to the story of Havelok: a woman, herself a queen and of independent mind and conduct, resists marriage to, as she thinks, a peasant, only to discover that the man she is in bed with is in reality a king. Here she is won over by sheer sexual attraction, though it is Ine's kingly identity that persuades her to marry him. In the character of Æthelburgh there are touches of other 'forward' heroines, such as Rymenhild, Yseult and Belisaunt in *Amis and Amiloun*.

In general the two episodes show something of the colouring of those twelfth-century Anglo-Norman romances, which supply foundation myths by reshaping local legends and pre-Conquest history into narrative fiction.[34] It is interesting in this case that it is within the field of ecclesiastical Latin history that the romance material occurs and that the assimilation of the imprecise history with romance motifs focuses on the uncertainties, the weak links in the historical sequence. These can be easily identified as the question of Ine's right to the throne and his marriage to an 'outsider'. Though the events sound like romantic fiction, the telling of the courtship story has some surprisingly naturalistic touches, perhaps because it is subordinated to the writer's other interest in Somerset church affairs.

No vernacular metrical romance on the theme of Ine and his queen was apparently written, though the material for such a work exists and one could

tepestae noctis silentio secum secretius agerent . . .', which Hunter, quoting Bede's phrase *intempestae noctis silentio*, emends and translates as 'In a secret interview in the deep silence of the night . . .'. I have translated it as I have on the basis that *intempestus*, 'unseasonable', and its derivative *intempestivus*, 'untimely', 'improper', seem to convey the sense of how 'irregular' the situation is.

33 The Wells recorder moves on after this to a list of Daniel's successors and to the later history of the diocese.

34 See Rosalind Field, 'Romance in England 1066–1400', *The Cambridge History of Medieval English Literature*, ed. David Wallace (Cambridge, 1999), pp. 155–62.

even provide suitable narrative closure by returning to the dramatic scene in which William of Malmesbury gives an account of their end. His interests lead him, like Bede, to see as the most interesting part of Ine's story his ending his reign by giving up power and going to Rome. The queen's plan to bring Ine to realisation of the vanity of the world, of which I quoted the beginning above, continues as follows:

> They had a noisy bout of royal extravagance at some vill. Next day, after their departure, the bailiff, with the queen's cognisance, used animal dung, piles of rubble, all the mess he could find to defile the palace. His master-stroke was to place a newly delivered sow in the royal bed. When they were a mile or more on their way, Æthelburh used her wifely wiles to beg him to allow them to go back. It was imperative, she said, and if he ignored her request it would be of much consequence. The king gave way easily enough, and found himself before the extraordinary sight of a place, only yesterday fit for the excesses of Sardanapalus, now deserted and turned upside down. He gazed for a while in silent thought, then looked back at his wife. She took her chance. With a pleasant smile she said: 'And where now, my lord and husband, are the revels of yesterday? . . . Where the elaborate vessels weighing down the very tables with their ponderous metal? Where the delicacies hunted down on land and sea to pander to greed? Are not all these things smoke and wind? Have they not all passed away? . . . Consider, I beg you, how miserably the flesh will decay, that is now fed on luxuries. Will not we who guzzle too freely rot the more wretchedly? . . . ' She needed to say no more: a tableau forced agreement from a husband who for many years had refused to listen to her whispered words.[35]

And so William brings Ine and Æthelburgh to a resolute Christian end as 'United thus by love for one another, at their appointed times they went the way of all mankind'. It is, in its way, as romanticised a close as the Wells chronicler's version of Ine's earlier biography, though here the narrative incident, like the expression, is self-consciously shaped by twelfth-century rhetorical artifice.

Comparison of the fragments in the *Anglo-Saxon Chronicle* to these twelfth-century enlargements of the story identifies at least two interesting ways in which art made its own sense out of history: William's high-style literary moralisation of the part of the history that interests him most, and the Wells ecclesiast's acceptance (because it supports his own special interest) of a less sophisticated, folk-tale version of the rise of a humble hero to great fortune and prosperous marriage. Both illustrate a cultural shift by which Ine's role as military leader, stabiliser of an extended kingdom (or, if viewed from the other side, enemy of the Britons), founder of institutions and lawmaker is either ignored or reduced by religious depreciation of secular achievement. It is not clear how soon after Ine's time this tale assumed its

---

[35] *Gesta Regum Anglorum*, pp. 53–5.

romantic, providential shape nor quite what was its basis in fact: Ine was a powerful Wessex king who ruled long enough to overcome uncertainty about his claim to regal power, whether the uncertainty was because he was a step-brother, foster-brother, illegitimate son, or simply, as his name suggests, an *in*-comer, an intruder. The only 'explanation' for the story of the ploughboy's convincing assumption of the royal role and his conquest of an exotic royal bride is that it was local Somerset tradition, providing some sort of rationale for what was unknown, which, as Freeman expressed it in 1872, 'though no doubt a creation of local vanity, is a creation not altogether without some ground work'.[36] Freeman suggests that bits from other histories, such as the story of Saul and David, have been worked into the tale; the later uncertainty about the succession after the death of Canute may have leaked into the post-Conquest form of the story. The legend of Ine's marriage to the proud 'Princess of Hunder', who did not think the king good enough because he had been a ploughman in his youth, continued to have currency in Somerset folklore until a much later period, though the form in which it survives is more decorous than its Latin forebear: the princess's liking for the young messenger sent from King Ine 'turned to love, and then to longing, until she told him her mind and asked him to marry her'.[37] It is only after the wedding that 'he took a crown and cloak from his baggage'. So her pride is humbled and then Ine in turn is taught to be humble by the queen. One can recognise the origin of all these touches: the folklore version has even taken in the reflections on worldly vanity.

These several episodes of Ine's story illustrate, in embryonic form, impulses towards historical fiction similar to the turning of Havelok into a local hero and patriotic leader and the combination in Guy of Warwick of chivalric hero and crusader; even in its undeveloped state the distance is evident between the appealing romance narrative and the incomplete and muddled jigsaw pieces that are the nearest that one can get to a 'truthful' contemporary record. But in this case the impulses towards English romance were never fulfilled.[38] Such a missed opportunity, as one might see it, is part of the unsatisfactoriness of the idea of the 'Matter of England': there are some romances that draw on English history, if in disguised forms, but there might have been more, and some tales, like that of Ine, were at least as much worth

---

[36] Freeman, 'King Ine', p. 20.

[37] See 'Ina the King', in Katharine M. Briggs, *A Dictionary of British Folk-Tales in the English Language* (London, 1971), Part B, Folk Legends, vol. 2, under 'Historical Traditions', pp. 77–8. The story was collected by Ruth L. Tongue: see 'Somerset Folklore' in *County Folklore* 8 (The Folklore Society, 1965).

[38] Though some reference in French to this period of history may be indicated by the inclusion of 'Cadewalan le ueyl' in the intriguing list of lays in Shrewsbury MS 7 (mid-thirteenth century) among other names from British history such as 'Glou degloucestre' (Glovus, founder of Gloucester), 'Le eir leycestre' (Lear) and Alfred; 'Cadewalan le ueyl' could be a reference to the death of Caedwalla and what followed. See Elizabeth Archibald, 'The Breton Lay in Middle English', *Medieval Insular Romance: Translation and Innovation*, ed. Judith Weiss, Jennifer Fellows and Morgan Dickson (Cambridge, 2000), pp. 55–70.

telling as some episodes from the sagas of Charlemagne and Arthur. Post-Conquest romance tends to lump together British and English history or to fail to make distinctions, as when Arthur is treated as the great white hope of the English, but Geoffrey of Monmouth, even if he confused matters by turning Ine from a Saxon into a Briton, did indicate how the split between Celt and Saxon might form the basis for narrative adventure.

Appendix

I am grateful to the Treasurer and Masters of the Bench of Lincoln's Inn for allowing me to examine the Register of the Priory of Bath (Hale MS 185) and to reprint the following extract from the Latin text in which Ine's story is told.

[fol. 96r] Fuit enim olim cum duo Reges regnassent in Anglia, unus trans Humbram et alter citra. Contigit quod Rex citra Humbram, completo dierum suorum numero, viam ingrederetur universae carnis; nullum relinquens haeredem. Unde in regno quod rexerat ortis justitio et injustitia, paci et justitiae nullus relictus est locus. Nam justum condempnabat injustus, fortis opprimebat imbellem, et qui plus poterat plus injuriae vicino proximo inferebat. Quid plura? Sic regni depopulatio fuit ejus pessima desolatio. Quod videntes regni primates et principes apud Londoniam Regem sibi quaerentes Dominum consuluerunt. Et recepto responso ut quaererent hominem qui vocaretur *Ina* ipsum facerent sibi Regem. Quod audientes regni principes statim plurimos circumquaque miserunt nuntios qui *Inam* quaererent et adducerent. Qui cum diutine quaerentes illum non invenissent, quidam eorum qui eum in occiduis provinciis quaesierant, Cornubia videlicet et Devonia, taedio affecti, et reversi, iter suum versus Londoniam direxerunt. Qui cum [per] provincias iter agerent et ad vicum quendam qui Somertona vocatur venissent, viderunt villanum quendam cum aratro suo in agro, voce magna clamantem, ac vociferantem *'Inam'*, ut veniret cum bobus patris sui qui erat socius villani. Quod audientes, nuntii sciscitaverunt a villano, quidnam vocaret. Qui respondit, quod Inam vocaverat filium socii sui cum bobus patris sui. Cumque nuntii vidissent Inam juvenem decorum, statura procerum, viribus robustum, *[fol. 96v]* gavisi sunt gaudio magno: 'Hic est,' inquiunt, 'quem quaerimus.' Cumque vellent eum ducere secum non s[in]unt[ur] a patre suo neque a vicinis, nisi data fidei cautione et securitate quod nichil mali in eorum ductu Ine contingeret. Quo facto, duxerunt eum Londoniam ad principes et regni majores. Qui videntes Inam, juvenem, et valde decorum, et ut videbatur valde strenuum, eum fecerunt sibi Regem, commisso sibi regno et omnibus quae ad regnum pertinebant: et ab episcopis consecratus est statim.

Et dum haec geruntur venit qui Regi diceret Regem trans Humbram nuper obisse et unicam filiam suam, ADELBURH nomine, haeredem reliquisse. Quod Rex audiens, missis regiis nuntiis, mandavit Adelburgiae quatinus nuberet, et fieret monarchia de duobus regnis eorum. Quod mandatum postquam Adelburh intellexerat, sprevit, et Regis nuptias contempsit, eo quod filius villani d[i]cebatur. Rex autem Ina, audito responso illius, credens se melius profuturum, iter arripuit, et faciens se Regis nuntium, ad A[d]elburgam usque pervenit, nuntians ei verbum et legationem quam ipsa prius audierat. At illa nichilominus, sicut ante, legationem refutavit, eo quod villanus eum progenuisset. Quod Rex ut intellexit, meditans sollicitus quod faceret, ut aliquo modo proficeret, aliquot diebus et mensibus remansit cum ea, veluti minister ministraturus ei. Contigit autem uti A[d]elburga convivium praesto fieri praeciperet primis et principibus regni sui. Ina vero, die convivii, jussus dominae in prandio fercula apponere. Qui cum apponeret, et indutus esset indumentis regiis, et praeterea prae astantibus forma speciosus, domina illum saepius et saepe respiciens, calefacta in concupiscentia ejus exarsit; et facto vespere lectum ejus in talamo proprio praeparari praecepit. Ina vero postquam accubuerat, lectum relinquens proprium, ad dominam pergens, eam non renitentem set nequaquam contradicentem cognovit. Cumque inte[m]pestae noctis silentio secum secretius agerent, Ina denuo legationem suam Adelburgae aperuit; set nullatenus exaudiri meruit, dum denique rex ei quisnam esset indicavit, et se Regem esse proposuit. Unde illa vehementer admirans, obstupuit, et petitionibus suis libens acquievit. Quo facto, rex inde discessit, et in patriam suam regressus, cum magno apparatu nuntios pro ea direxit: quam, ubi venit ad villam tunc temporis quae Cideston, nunc autem Wella vocatur, solempniter desponsavit; episcopo Daniele ministerium desponsationis feliciter consummante[m]: qui, Regina mediante, impetravit a Rege dari sibi villam eandem ad transfer[e]ndum illuc sedem pontificalem. Daniel vero sine mora de Kunigresburia transtulit ad Wellam cathedram pontificis.

4

The King Over the Water:
Exile-and-Return Revisited

ROSALIND FIELD

On 12 March 1194, Richard I returned to England from exile in the emperor's prison, to reclaim his throne in the teeth of his brother's attempted usurpation. As he landed in Sandwich the chroniclers reported bright sunlight. Accompanied by his mother, Eleanor of Aquitaine, greeted by loyal supporters and vast crowds, he made his way through Kent, reaching London on 23 March, 'where to the great acclaim of both clergy and people he was received in procession through the decorated city into the church of St Paul's to give thanks for his restoration'.[1] A week later at a Great Council in Nottingham he was joined by more supporters, including William Marshal.[2] There were deliberations over punishment, confiscations for John and his followers, and rewards for Richard's loyal supporters. The king also went hunting in Sherwood Forest. In mid-April Richard staged a second coronation or formal crowning ceremony in Winchester Cathedral when he received the crown from the Archbishop of Canterbury, to purge himself of the stain of imprisonment. After changing his clothes the king attended a celebratory banquet.[3]

Such an account of Richard's return would already seem familiar to readers of those insular romances of the twelfth century that deal with the theme of the return of the exiled ruler. The exile-and-return tale type is so familiar as to have remained largely unexamined in romances scholarship. This paper aims to go beyond the simple awareness of its ubiquity to ask why it occurs in such a noticeable cluster in insular romance of the Anglo-Norman period.

The exile-and-return narrative does not sit as easily within folk-tale tradition as is sometimes assumed. Although romance criticism has habitually taken it as a shorthand term for a romance type – '*Horn* is immediately recog-

---

[1] Alison Weir, *Eleanor of Aquitaine* (London, 2000), p. 306, citing Ralph of Diceto, *Imagines Historiarum*, ed. William Stubbs (Rolls Series, 1876), vol. 2, p. 114.

[2] David Crouch, *William Marshal: Court, Career and Chivalry in the Angevin Empire 1147–1219* (London, 1990), pp. 72–4.

[3] Roger of Hoveden, *Gesta Regis Henrici Secundi et Gesta Ricardi 1*, ed. William Stubbs (Rolls Series, 1867), 51–3, pp. 247–8.

nisable as a folk-tale of the exile-and-return type'[4] – and although there are several fragments of the traditional tale-type of abandoned children and the return of the culture hero, there is nothing that adds up to a developed folk-tale type equivalent to, for example, the *Romance of Horn*.[5] Deutschbein's 1906 study [6] is frequently credited with the discovery of a northern exile-and-return type, but on closer investigation it turns out that his evidence for this ancient tale is supplied by the romances of Horn, Havelok, Tristan, Bevis, Guy – in other words we are enmeshed in a classic circular argument in which the existence of these romances in Anglo-Norman and later English tradition is taken to prove the prior existence of the tale-type. A fuller analysis, less concerned with origins, has recently been provided by Diane Speed:

> The most common narrative base of medieval romance [is] the exile-and-return, or its variation, the chivalric quest. For a limited time the hero undergoes displacement from his home and the security of self-definition in relation to familiar circumstances, and his society experiences corresponding loss or diminution. In unfamiliar territory, which is testing or threatening, he goes through a process of learning and maturing. His eventual restoration at the end of that process marks a return to order for himself and his society and usually for both an improved security based in an expectation of no worse than natural death, together with perpetuation of the dynasty and eternal salvation of the pious individual. In reaching this kind of conclusion, medieval romance foreshadows the modern nationalism, articulated in the novel.[7]

This is a perceptive analysis, but I would like to distinguish further between the exile-and-return romance and the chivalric quest, the latter being both more individualistic and more unpredictable. While chivalric questers seek to escape or surpass the father, and in so doing often to defy him, exiled heirs seek to avenge and equal the father, and right the wrongs done to him. As I will argue, exile-and-return does not guarantee a positive conclusion and its interrogation of the hero's society can be more stringent.

So without wanting to deny the existence of culture-hero myths of returning rulers and the ubiquity of the romance of the displaced hero, I want to start by looking again at the exile-and-return romance as found in insular

---

[4] W. R. J. Barron, *English Medieval Romance* (London,1987), p. 65.
[5] As Julie Burton pointed out some years ago, exile-and-return is not actually represented in Stith Thompson's *Index of Folk Tales*: Julie Burton, 'Folktale, Romance and Shakespeare', *Studies in Medieval English Romances*, ed. Derek Brewer (Cambridge, 1988), pp. 176–97 (pp. 177–8). Stith Thompson, *Motif-Index of Folk Literature*, 5 vols, FF Communications 106–9, 116 (Helsinki, 1932–5) gives the following motifs: L111.1 Exile returns and succeeds; A516 Expulsion and return of culture hero; S140 Cruel abandonment and exposures; S300 Abandoned or murdered children; S350.2 Child driven out, brought up in secret; S141 Exposure of woman and/or child in boat.
[6] M. Deutschbein, *Studien zur Sagengeschichte Englands*, vol. 1 (Cothen, 1906).
[7] Diane Speed, 'The Construction of the Nation in Medieval English Romance', *Readings in Medieval English Romance*, ed. Carol M. Meale (Cambridge, 1994), pp. 135–59 (p. 146).

literature and in its *particular* cultural and historical context. The project of defining and characterising insular narrative for the twelfth century has tended to focus on that which distinguishes it from continental narrative. This topic suggests it is also possible to identify themes and characteristics that are intrinsically, rather than reactively, insular. In this case it is the return by water, so obvious that we tend not to notice it, but an unavoidable concomitant of the island setting and one that becomes a defining feature of a truly insular tale type.

If to lose one heir may be regarded as a misfortune, and to lose two looks like carelessness, then the loss of seven would seem a catastrophe that needs further investigation. The cluster of exile-and-return tales in the Anglo-Norman romance of the late twelfth to early thirteenth century is remarkable. To Deutschbein's list of *Havelok, Horn, Boeve* and *Gui* can be added *Protheselaus, Waldef* and *Fouke Fitzwarin*. I do not include *Tristan* for reasons given below. From the range of material available to twelfth-century romance writers a clear pattern of choice emerges from which we can identify the structure of the fully developed 'classic' type:

It opens with the male protagonist as a young boy. The initial stasis is broken by a violent crisis in which the father is killed. The boy, now heir to his father's lands, is exiled across water by the usurper, often after cruel treatment. In exile, disguised or otherwise deprived of his identity, he is often in danger as he reaches maturity. Aided by friends and/or love, he may become a leader in his new land. He returns – across water – often with an army. He finds a welcoming party, often hidden allies from his father's generation. He defeats and kills the usurper, thus avenging his father's death. He regains the lands to general acclaim and establishes a dynasty.

Some of these romances are well known, some less so. In these simplified synopses I have emphasised the exile-and-return narrative and omitted most other narrative elements.

Havelok – Gaimar's Haveloc episode (1135–40) and *Lai d'Haveloc* (1190–1220)[8]

Gaimar begins with the situation in England with the orphaned Argentille of Norfolk forced into marriage with the scullion Cuaran by her uncle, the usurper Edelsi of Lincoln. *Lai* begins with the hero and the parallel situation in Denmark. In both, Haveloc's father Gunter is killed by a treacherous noble, Odulf, working with the invading Arthur. The child heir Haveloc, two years old, flees with the assistance of Grim. After growing up in Grimsby as a member of Grim's family, Haveloc works in Lincoln for Edelsi as a cook.

---

8   Geffrei Gaimar, *L'Estoire des Engleis*, ed. Alexander Bell, ANTS 14–16 (Oxford, 1960); *Le Lai d'Haveloc*, ed. Alexander Bell (Manchester, 1925), trans. J. Weiss, *The Birth of Romance* (London, 1992).

After the forced marriage to Argentille, Haveloc discovers his identity and returns to Denmark disguised as a merchant. He encounters Sigar, who recognises him and organises resistance to Odulf. Odulf is killed. After three years of peaceful rule Haveloc leads an army to England and claims the land in Argentille's name. The English under Edelsi resist but are defeated in battle. Edelsi dies and Haveloc becomes king of Lincoln and Norfolk as well as Denmark.

This is an early, but complex double form of the exile-and-return pattern with the potential for further development. It raises interesting issues of identity – in that the hero is unaware of his true identity, not just disguising it. There are gender-specific ways of handling the return of the heir which are discussed further below. The recognition of the true heir is just that – Sigar dramatically recognises Haveloc as his father's son when he sees him in action in the fight in Denmark – but it is backed up with marvellous proofs, the flame and the horn.

Romance of Horn[9] (c.1170)

Aaluf, Horn's father, king of 'Suddene' is killed by invading Saracens who send the boy Horn and his companions to sea in a rudderless boat. They land in Brittany where Horn grows up. He is again exiled, this time alone, and in Ireland adopts the disguise of 'Gudmod'. After saving Ireland from the Saracens he leads an army to Suddene. He is welcomed in Suddene by the seneschal Hardré, representative of his father's generation, and also by his mother who has survived in hiding. He defeats the Saracens, kills his father's killer and restores Christianity. Returning to Suddene he saves Rigmel, marries her and unites the two kingdoms.

Here, unusually and probably accidentally, the kingdom of Suddene is unidentified. In all other respects the career of Horn provides a template of the type. The presence of Saracens gives the exile-and-return pattern a crusading gloss and avoids the more usual narrative of civil strife.

Boeve[10] (late twelfth to early thirteenth century)

In the *enfances* section the eight-year-old Boeve defies his mother's lover, the Emperor, who has murdered his father the Earl of Southampton. Boeve is sold to Saracen merchants and taken to Egypt. As an adult he returns with his wife and an army to regain his lands with the help of his tutor, Sabaoth and is welcomed by the burgesses of Southampton. His lands are restored, but after a quarrel with king he leaves for Egypt. He returns to England to regain lands

---

[9] Thomas, *The Romance of Horn*, ed. M. K. Pope, ANTS 9–10, 12–13 (Oxford, 1955, 1964), trans. J. Weiss, *The Birth of Romance* (London, 1992).

[10] *Der anglonormannische 'Boeve de Haumtone'*, ed. A. Stimming (Halle, 1899).

not for himself but for the next generation and marries his son to the king's daughter. He returns to Egypt to die.

Here the hero is not a king but the pattern of regaining his patrimony fits the type. Kings and emperors are the enemy, and the hero is twice exiled from his lands – and from England – and twice returns. This double exile-and-return is worked out over two generations; in the first Boeve fills the role of the child, in the second of the father. The motif of the father seeking to reunite the divided family may derive from the Apollonius of Tyre narrative.[11] *Boeve* is pessimistic about the problems of holding lands from a dishonest king.

Protheselaus[12] (before 1189)

As Hue de Roteland's sequel to his *Ipomedon*, this concerns regaining patrimony and equalling the father. After the death of Ipomedon, his eldest son Daunus disinherits his younger brother, Protheselaus. There follows a chivalric account of regaining lands, in which the hero is in disguise and aided by various love-sick queens, who, more than the lands themselves, are the father's legacy to his son. By the end Protheselaus has married Medea of Sicily and on the death of his brother rules the triple kingdom of Sicily, Apulia and Calabria. As we might expect from Hue, this does not run true to type, but suggests knowledge of the type.

Waldef[13] (1200–1210)

As an infant, Waldef of Norfolk is disinherited by Frode, the seneschal who marries his mother, the sister of the Duke of Normandy. Frode arranges for Florenz, a courtier, to kill the child but Florenz flees to Normandy with Waldef. They remain in Rouen in disguise until Waldef is sentenced to death for the accidental killing of the mayor's son. He is saved when recognised as the duke's nephew. When he comes of age, Waldef returns with Florenz, is recognised by his lords and kills Frode.[14] He becomes king of Norfolk. Later the enmity of the king of London leads to further exile from which Waldef returns to die in battle. His two sons gain European crowns.

Here the hero's identity is expressive of a bond between England and Normandy. The return of the young heir fits the type, and Waldef is another hero who grows to take on the role of the father of a divided family. Later the enmity of the king leads to the death of the hero in a thoroughly pessimistic account of warring kingdoms.[15]

11 Burton, *Folktale, Romance and Shakespeare*, p. 178.
12 Hue de Roteland, *Protheselaus*, ed. A. J. Holden, ANTS 47–9 (London, 1993).
13 *Le Roman de Waldef* ed. A. J. Holden, Bibliotheca Bodmeriana, Textes 5 (Cologny-Geneva, 1984).
14 In an interesting precedent to the clumsiness of Orfeo's steward in *Sir Orfeo*, Waldef's lords knock over the tables in their haste to greet him: *Waldef*, ll. 3109–16.
15 I have discussed this in more detail in '*Waldef* and the Matter of/with England', in *Medieval*

Gui[16] (1232–42)

A later variant on the exile-and-return pattern. There is no patrimony to claim here, but the hand of the hero's social superior, Felice. Gui's later self-imposed exile is penitential not political. But there is disguise and danger, and he returns to save England from the heathen. His son, Reinbrun, becomes a hero of his own, more conventional, exile-and-return narrative.

Fouke Fitzwarin[17] (thirteenth/fourteenth century)

Fouke III, having been honoured by Henry II and Richard, is disinherited by King John. He turns outlaw and takes to the forest. He later takes refuge in France whence he is expelled. Twice he embarks on sea voyages to return to England and confront John. Finally, with the support of Ranulf of Chester and Hugh Marshal, Fouke is reconciled to the king and reinstated in his lands.

This is the most historically factual of the romances, dealing with near-contemporary figures, although well-laced with romance marvels. It also incorporates Gaufredian Matter of Britain material, opening with the defeat of Gogmagog.

This is the Anglo-Norman cluster of exile-and-return romances. As is well known, these romances continue into the Middle English period with extant versions of *Havelok*, *Horn*, *Bevis* and *Gui*, and probable lost versions of *Protheselaus*, *Waldef* and *Fouke Fitzwarin*. We could add new variants to this list, including *Gamelyn* and *Sir Orfeo*, which show modified treatment of the essential motifs.[18] The story of Tristan does not belong here despite its inclusion in Deutschbein's list. The Tristan story is a genuinely ancient one and as such resists the normalising tendencies of medieval romance in many ways. Just as it resists the courtliness and socially positive morality of most twelfth-century romance, so it resists the patterning of the standard exile-and-return narrative. Tristan is not a dispossessed heir, he is not concerned to equal or avenge his father. His movements are dictated by his role as a passionate lover and have little or no impact on the wider political scene; however, as a lover he surpasses the somewhat calculating affections of the standard exile-and-return hero. For Tristan, the personal is not political.

Exile-and-return would therefore seem to be a tale-type that achieves its

Insular Romance: Translation and Innovation, ed. Judith Weiss et al. (Cambridge, 2000), pp. 25–40.

[16] *Gui de Warewic: Roman du XIIIe siècle*, ed. A. Ewert (Paris, 1932–3).

[17] *Fouke le Fitz Waryn*, ed. E. J. Hathaway et al., ANTS 26–8 (Oxford, 1975–6), trans. Stephen Knight and Thomas H. Ohlgren in *Robin Hood and Other Outlaw Tales*, TEAMS Medieval Texts (Kalamazoo, 1997). The surviving prose version dates from the early fourteenth-century, but is based on a late thirteenth-century verse original. See Hathaway et al., Introduction, section 3.

[18] Since Gollancz's study in 1898, *Hamlet* has been recognised as drawing on this type. Act IV sets up an exercise in the tragic denial of expectations, with the heir's exile to and return from England. There is no welcoming party. The joining of the two kingdoms is left to his rival, Fortinbras.

classic form after the Conquest. *Beowulf* offers the example of another tale in which the hero leaves his homeland and returns to it, but there is no feeling of exile to Beowulf's voyaging, no triumphant return to challenge tyranny and no need to avenge the father. The potential for an exile-and-return narrative is there, but it remains unrealised. Furthermore, exile-and-return is inherently patriarchal, with a masculine protagonist and a narrative of inheritance, both personal and dynastic. It relies on an acceptance of primogeniture by which there can only be one true, preferably male, heir. This system became established in Norman England, but not in pre-Conquest England. The sort of confusion depicted in the various narratives of the Conquest, set up by the uncertainty over the inheritance of Edward the Confessor, makes for bad romance structure as well as disastrous political events.

In its fullest form, in the narratives of the twelfth and thirteenth centuries, exile-and-return encodes feudal ideology and shows the feudal system operating to the advantage of the aristocracy as much as the crown. The emotional relationship of father and son is displaced into territorial expression, for the relationship itself can only be glimpsed, if at all, in the initial moment of fortunate stasis before the father's death. The father–son relationship is not one of psychological depth and while the son must surpass the father, there is little sense of personal competitiveness.[19] However, the moment of recognition, when the son matures into the physical replica of his father, can be an important turning point in his relationship to his followers.[20] The returning heir makes gains, often beyond the competence of the father he follows. The experience of exile gains allies and often expands territory for the lost heir. The importance of friends in exile and allies on his return emphasises the interdependence of lord and follower. The situation flushes out opportunistic traitors, the Prince John type. It tests and confirms loyalties, both political and personal. The loyalty is of two layers – to the past, in that loyalty to the returning heir is in effect loyalty to the memory of his father, and trust in him for the sake of his father; and to the present in that the returning heir gathers around him a new generation of followers, and often a love, who follow him for his own sake and not for that of his father – so his return brings together past and present, two generations. It also measures the time between the first reign, that of the father, and the second, that of the restored son (using reign does not denote royalty) in such a way as to convey progression – more lands, increased contentment, enemies scattered, a political *felix culpa*. But it is not optimistic for long, and where it breaks down the departure from the norms established by the narrative type exposes the evident fickleness and power-abusing habits of tyrannical kings. Such kings are resisted, but there is

---

[19] A theme well known elsewhere in twelfth-century romance – e.g. Marie de France's *Milun*.

[20] It is important that others perceive the likeness. This differentiates the handling of this motif from the more individualistic, even oddly narcissistic, variant found in Disney versions of the lost heir, where the son looks in water and sees himself as his father (*Bambi, The Lion King*).

no easy guarantee of success – these romances are unexpectedly clear-sighted when it comes to the workings of power in feudal society.

The processes of exile and return from exile serve to objectify the land. The home territory, which is virtually invisible, worn like an old garment while the hero lives there, becomes something lost and viewed with longing and possessiveness, to be regained, and increasingly to be named. In this respect, the land is gendered feminine in relationship with the male protagonist, a relationship that mirrors, and even competes with, that with the heroine. An early expression of this is provided by Henry of Huntingdon's poetic dramatisation of the rescue of England by Henry II in 1153:

> 'Duke Henry, greatest descendent of great Henry, I am falling into ruin – I noble England am falling. . . . I would cry, 'Have mercy! Come, help, stop! Rightfully I belong to you, so you have the power, raise me from my fall. . . . He comes. Who? He who is the commander of commanders, a boy in years, an elder in mind. Hail jewel of manhood! . . .'
> 'Through bloodshed I seek peace for you, my dear foster-daughter for whom I have taken on such great dangers. May I gain possession of you only if, through me, you gain peace. If not, may I die, rather than see you dying.'[21]

It can further be seen that this is a triangular narrative, not a simple opposition between protagonist and antagonist. The important third party without whom the narrative is incomplete is the 'welcoming party', sometimes one representative individual (Hardré, Sigar/Ubbe, Saboath), then a group of supporters. This draws attention to the mutuality of king and subjects and to the dependence of king or lord on loyalty. We can see this working in the later Middle English rehandling of the Orfeo story. In *Sir Orfeo* the exile is self-imposed and the crisis is deeply personal, but is reiterated in the theme of loyalty and of the welcoming party. The forest of exile, the disguise of the hero, the rescue of the beloved all lead inevitably to the triumphant reception by the loyal followers and the implied ritual of resuming the crown – bathing, reclothing and processing.

So a successful exile-and-return requires allies, the political will to return to rightful rule, respect for the memory of the father and recognition of the claims of the son – who in turn must recognise the rights of his people. Returning or restored kings-to-be are greeted with hope for the overturning of misrule. But it can also be noticed that exile-and-return nearly always implies a potential challenge to the king. The false king, the usurper or the king who confiscates the hero's lands, is characterised by criminality, illegality, in short, tyranny. The contrast between the false and true kings is demonstrated,

---

21 Henry of Huntingdon, *The History of the English People 1000–1154*, trans. Diana Greenway (Oxford, 2002), p. 89. Greenway points out Henry's debt to Lucan, *Civil War* I, 210–21, where Caesar encounters the female spectre of Rome, although the comparison shows that Henry's treatment of the scene is more positive and contains the potential romance themes of rescue and an emotional relationship.

not by arguments about hereditary right, but by the state of the kingdom, the upholding of laws, the opinions of good and honest men. The community of the realm claims its place as an active agent in the drama of succession.

From *Boeve* onwards the lands to be restored are as likely to be baronial fiefdoms as kingdoms, as the type explores the conflict between the crown and individual lords, a conflict that often involves the entire kingdom in its resolution. To some extent geography provides a marker for this; exile-and-return across the sea leads to the restoration of a kingdom, but where the action concerns the patrimony of an individual lord or landowner it is land-locked, and the exile is to the forest – giving the romance of the outlaw, as in *Fouke Fitzwarin, Gamelyn* and so on into the Robin Hood tradition. The sea and the forest are equivalent symbols for separation, chance and danger, but only the sea encompasses an island kingdom. The status is different, but the issues are similar – law, justice, good rule. Even where the patrimony is some-thing smaller than the kingdom and the primary adversary is the usurping brother, the rule of the forest stands metonymically for the rule of the kingdom and the quality of the king's rule is under scrutiny.

This narrative type reconfigures the relationship of the king to the land – it is being returned to its rightful owner, not given as a gift. It articulates a chal-lenge to the feudal claims of monarchy to be the fount of land and honour, a live issue in the political scene during the reign of Henry II.[22] The choice of the legendary geography of pre-Conquest England as the locus of action for many of these romances neatly conflates the narrative preference for kingship with the smaller units of actual aristocratic inheritance. The kingdoms of 'Suddene' or Lindsay merge easily with the concept of later counties – as various descriptions of England make clear.[23] Boeve's son is to inherit England and Gui will fight for England against the heathen, but it is not until the Middle English *Havelok the Dane* and more surprisingly, the Auchinleck *Sir Orfeo*, that we find heroes claiming the English throne.

We are left with the question of why there should be such an enthusiasm for this tale-type from the mid-twelfth-century onwards. Some of this may be based on the legendary constructions of insular history, according to which lands are always regained, never conquered. As G. A. Loud has shown, the Normans saw themselves as part of the Trojan diaspora: 'The legend of Norman descent, via the Danes and Dacians, from the Trojans, promulgated by Dudo, copied by William of Jumièges [was] accepted to a greater or lesser extent by their successors.'[24] John Niles has recently shown that in the *Historia* Geoffrey of Monmouth used the prophecies of Merlin to adumbrate

---

[22] See M. T. Clanchy, *England and Its Rulers 1066–1272* (London, 1983), pp. 120–3.
[23] A. Bell, 'The Anglo-Norman *Description of Britain*: An Edition', *Anglo-Norman Anniversary Essays*, ed. Ian Short, ANTS Occasional Publications Series 2 (London, 1993), pp. 31–48.
[24] G. A. Loud, 'The Gens Normannorum – myth or reality?' in *Proceedings of the Battle Conference 1981, Anglo-Norman Studies IV*, ed. R. Allen Brown (Woodbridge, 1982), pp. 104–16 (p. 113).

the Norman Conquest as restoring the land to its rightful owners, the British and by extension the Normans, after the misrule of the usurping English:

> Eventually a new race of people will take control of the land and will restore dwellings to their former owners. . . . This island shall be called by the name of Brutus, and the title given to it by the foreigners shall be done away with. . . .[25]

So not only the Britons but also apparently the Normans can claim to be returning to their lands, not conquering them. Such a perception of the legendary foundation of Britain may have inspired the curious feature of the Anglo-Norman romances that occlude possession of lands by conquest, so that the Norman Conquest and its associated land-grab is metamorphosed into a return, and acquires the accompanying theme of providentially inspired restoration. Thus for the mid-twelfth century, the exile-and-return narrative establishes a strong claim to ownership by which land can be claimed without dissent, although not, as we have seen, without negotiation.

The initial impulse may well have arisen from a more pressing sense of current events. The loss of the White Ship in 1120 saw the death by drowning of Henry I's only legitimate son, and the body was never recovered.[26] It was a death that rendered inevitable the civil war between Stephen and Matilda, and may have given rise to the compensatory fantasy that the heir might return from the sea and save the land from misrule. It is noticeable that, with the exception of *Horn*, the enemy in exile-and-return narrative is domestic not foreign, the threat to the kingdom is treachery not invasion, those to be defeated are similar not alien. Like the Matter of Britain, with its roots in Geoffrey's 1136 *Historia Regum Britanniae,* these romances deal with the dangers of civil war.[27]

The exception to the rule of the male protagonist is of course the Argentille/England strand in the double lost-heir structure of the Havelok story. This produces interesting variants, going beyond repetition to examine the different circumstances applying to a female heir. Most discussions of the Havelok story are concerned with the later Middle English *Lay of Havelok the Dane*[28] and its thirteenth-century context. However, if we are considering the tale as it occurs in Gaimar's *Estoire* written in the 1130s or even in the *Lai,* dating from the late twelfth century, the pertinency of the question of female inheritance becomes clearer.[29] Neither Gaimar nor the *Lai* give us a totally passive heroine – Argentille is certainly more intelligent than Havelok and a

25 John D. Niles, 'The Wasteland of Loegria: Geoffrey of Monmouth's Reinvention of the Anglo-Saxon Past', *Reinventing the Middle Ages and the Renaissance*, ed. William F. Gentrup, Arizona Studies in the Middle Ages and the Renaissance, 1 (Turnhout, 1998), pp. 1–18 (p. 12).

26 William of Malmesbury, *History of the Norman Kings*, vol. 3, 1120.

27 I develop these ideas further in 'Children of Anarchy' in the forthcoming collection of essays, *Writers of the Reign of Henry II*, ed. Ruth Kennedy and Simon Meecham-Jones.

28 *Havelok the Dane*, ed. G. V. Smithers (Oxford, 1987).

29 Between 1135 and 1189 all rulers of England were either female (Matilda) or ruled by claims through the female line (Stephen, Henry II).

more active agent in the narrative; she makes things happen, he is the one who responds to events. However, she does need to be rescued and can only be rescued by a providential marriage. The returning heir is treated very differently according to gender. For Havelok the key is his resemblance to his father and the discovery of allies among the remnant of his father's followers, helped by some marvellous pointers to his true identity. When Argentille returns to England, there is no doubt of her identity, but because she cannot resemble her father there is no climactic drama of recognition. Her rights have to be fought for and negotiated. This difference is effectively developed by the Middle English adaptor who uses it to examine the workings of law and good rule in England. The presence of a female heir moves the emphasis from simple success in battle to success through negotiation.

So exile-and-return is a tale-type by which the rightful heir comes into his own, tyranny is identified and overthrown, and the community of the realm claims its place as an active agent in the drama of succession. And it is an insular tale-type – the setting of kingdoms separated by water, with the sudden appearance of the heir on the shore, is deeply ingrained, not superficial.[30] Typically the action moves freely around the littoral lands bordering the North and Irish seas or the Channel. By contrast we can perhaps see the continental and republican version as being exemplified by Cincinnatus, the legendary Roman awaiting the call of his country's need in his country estate.[31]

For an English or British audience of any date the island kingdom is not a fictional construct, and tension between good rule and tyranny is a constant. So this narrative provides a stereotype that governs the interpretation of historical events. From Henry II and Richard I to Bolingbroke and on to both Charles Stuarts, it provides a framework by which history is mythologised. The secret Jacobites whose coded toast gives me my title were drawing on well-established insular tradition.[32]

In the late twelfth century, the historical scene provides its own version as we saw earlier, in the return of Richard I from exile in the Emperor's prison. We can recognise the additional and expected ingredients: the welcoming party is very important here, the loyal barons of England led by William

---

30 The persistence of the King over the Water type in traditional narrative is rather oddly exemplified in J. R. R. Tolkien's *Lord of the Rings*. In the third volume, entitled *The Return of the King*, the climax of the heroic thread of the narrative is reached with the return of the exiled Aragorn to his rightful place as king of Gondor. To achieve this the narrative leads him by some very contrived journeying to an otherwise unremarked river and the seizure of ships from a previously unmentioned tribe so that he can make a triumphal entry on to the battlefield by water; 'Thus came Aragorn son of Arathorn, . . . borne upon a wind from the Sea to the kingdom of Gondor', *The Return of the King* (London, 1955), p. 123. It would seem that Tolkien, always alert to the patterns of traditional narrative, has manipulated his material to make Aragorn return across the water.

31 The parallel has been drawn with the recall of Charles de Gaulle from retirement in Columbey les Deux Eglises to lead the Republic of France in 1958.

32 See Sir Walter Scott, *Redgauntlet*, Letter V: 'My father . . . so far compromised his loyalty as to announce merely "The King," as his first toast after dinner, instead of the emphatic "King George". . . . Our guest made a motion with his glass, so as to pass it over the water-decanter which stood beside him, and added, "Over the water".'

Marshal, the supporter of his late father, and his mother, Eleanor of Aquitaine. Both were figures who remained loyal through the long years of exile, like Hardré and Queen Samburc in the version of *Horn* that may have been performed for the court of Henry II.[33] The rituals of reconsecration and the return of legitimate justice follow on smoothly. It is a measure of the legendary force of the narrative that there remains little realisation of the fact that Richard chose to leave the country, finally, two months later and the villain of the piece became his only heir.

Two hundred years later, in 1399, the events of Bolingbroke's quarrel with Richard II follow a familiar pattern of feudal disruption. Disinherited by the king on his father's death (with the implied insult to his father, the king's uncle), Bolingbroke's exile at a powerful foreign court and his return to the coast of England, moving inland and gathering allies – all suggest that Richard, apparently an enthusiastic reader of Arthurian romance,[34] would have been advised to turn the leaf and read another tale, one from the insular *exempla* of challenges to tyrannical kings. Bolingbroke found his welcoming party among his own followers and those of his father, and in gaining the throne both justified and exceeded his father's reputation. Chaucer is our witness that contemporaries perceived the legendary link with legalistic precision:

> O Conquerour of Brutes Albyon,
> Which that by lyne and free eleccion
> Been verray kyng. . . .[35]

Later writers were to make use of the implications of the tale. Helen Cooper has shown how Elizabeth I was foreshadowed in the figure of Argentile in William Warner's version of the Havelok story, *Albions England*.[36] In *Cymbeline* Shakespeare rewrites his source to have the Romans land at Milford Haven in a clear reference to Henry Tudor.[37] Dynastic change, restoration, challenges to the throne throughout English[38] history have been perceived or enacted according to this pattern.

This suggests that the Anglo-Norman romance of the twelfth and early thirteenth centuries saw the formulation of the classic form of the exile-and-

---

[33] See Judith Weiss, 'Thomas and the Earl: Literary and Historical Contexts for the *Romance of Horn*', *Tradition and Transformation in Medieval Romance*, ed. Rosalind Field (Cambridge, 1999), pp. 1–14.
[34] Edith Rickert, 'Richard II's Books', *The Library*, 4th series, 13 (1933).
[35] Geoffrey Chaucer, 'To His Purse', ll. 22–4, *The Riverside Chaucer*, ed. Larry D. Benson (Oxford, 1988).
[36] Helen Cooper, 'The Elizabethan Havelok', *Medieval Insular Romance*, ed. Judith Weiss, Jennifer Fellows and Morgan Dickson (Cambridge, 2000), pp. 169–83.
[37] I am indebted to Helen Cooper for drawing my attention to this. It has since been discussed by Gary Taylor in his analysis of the construction of British history in *Cymbeline*: 'Made in Rome', *The Guardian*, 30.07.03 (G2, pp. 10–11).
[38] English, as distinct from British, for reasons of geography and of traditional literary constructions. For a recent discussion of the geographical identity of the Matter of Britain, see Michelle Warren, *History on the Edge* (Minneapolis, 2000).

return narrative. It is a narrative repeated and reworked, less because of a nostalgia for earlier narrative than for its chiming with contemporary concerns and the perception of the same motif in the English political scene from Henry II to Henry IV and beyond.

The classic narrative structure shows an insular tale-type, set in kingdoms separated by water and with the return of the heir encoding specifically feudal ideas of mutual dependency between king and supporters. It is a tale-type with a strong sense of time and place, of the objectified land and of social loyalty. In constructing a political norm it provides a means for identifying and challenging tyranny.

It is best understood not as an essentialist folk tale, but as a specific political myth, capable of renewal and reapplication and moving between literature and the ritualised perception of political actuality. Once the pattern is familiar it reappears on the political scene every time the rulers of England look over their shoulders at the challenger landing on the shore.

5

Ineffectual Monarchs:
Portrayals of Regal and Imperial power in
Ipomedon, Robert le Diable and *Octavian*

JUDITH WEISS

In a recent article I ventured some ideas about the divergent views of emperors encountered in Anglo-Norman chronicle and romance. Looking at both Arthurian and non-Arthurian narrative from the twelfth to the mid-thirteenth century, I was struck by the depiction of emperors as the scourges, or alternatively, as the saviours, of humanity, very wicked on the one hand, very good on the other. I made some connections between these portrayals and historical events, and also linked them to pro- and anti-imperial propaganda. Finally I looked at thirteenth-century romances where emperors were no longer powerful but increasingly powerless, reliant on the help of heroes, and I tentatively connected this to the waning of imperial power that is a feature of the period.[1]

This ineffectuality of the monarch – I use the term 'monarch' because in romance the distinction between an emperor and a top-ranking king is slight[2] and the terms are used interchangeably – is what I now would like to pursue further, in three romances that express three differing reactions to regal and imperial power, but which all depict it as shown up or sidelined by a hero. This seems to become a *topos* in romance from the 1170s onwards – though it has perhaps already been anticipated by a few *chansons de geste* in the *Guillaume* cycle. To some extent too, it is a recurrent motif in popular story, perhaps first appearing in the Bible via the story of Saul and David.

Two of my texts are from the twelfth century, one from the thirteenth. Two seem rather neglected by critics, while one has received plenty of attention. This last is Anglo-Norman: Hue de Rotelande's *Ipomedon*, c.1180. The other two, strictly speaking, are Continental French: *Robert le Diable*, late twelfth

---

1   Judith Weiss, 'Emperors and Antichrists: Reflections of Empire in Insular Narrative, 1130–1250', *The Matter of Identity in Medieval Romance*, ed. Phillipa Hardman (Cambridge, 2002), pp. 87–102.
2   Alexander is called by both terms in Thomas of Kent's *Roman de Toute Chevalerie*.

century, and *Octavian*, thirteenth century.[3] It is of course difficult, even absurd, to try to keep insular and Continental romances in mutually exclusive boxes. Robert's story starts in Normandy, at a date when that duchy belonged to the Plantagenets, and its protagonist is heir to the duke, with a name borne by several Norman dukes, including the father to William the Conqueror. It is a story that was popular in England, since it appears in two later English versions, *Sir Gowther* and (more remotely) *Roberd of Cisyle. Octavian* was also popular with insular audiences since it gave rise to the two English *Octavians*; its original Picard version was copied by one or more Anglo-Norman scribes. One of these copies seems early on to have belonged to a priory in Dover.[4] These romances, like most romances, travelled between England and France, becoming everyone's property; it is only for our convenience that we allocate them firmly to one country rather than another.

These three texts are very different, but they are also connected to each other in ways that will become clear, and which their plot summaries show. They illustrate perfectly that intertextuality so characteristic of romance from its inception, in that they share narrative motifs and vary them according to their own agendas.

If, as I have postulated, the inert or ineffectual monarch becomes a recurrent topos in narrative from the mid twelfth century, this is perhaps surprising, since from 1154 to 1223 the Western European stage was dominated by a number of powerful rulers who took care to enhance their power by some impressive propaganda. It is simplistic to assume, of course, that literature responds directly or even contemporaneously to the events of history. Nevertheless I think it does respond, often through utilising age-old story-patterns. One of my texts – *Octavian* – I fancy responds to some thirteenth-century events and concerns. The other two are rather more complicated in their reactions.

The monarchs I have mentioned are Henry II of England (1154–91), Philip Augustus of France (1179–1223) and the Holy Roman Emperor Frederick Barbarossa (1152–91). Their reigns overlap. They were certainly competitive with each other, and their countries were vying for top international status before their reigns even began. German rulers, from the Ottonian emperors on, tried to assume the mantle of imperial greatness from Charlemagne and constantly boosted the image of the Holy Roman Emperor by associating him both with Charles and with the legend of the Last World Emperor, who would save the world just before the advent of the Antichrist. French rulers made

---

[3] Hue de Rotelande, *Ipomedon*, ed. A. J. Holden (Paris, 1979); *Octavian*, ed. Karl Vollmöller (Heilbronn, 1880); *Robert Le Diable*, ed. E. Löseth (Paris, 1903). Gaston Paris disagreed with the reasons Vollmöller gave for dating *Octavian* to 1229–44 and thought it later; he believed there was a twelfth-century French original (Gaston Paris, *Romania* 11 (1882), pp. 609–14). But there are perhaps grounds for dating it to the early thirteenth century: see below, n. 18.

[4] *Octavian Imperator*, ed. Frances McSparran (Heidelberg, 1979), p. 28; Gaston Paris, review of Vollmöller's edition of *Octavian, Romania* 11 (1882), pp. 609–14; K. V. Sinclair, 'Evidence for a lost Anglo-Norman copy of *Octavian*', *Neuphilologische Mitteilungen* 79 (1978), pp. 216–18.

sure the memory of Charlemagne was kept alive, especially as ancestor to the Capetian kings, and associated him too with the Last World Emperor; the latter's journey to Jerusalem was imitated in Charlemagne literature. Britain was the birthplace of the legend of King Arthur, deliberately, in Geoffrey's *Historia Regum Britanniae*, made the grandson to a Constantine (thereby evoking Constantine the Great) and an equal to Charlemagne, with characteristics of the Last World Emperor. Rulers in all three countries were also intent on appropriating aspects of classical Roman emperors, especially the one who above all was linked both to power and to spirituality: Augustus Caesar, whose original name was Octavius. Through the Church's interpretation of Virgil's fourth Eclogue, Augustus was favourably depicted in that his reign saw the birth of Christ, and a long-established legend portrayed him as receiving a vision of this birth through the agency of the Tiburtine Sibyl. Henry I, Frederick Barbarossa and Philip all called themselves 'Augustus', while Henry II, calling himself 'fitzempress', claimed imperial grandeur through his mother Matilda, the *imperatrix augusta*.[5]

The propaganda for imperial and other similarly powerful rulers in the twelfth and thirteenth centuries is thus substantial. We can bear this in mind when looking at the earliest of my three romances to depict a ruler as ineffectual. *Ipomedon*, one of two poems by Hue de Rotelande, who lived near Hereford and was an older contemporary of Chrétien, is a highly sophisticated work: Hue was apparently very familiar with both insular and continental romance. A summary of its plot is below; what I want to examine in detail is an episode from it that is reminiscent of a recurrent scene in Arthurian narrative.

Ipomedon, son of the king of Apulia, hears about the beautiful La Fiere, queen of Calabria and niece of Meleager, king of Sicily, and decides to visit her court incognito. Here La Fiere falls in love with him and he with her; nevertheless he conceals his true valour in favour of his skills as huntsman. He quits the court in order to gain renown through prowess elsewhere, while La Fiere is urged by her barons to marry. She gets her uncle to proclaim a three-day tournament whose victor she promises to wed. Ipomedon, hearing this, anonymously offers his services to Meleager on condition he can serve the queen, be entitled her 'dru' (lover) and kiss her twice daily. Again Ipomedon devotes himself to hunting, to the despair of those who love him, such as the queen and Capaneus. However, come the tournament, he participates successfully in it each day, under different colours, while in the

---

5   Weiss, 'Emperors and Antichrists', pp. 91–4; Gabrielle M. Spiegel, '*The Reditus Regni ad Stirpem Karoli Magni*: A New Look', *French Historical Studies* 7 (1971), pp. 145–74 (pp. 158–160); Gerhard Rauschen (ed.), *Die Legende Karls des Grossen im 11.und 12. Jahrhundert* (Leipzig, 1890), pp. 97–100, 142–3; Robert Folz, *Le Souvenir et la Légende de Charlemagne* (Paris, 1950); Dominique Boutet, *Charlemagne et Arthur* (Paris, 1992), pp. 469–71; K. H. Leyser, *Medieval Germany and its Neighbours, 900–1250* (London, 1982), pp. 197–200. For an early fifteenth century depiction of Augustus hearing of Christ's birth from the Sibyl, see the Limbourg brothers' *Très Riches Heures* for Jean, Duc de Berry, fol. 22r.

evening still playing the buffoon at court. At the end, he leaves without claiming La Fiere's hand. His father has meanwhile died, but Ipomedon refuses to be crowned and embarks on new adventures. Then he learns that La Fiere is being forcibly courted by a princely pagan giant, Leonin, and needs a champion to defend her. Returning to Meleager's court, he gets the king to promise he may undertake the next adventure to come along, and when La Fiere's confidante arrives asking for help for her mistress, he volunteers while the rest of the court remains silent. He follows her, despite her jeers and insults, and defends her from attacks, which finally wins her over. Defeating La Fiere's suitor, he nevertheless pretends to be Leonin, and victorious, which drives La Fiere to despair; she proposes to go into exile. The two lovers are only united through the efforts of Capaneus, who also turns out to be Ipomedon's long-lost half-brother. Wedding and coronation follow.

When Ipomedon enters the hall of Meleager as La Fiere's champion, he is disguised as a fool, shaven and tonsured, with rusty sword and dirty armour, and on a lame nag. The king's best knight, Capaneus, is away. To universal derision, the fool asks the king to retain him. At this juncture La Fiere's confidante, Ismeine, arrives at court. To her astonishment, neither the king nor his knights respond to her request:

> 'Vus estes del mund sire e reis,
> Li plus hauz e li plus curteis,
> Li plus pöestis, li plus fers,
> E plus avez bons chevaliers
> Ke nuls reis ke or seit en vie;
> El ne savreit ou quere aïe
> Se ele endreit vus devreit faillir.
> Reis, sucurrez la de murir!'
> Li reis entendi sa resun,
> Esgarde envirun sa meisun
> E n'ot nul d'eus un sol mot dire,
> En pes se set, pense e suspire,
> E la pucele le hasta
> E piteusement demanda:
> 'Sire, ne avrai autre respuns
> Ne de vus ne de voz baruns?
> Tant en vei de bons chevalers
> E ja est si granz li mesters;
> J'irray saunz respunce issy?'
> En pes sunt, nul ne respundi.   (*Ipomedon*, 8027–46)

['You're lord and king of the world, the highest and most courteous, the most powerful, the strongest, and you have more good knights than any king now alive. She would not know where else to seek help if she were to fail to get it from you. King, help her avoid death!' The king heard what she said, looks around his hall and does not hear anyone say a single word; he sits motionless, sighing and thoughtful, and the girl pressed him hard and pitifully asked: 'Lord, shan't I get any other reply from either you or your barons? I see so many good knights, and the need is so great – shall I depart in this way, without a reply?' They sit quiet, not one replied.]

Only the fool takes up the challenge. Ismeine rejects him and has a contemptuous final word for Meleager as she sweeps out:

> . . . Jo m'en irrai,
> De mut feble sucurs ai;
> Mut m'esmervail de ceste curt . . .
> Vois m'en quant vostre curt me faut.   (8075–7, 8092)

[I'm going; very feeble help I've got from you. I'm astonished at this court . . . I'm going, since your court has let me down]

The elements of one of the early scenes in Chretien's later *Conte del Graal* (between 1181 and 1191) are already anticipated here. Though Hue de Rotelande, by locating his romance a long way from Britain and in a pagan world, and by adopting the names from the *romans antiques* for his characters, is ostensibly distancing himself from Arthurian story, he is actually displaying how brilliantly he can handle what is obviously becoming a stock Arthurian motif: Arthur the inert and fallible king, the *roi fainéant* whose lassitude has infected all his court, so that neither he nor they can respond to a challenger. Chrétien's previous Arthurian romances, *Yvain* and *Le Chevalier de la Charrette* (between 1177 and 1181) were working towards this picture of regal decadence; Hue may have taken the hint from them. From the start of his romance he has depicted Meleager as, in Holden's words, 'the venerable king, arbiter of proprieties and fountain of wisdom, brave and energetic in theory',[6] with a valiant nephew, Capaneus (clearly the Gawain figure), and a boastful, rude steward, Caemius, whose name sounds like Kay: the Arthurian pastiche is clear. But he has also teasingly insinuated that the old king with a young wife may be impotent – is that not one reason for Ipomedon's 'job' as *dru la reine*? – and in a three-day tournament, has portrayed him as trounced and in flight (6285–6).

The non-Arthurian body of material expertly exploited by Hue for this episode is the Tristan story, notably that portion of it (as in the *Folies Tristan*) that deals with Tristan's disguise as a fool or madman when he returns to king Mark's court to see Iseut. Both *Ipomedon* and the *Folies Tristan* play with the paradox of the wise fool, who speaks the truth while derided and maltreated by king and court, thus exposing the actual folly of those who think themselves wise. Similar ideas are, once again, contained in Chretien's *Conte del Graal*.[7]

---

6 *Ipomedon*, ed. Holden, p. 52.
7 Holden has noted the 'Arthurian model' and the influence of the *Folies Tristan*, p. 51.

Hue's romances have a strongly ironic tone, which on occasion descends to the comic, even the obscene; his handling of popular romance topics seems primarily intended to make us laugh. His sophisticated version of the theme of the ineffectual monarch is a humorous response to the creation, earlier in the century, by Geoffrey of Monmouth and Wace of the all-conquering Arthur, rival and potential successor to the Roman emperor, and in particular to the scene where Arthur receives the Roman ambassadors, takes counsel, and provides an articulate and energetic reply. But here Meleager has no reliable counsellors; the only one who might have corrected him – Capaneus – is away. By his silence, he allows the coercive behaviour of Leonin free rein.

My second romance is *Robert le Diable*, written perhaps a few years later. Whereas *Ipomedon* was deliberately secular (and deliberately resistant to profound interpretation), *Robert* is from the start structured to show us the deficiencies of worldly achievement and the superiority of divine power. Robert turns out to be a rapist, arsonist and murderer because his mother, frustrated by God's apparent inability to give her a child, accuses Him of possessing no power, and prays to the Devil instead. The conclusion of the romance shows us where true power lies, through Robert, the 'chevalier Jesu Christ' and ultimate saint – and also the only character to possess a name.

> The duke of Normandy and his wife are childless despite their prayers. She dares to pray to the devil instead, whereupon pregnancy ensues. After a turbulent youth, Robert inspires so much fear that he finally begins to wonder about the source of the anger which drives his crimes, and questions his mother. He is determined to serve God and expiate his crimes, so journeys to Rome. Here the Pope directs him to a hermit in a forest, who receives divine guidance on what penitence Robert should undergo in order to be absolved. He must behave like a dumb madman or fool, eat only the leavings of dogs, and incite the populace to attack him every day. Pursued by the crowd, Robert takes refuge in the emperor's court, but he will eat nothing that is not given to the dogs and lies on straw next to them. The emperor is under siege from his powerful seneschal, who wants to marry the beautiful but mute princess. The Turks learn of the emperor's straits, and invade. Robert prays to God for help. A white knight, divine messenger, appears to offer Robert his armour and horse. He routs the Turks and returns to resume his ragged clothes. The princess has seen and understood what he has done and at a great feast vainly tries to indicate to her father that Robert is their saviour. She is rebuked and derided, while Robert's antics with the dogs attract universal hilarity. The Turks attack twice more but Robert continues victorious; the emperor offers to reward anyone who can produce the white knight. After the third attack, an ambush is set by the emperor for Robert as he returns, and he is wounded in the thigh by a knight anxious for the reward. He nevertheless escapes and takes his usual place in court. The emperor proclaims that he will give his daughter to the white knight. The seneschal pretends to be him, wounding himself to support his claim. The distraught princess suddenly finds the power of speech and reveals this act of treachery.

Robert is sent for but remains mute. Only the hermit can persuade him to speak. Four Norman barons appear to tell him his father has died and implore him to return to govern his lands, but he rejects their offers, like those of the emperor, only asking to be carried to the hermit's hut. Accompanied by all Rome, he retires there and ultimately succeeds the hermit, dying in the odour of sanctity. Buried in Rome, the body is stolen by a wealthy man from Le Puy who reinters it there in an abbey.

The heart of the romance lies in Rome, seen as both seat of the Empire and of the Christian church: the Pope is – literally – hand in hand with the emperor on all occasions of note (1600–1). When Robert, stricken with remorse, makes his way to Rome, he encounters an emperor with good intentions and reactions: he is a kindly man who takes the beleaguered fool under his protection and is concerned for his welfare. But like Meleager in *Ipomedon*, he is totally taken in by the hero's disguise, so finds his voluntary degradation to the level of the palace dogs merely amusing, as does the whole court (1366–9, 1378–84). Here again we can see similarities with the scene from *Ipomedon*, in the play on madness versus wisdom, and truth rejected as folly, but the themes are treated in a more serious manner. There are two apparent fools in *Robert le Diable*, both mute, whether voluntarily or involuntarily: the hero himself, and the emperor's daughter, and their parallel situations are frequently noted. Towards both the emperor is depicted as inadequate, unable to see truths beneath surfaces or believe them when under his nose, and though in charge of the whole Christian world (for Rome is its head) he is helpless.

The emperor has an insubordinate seneschal who desires the princess and besieges Rome because he can't get her. As a result, both emperor and people are confined to the city, powerless, and the news of Rome's decline spreads throughout the world, attracting three attacks from the Turks.

> Les nouvelles mout loing en vont;
> Il n'a contrée en tout le mont
> C'on ne parot de cheste guerre
> *[missing line]*
> Et c'on n'en sache la novele,
> Que Rome plus ne se revele,
> Et qu'ele est si fort abaissie
> Et si vencue et si plaissie
> Que Romain sont mis en prison,
> En Rome a poi de garison,
> Et qu'il n'ont mais qu'a deus ans vivre.   (*Robert*, 1427–37)

[The news travels far and wide; there's no land in the whole world where this war is not talked of and where it's not known that Rome no longer makes merry, and that she is brought so low and is so defeated and tamed that Romans are as if in prison, there's no safety in Rome, and they've only got two years to live.]

Here is another reminiscence of *Ipomedon*: there, the three-day tournament gave the hero, disguised successively as a white, red and black knight, the opportunity to distinguish himself. Here, in Rome, the weeping emperor and his troops are only saved from annihilation by Robert, disguised as a white knight for all the attacks, and as determined as Ipomedon not to be discovered.[8]

Here it is not that the emperor has no counsellors: rather he chooses to believe the wrong ones. Three times his daughter points out the fool as the saviour of Rome; three times, ashamed and embarrassed by what he sees as her madness, he refuses to believe her. Even more humiliatingly, he is lied to by a knight who owes him the truth, and duped by his former counsellor, the seneschal, pretending to be the recent scourge of the Turks. It is only at this point that the princess, in danger of being forcibly married to a fraud, miraculously regains her speech: she, a wise fool (2898), publicly reveals the *chevaliers preus et sages*, whom the Turks believed to be St George himself.

The weak and foolish emperor was on the point of becoming a tyrant. But he does at least finally make a sensible gesture: recognising that real power lies with the humble and weak, he offers to unite the princess and Robert, and give them his empire. But Robert refuses. Even when invited to return home, he chooses paradise over his duchy (4939) and the safety of his 'wretched soul' (4936) over the pomp of the world (4979–86). He follows his hermit-counsellor back to the forest, replaces him when he dies, and is recognised at his own demise as a miracle-working saint.

In this self-abnegation and denial of power, Robert paradoxically achieves it – as earlier, his surrender of human behaviour and expectations in order to live like a dog had empowered, not weakened, him. We are reminded of slightly later heroes, in *Waldef* and *Gui de Warewic*, who abjure fame, possessions and family in favour of a severely ascetic life. The emperor and his empire (along with his companion the Pope) are portrayed as ineffectual if well-meaning. It is an orthodox religious view of the vanity of worldly dominion and one not confined to the late twelfth century when *Robert* was written.[9]

But the romance has a sprightly, even anti-climactic, coda. After telling us of Robert's death, and burial in Rome, the author relates the theft of his remains by a 'riches hom' from Le Puy en Velay. The saintly body, transported to its new provincial home, a specially constructed 'abbey of St Robert', continues to be no less efficacious than in Rome. It is hard not to see in this a final thumbing of the nose to the greatest powers in Christendom.[10]

---

8   This is not to imply any direct influence: as Holden (p. 46) points out, the motif of the three-day tournament is popular in the folklore of many lands, as well as receiving several literary treatments.

9   See Georges Duby, *The Early Growth of the European Economy: Warriors and Peasants from the 7th–12th Century*, trans. Howard B. Clarke (London, 1974), p. 259.

10   It is also a fictitious account of a common occurrence, i.e. the theft of relics and their removal to a new location in order to give it the protection of the saint, an increased sense of identity, and

If, in *Robert*, only the hero-saint was significant enough to merit a name, in *Octavian*, my last text, most characters are named and many of those names have important connotations. The romance bears a title, in red, at the beginning and repeated at the end, which tells us it is about *Otheuiens empereor de Rome*. This spelling reminds us both of Octavian, alias Augustus, formerly Octavius, and of the Ottonian emperors: Ottos I, II and III, who took care to associate themselves with their famous classical predecessors by entitling themselves *romanorum imperator augustus*.[11] The 'Otheuien' of the romance thus has a lot to live up to. But just like the emperor in *Robert*, though loving and sensitive, he is also misled and deceived, preferring his mother's wicked counsel to that of his sensible subjects.

The romance starts with the coronation of Dagobert in Rheims and then moves to Otheuien, the childless emperor of Rome, and his wife. When twins finally arrive, the empress is accused by her wicked mother-in-law of adultery, and exiled. One of her boys, Florent, is stolen en route to Jerusalem, and ends up bought by Climent, on pilgrimage to Syria. Climent and his wife bring up their foster-son in Paris hoping he will become an apprentice to a butcher and learn about money, but his preference for hawks and horses reveals his birth. Meanwhile, Saracens (Turks) arrive, headed by the Soudan and his beautiful daughter, Marsabille. Dagobert summons his allies including Otheuien, who relates his sad family history. The Saracen king of the giants proposes a fight for the love of Marsabille; all others declining, Florent volunteers. He wins the contest, and the girl's love, and presents the giant's head to Dagobert, who knights him. Climent attacks the minstrels at the dubbing feast and takes the knights' cloaks as insurance that they will foot the bill, not him. His knowledge of the Saracen language enables him to penetrate the pagan camp and snatch the Soudan's marvellous horse, which he presents to Dagobert. Florent has meanwhile abducted Marsabille, then rushes to the aid of Otheuien, overpowered by Saracens; they are captured, but the day is saved by St George. The empress, in Jerusalem, is questioned about her identity; the king of Acre offers to send her, her son the younger Otheuien and a body of knights to France in order to secure a reunion. En route they encounter the fleeing Saracen army and Otheuien captures the Soudan, who promises to convert. He is presented to

greater economic vitality. Apparently by the eleventh and twelfth centuries, the vogue in France for stealing Roman martyrs had declined in favour of the remains of Frankish saints. See Patrick J. Geary, *Furta Sacra: Thefts of Relics in the Central Middle Ages* (Princeton, 1990), pp. 19, 77. Why the romance should promote Le Puy en Velay is not clear. It was the greatest Marian shrine of the period and a major cult centre, so an essential stop on the pilgrimage route to Compostela. The Polignac family were the vicomtes of Velay; their lands were contiguous to Le Puy and they made gifts to the churches there. But since the MSS and original author of *Robert* are all assigned to north or north-eastern France, the Polignacs cannot be its patrons. See Christian Lauranson-Rosaz, *L'Auvergne et ses Marges (Velay, Gévaudan) du VIIIe au XIe Siècle* (Le Puy-en-Velay, 1987), pp. 107, 129; Löseth, *Robert Le Diable*, pp. xlvi–xlvii. I am indebted to Prof. Jonathan Riley-Smith for his help on this subject.

11 Timothy Reuter, *Germany in the Early Middle Ages* (London, 1991), pp. 177, 274; Boyd H. Hill, *Medieval Monarchy in Action: The German Empire from Henry I to Henry IV* (London, 1972), p. 51.

Dagobert and baptised. The emperor's family is reunited, and together with Climent returns to Rome.

The emperor, whose foolish actions set the plot going, is in fact put in the shade by three other characters. The first of these shares the honours of the romance's final title: '*ici finist le romance de Otheuiens empereor de Rome et le roi Dagonbert de France*'. Unlike the English *Octavian*, the French one starts with Dagobert, portrayed as an efficient ruler and as the pious founder of the abbey of St Denis (19–20), something that was early on incorrectly attributed to the seventh-century Dagobert: the name and deeds (accruing down the centuries) of this monarch were constantly invoked for the purposes of political legitimation by his successors, including Philippe Auguste.[12] Dagobert in the romance comes across, unlike the emperor, as prominent, active and sensible. Most of the poem's action takes place in his kingdom and outside his capital city, which he has to protect from Saracen attacks; he summons Otheuien to help him (along with many other Western potentates), and he rebukes him for his behaviour to his wife. France therefore, and especially Paris, is more important than Rome, even if Rome is where this story ends.[13]

The emperor is also sidelined by the younger generation, his two sons, especially Florent. They are brave, resourceful, and responsible for defeating the Saracens- though some credit should be given to St George here, appearing with a force on white horses from Montmartre – assimilating converted pagans into Christian society and reconciling and reuniting their own scattered family. The chivalrous aspirations of young Florent are, however, presented with some humour, suggesting that the poet does not wholeheartedly subscribe to them. I am supported in this view by the romance's most interesting creation – Climent, Florent's foster-father.

Climent is a wealthy Parisian bourgeois – though labelled a *vilain*, a word to which I shall return – with a battlemented and turreted mansion in St Germain-des-Pres.

> 'Sire, dist il, ne uos ennuit,
> Cui est cil palais que la uoi?
> Amis, par la foi qe uos doi,
> Il est es murs tre bien fermes,
> Et s'est deuant tre bien quarnes.
> Qui en est mestres heritiers,
> Est il serjans ou cheualiers?'
> 'Nenil, sire', ce dist li rois,
> 'Ains est un mens uilains, Climens,
> Que molt est sages e uaillans.' (*Octavian*, 1610–20)

---

12 Laurent Theis, *Dagobert* (Paris, 1982), pp. 32–6, 74, 95, 99.
13 It may or may not be significant that Otheueien is repeatedly entitled *roi de Rome*, despite the romance's title.

['My lord,' he (Otheuien) said, 'excuse me, but what is this palace I
see over there? My friend, by the loyalty I owe you, it is enclosed by
very strong walls and in front is very well battlemented (?). Who is its
chief owner? Is he a soldier or a knight?' 'No, my lord,' said the king,
'he is neither knight nor burgess, but is one of my peasants, Climent,
who is very wise (prudent?) and brave.']

Climent represents the new economy of money intruding into the aristocratic
world, sending his son and foster-son with his *livres* and *deniers* to the city's
money-changers, and appalled when Florent, true to his noble nature,
exchanges them for a horse.[14] Suspicious of knighthood, he tries to stop
Florent receiving it and refuses to be knighted himself on pragmatic grounds:

'Voire,' dist Climens, 'par diables,
Sire rois, laisses moi estier!
Ie n'ai cure d'armes porter,
Li escus me seroit pesans,
Et li cheuaus est trop corans,
Heaume ne porroie souffrir,
[N]e la lance mie tenir.
[S]i aime molt mex repouser,
Et mes deniers souent conter,
Mangier cras chapons et pertris
Et boiure souent de bon uins,
La nuit deduire a ma mollier,
Souent acoler et baisier.
Foi que uos doi, biax sire rois,
Vos me dites come cortois
Et come prodom et senes.
Autre chose ne requeres!
N'ai que fere d'aler en ost,
Mes cheuaus me portera tost,
Le col me puisse tot brisier
Au ior que seroi cheualier.'
Li cheualiers grant ioie en ont,
Quant le uilain entendu ont.   (*Octavian*, 2958–80)

['Truly,' said Climent, 'let me be, my lord king! I've no wish to bear
arms: I'd find the shield too heavy and the horse too fast; I wouldn't be
able to bear the helmet or hold the lance. I like taking my ease much
better, and often counting my money, eating fat capons and partridges,
and often drinking good wines, enjoying my wife at night, often
hugging and kissing. By the loyalty I owe you, my fine lord king, you

---

14 See Jacques Le Goff, *The Medieval Imagination*, trans. Arthur Goldhammer (Chicago, 1988), pp.
151–65: 'the two estates [of merchants and money-changers] were the most typical of the new
medieval city'. The money-changers of Paris were situated chiefly on the Grand Pont, which
connected the Cité with the commercial quarter on the right bank. See John W. Baldwin, *Masters,
Princes and Merchants:The Social Views of Peter the Chanter and his Circle*, 2 vols (Princeton,
1970), vol. 1, p. 291.

speak to me like a courteous, worthy and wise man. Don't ask me anything else! I've no business joining the army: my horse would soon carry me off and quite break my neck, the day I became a knight.' The knights, hearing the peasant speak, enjoyed themselves greatly.]

The few critics who bother to discuss the French *Octavian* comment on the 'comic possibilities' of Climent,[15] but I think he represents an increasingly ambivalent view of the rising bourgeoisie, presumably shared by poet and audience. If his incomprehension of aristocratic values appears funny, so too does the naiveté of Florent, who is easily conned into paying much more than a horse is worth. From the city walls, the Parisians mock Florent as he rides by in his rusty armour on the way to fighting the Saracen king: they sarcastically compare the armour to Arthur's and assert the young man could be more correctly termed 'li fiuz Audegier, sant faille' (2285). *Audigier* is a fabliau which parodies a *chanson de geste*; the allusion suggests Florent is not the genuine article. Temporarily, the Parisians are the mouthpiece for a derisive view of him and what they see as his pretensions.

Climent, meanwhile, may be ridiculed for worrying about the costs of Florent's dubbing feast – he suspects the knights won't all pay their share and he will have to foot the bill – but he is the only person with the audacity, and with a merchant's knowledge of foreign languages, to capture the Soudan's marvellous horse, the weapon that Dagobert uses successfully against his foes. Saluted as 'molt hardis e uaillant' (4319), Climent significantly accompanies the emperor's reunited family back to Rome. He has become indispensable to it.

Many historians have remarked upon an élite of wealthy mercantile families that emerged in French towns in the thirteenth century, and have observed the aristocratic habit of labelling as *serf* or *vilenaille* those who did not belong to the ranks of the nobility. Indeed Duby has identified an increasingly popular theme, in literature of the late twelfth century on, of the wealthy upstart villein, aping the manners of his betters and taking their place through his possession of cash. He links it to the anxieties of a nobility increasingly indebted to the rich bourgeoisie.[16] Others have commented upon Philippe Auguste's predilection for competent burgesses and minor gentry in his administration, rather than great lords: he increasingly confided his governent to 'a new entourage of lesser men', and when he went on crusade asked six prominent Parisian bourgeois to handle the financial affairs of the capital.[17]

---

[15] *Octavian Imperator*, ed. McSparran (Heidelberg, 1979), p. 46.

[16] A good illustration of Duby's perception can be found in the beginning of the early thirteenth-century fabliau, 'Berenger au Long Cul'. See *Chevalerie et Grivoiserie: Fabliaux de Chevalerie*, ed. Jean-Luc Leclanche (Paris, 2003), no. II, ll. 13–35.

[17] R. H. Hilton, *English and French Towns in Feudal Society* (Cambridge, 1995), p. 99; Le Goff, *Medieval Imagination*, p. 165; Georges Duby, *The Chivalrous Society*, trans. Cynthia Postan (London, 1977), p. 182; John W. Baldwin, *The Government of Philip Augustus* (Berkeley, 1986), pp. 100–2. One of the six bourgeois was a money-changer, Errouin Le Changeur: see Jacques Boussard, 'Philippe Auguste et Paris' in *La France de Philippe Auguste*, ed. R-H. Bautier (Paris,

In *Octavian*, then, the figure of the emperor is eclipsed by several figures: his own sons, a national king and, most insultingly, by a successful bourgeois. And he ignores the advice of those best fitted to counsel him. We could read this as a protest against the misuse of both regal *and* imperial power. Some have seen early thirteenth-century chronicles as articulating aristocratic anger at the expulsion of the magnates from Philippe Auguste's government.[18] One of the king's 'new men' was Henri Clement, a 'petit chevalier' who became Philippe's marshal.[19] Our romance perhaps recalls this figure and is resentful of power given to the 'lesser men'. On the other hand, perhaps the figure of Dagobert is there to glorify Philippe Auguste rather than denigrate him, and the romance nicely expresses the mixture of attitudes felt about those he promoted. At any rate, it is clear that the depiction of Dagobert, so much more active than the emperor, fits developments in the thirteenth century: the empire was waning and new national states were emerging that recognised no superior in temporal affairs.[20]

To sum up: our three texts can be read as exhibiting broadly similar reactions to monarchical power. *Ipomedon* debunks the legend of the powerful king-emperor Arthur. Hue may be attacking the Plantagenets and their blatant appropriations of the story of Arthur, but the 1180s are a little early for this. On the other hand, Henry II's writer of propaganda, Stephen of Rouen, had by 1167 composed *Draco Normannicus*, which compares Arthur and Henry, to Arthur's discredit, and it could be that Hue was joining this particular band-wagon. Or maybe he had no other end in mind than to burlesque and entertain. His hero may emerge temporarily as better than an ineffectual king, but is in turn undermined by his own desire to renege on responsibilities. *Robert le Diable* represents imperial rule as surpassed by the world of the spirit – but only after the physical success in battle by Robert, a provincial nobleman, Normandy eclipsing Rome. And the coda may be a further dig along these lines, in the triumph of Le Puy over both Normandy and Rome. Finally, in

---

1982), pp. 323–40 (p. 333). Climent's anxiety that knights will not pay for Florent's dubbing-feast is illuminated by Duby's comments on knights' financial difficulties over getting their sons dubbed and armed: Duby, *Chivalrous Society*, p. 183.

18 Gabrielle M. Spiegel, *Romancing the Past: The Rise of Vernacular Prose Historiography in Thirteenth-Century France* (Berkeley, 1993), p. 17; she remarks that thirteenth-century historiography sought to deny and mask the consequences of recent transformations in political power and the social status of its aristocratic patrons (p. 10).

19 Baldwin, *Government*, pp. 107–23. Clement died soon after 1214. The *Chronique Française des Rois de France* by the anonymous writer from Béthune mentions him as one of Philippe Auguste's 'conseilliers' 'qui molt ert bien de lui: car molt l'avoit bien servi en ses guerres' and who in reward was in June 1204 given Argentan. He is twice mentioned as advising and helping Prince Louis. See Léopold Delisle, *Recueil des Historiens des Gaules et de la France*, 24 vols (Paris, 1904), vol. 24, pp. 764, 767.

20 B. Tierney, *The Crisis of Church and State 1050–1300* (New Jersey, 1964), pp. 159–61 and document no. 92. It may be relevant that Emperor Otto IV – depicted by Guillaume le Breton as a Roman emperor – was defeated by the French at the battle of Bouvines in 1214: Baldwin, *Government*, pp. 217–19.

Octavian national power outshines imperial inert magnificence, while due credit is given to a new rising power: money. Of all three texts this, I think, has its ear most firmly to new trends, while all three could broadly be said to represent a detached, even critical, attitude towards traditionally powerful rulers, at a time when the balance of forces in Western Europe is shifting.

6

English Identity and the Law in *Havelok the Dane, Horn Childe and Maiden Rimnild* and *Beues of Hamtoun*

ROBERT ROUSE

The law occupies a crucial role in the mythology and ideology of a people.[1]

During the great rebellion of 1381 the tenants of St Albans Abbey, led by one Walter Grindcobbe, petitioned the abbot to deliver to them charters held by the abbey that related the liberties of the vill. The Abbot produced these charters, but as Stephen Justice has suggested, they seem to have lacked the confirmation of the freedoms that the rebels desired.[2] These deficient charters were then burned, and the rebels demanded that the abbot produce one particular 'ancient charter . . . with capital letters, one of gold and one of azure'.[3] This charter, Walsingham tells us, was believed to confirm a series of liberties and privileges that had been granted to the townsfolk in the time of King Offa for their services in building the monastery.[4] These privileges, they claimed, had once been enjoyed by the town, but had been slowly eroded over time by the abbot and the monks. The abbot, faced with pressure to produce the rumoured Anglo-Saxon charter, repeatedly denied its existence. Despite these denials the rebels would not accept that the charter did not exist, and

---

[1]   R. R. Davies, 'The Peoples of Britain and Ireland, 1100–1400: III, Laws and Customs', *Transactions of the Royal Historical Society* 6th series, 6 (1996), pp. 1–23 (p. 6).

[2]   Stephen Justice, *Writing and Rebellion: England in 1381* (Berkeley, 1994), p. 47. See also Paul Strohm, *Hochon's Arrow: The Social Imagination of Fourteenth-Century Texts* (Princeton, 1992), pp. 4–5.

[3]   Thomas Walsingham, *Gesta abbatum monasterii Sancti Albani*, ed. Henry Thomas Riley, 12 vols (London, 1862–76), vol. 3, pp. 307–8, cited in Justice, p. 47.

[4]   Walsingham, vol. 3, p. 365. It is an interesting fact that the liberty of St Albans, a zone of legal privilege centred on and controlled by the abbey itself, was also founded upon a forged charter that claimed its authority from King Offa. The rebels were, perhaps unwittingly, conforming to a model of legal appeal that underlay the very privileges of the institution that they were opposing. For a discussion of St Albans Abbey and the charter of King Offa, see Julia Crick, 'Liberty and Fraternity: Creating and Defending the Liberty of St. Albans', *Expectations of the Law in the Middle Ages*, ed. Anthony Musson (Woodbridge, 2001), pp. 91–103.

eventually the abbot was forced to write out a new charter confirming King Offa's privileges.[5]

The actions of the rebels in the St Albans case highlight an intriguing aspect of English law in the fourteenth century: the rebels' claim to legal privilege is based upon a charter that was believed to have originated in the distant Anglo-Saxon past. As Rosamond Faith has observed, the legend of Offa's charter to the town is a 'striking piece of local political tradition'.[6] However, this tradition is not only political, but also legal. Offa's charter represents a belief that the rebels would have found what they considered to be justice in the form of ancient law. Anthony Musson sees in the rebels' demands for such ancient charters a manifestation of the 'pride [that] was increasingly taken in the Anglo-Saxon legal past'.[7] This pride, Musson suggests, was a consequence of the keen interest in legal history that seems to have been a characteristic of late medieval English society. This interest 'was exhibited in a practical sense . . . both in the form of "community memory" and in the growing recourse to written sources'.[8] Surveying the use of the Anglo-Saxon past within a variety of late medieval legal and pseudo-legal texts, Musson concludes that

> if the recorded notions of some are representative of the majority of people in the thirteenth and fourteenth centuries, it would appear that the Anglo-Saxon past appealed to them specifically and that a so-called 'Golden Age' could be located under the codes of legislative icons such as Alfred, Cnut and St Edward the Confessor (a cult devoted to the latter was particularly strong in royal circles during the period).[9]

Musson's wide selection of written sources, which range from statutes to chronicles, legal records to romances, suggests that the idea of the Anglo-Saxon past as a Golden Age of the Law was influential and widespread in late medieval England.

The reasons that underlie late medieval English society's interest in the Anglo-Saxon legal past are many and varied. Musson identifies three key cultural impulses that may account for the phenomenon:

> From the various forms of expression, however, we can draw together three interlinking motives. First there was an appeal to the past as a legitimising agent: the idea familiar to many historians of the common law that authority came (or was provable) through antiquity, tradition or long usage. The second, not dissimilar from the first, was the appeal to the past in order to

5   Rosamond Faith, 'The Great Rumour of 1377 and Peasant Ideology', *The English Rising of 1381*, ed. R. H. Hilton and T. H. Aston (Cambridge, 1984), pp. 43–73 (p. 64).
6   Ibid., p. 64.
7   Anthony Musson, 'Appealing to the Past: Perceptions of Law in Late-Medieval England', in *Expectations of the Law in the Middle Ages*, pp. 165–79 (p. 176).
8   Ibid., p. 165.
9   Ibid., p. 178.

inform or transform the legal present. Third and finally, it is possible to perceive an appreciation of and reliance on the legal past as a means of achieving identity, be it personal, corporate, regional or national.[10]

Here I wish to concentrate upon the last of these three cultural motives: the role of the law in English identity formation.

Musson notes that 'scholars working on written law-collections have shown that by emphasising their law's ancient origins and perhaps identifying a fundamental "law-giver" people could engender and further a sense of community and collective identity . . . '.[11] This connection between law and social identity is also evident in the romances: Susan Crane has noted that the 'legal preoccupations' of the romances become increasingly concerned with the negotiation of English identity.[12] I have argued elsewhere that the Anglo-Saxon past operates as a 'theatre of English identity' within the Matter of England romances, and here I will consider how the 'legal preoccupations' of *Havelok the Dane, Horn Childe and Maiden Rimnild* and *Beues of Hamtoun* act both to construct and redefine notions of English identity in relation to its Anglo-Saxon past.[13]

That the Matter of England romances are subject to 'legal preoccupations' is well established. Thorlac Turville-Petre writes of *Havelok*: 'Above all, the poet lays great emphasis upon legal practices and social institutions.'[14] Crane also notes the widespread legal fixation of the romances: 'A concern for just procedure often transforms crises that could be occasions for warfare into lessons in legality. . . . Crises in which heroes and villains act as litigants abound, emphasizing the preoccupation with law and custom that characterizes the romances of English heroes.'[15] These romances seem to be singularly interested in the nature and operation of law, raising questions regarding both the legal fluency of their audiences and their concern with the just operation of law.

It may be the case that the romances are operating as one medium through which communal concern regarding legal innovations could be articulated. Richard Firth Green notes that 'the prominence given to archaic legal forms, such things as ordeal and trial by battle, in the literature of the late Middle Ages is very striking, and it can be only partly explained by the dramatic

---

10 Ibid., p. 165.

11 Ibid., p. 172. See also Susan Reynolds, *Kingdoms and Communities in Western Europe, 900–1300*, 2nd edn (Oxford, 1997), pp. 250–76.

12 Susan Crane, *Insular Romance: Politics, Faith, and Culture in Anglo-Norman and Middle English Literature* (Berkeley, 1986), p. 86.

13 Robert Rouse, 'Expectation vs Experience: Encountering the Saracen Other in Middle English Romance', *SELIM, The Journal of the Spanish Society for Medieval Language and Literature* 10 (2000), pp. 125–40 .

14 Thorlac Turville-Petre, '*Havelok* and the History of the Nation', *Readings in Medieval Romance* (Cambridge, 1994), pp. 121–34 (p. 122).

15 Crane, p. 87.

potential inherent in such procedures'.[16] 'Literary responses to the perceived degenerate state of the law in the late Middle Ages generally took one of three forms: predictably some writers turned to satire, while others chose to romanticize opposition to the law in the person of the outlaw; a third group reveal their unease in a nostalgia for the old folklaw and its ways.'[17] The Matter of England romances, situated as they are in the Anglo-Saxon past, are highly suitable candidates for Green's third category of cultural response to legal change. If Green is correct in his assessment of this late medieval literary reflex, we might expect to find in these romances a critique of their contemporary legal environment in contrast to an imagined Anglo-Saxon Golden Age of law and justice.

Diane Speed, like Susan Crane, identifies law and justice as an important concern of the romances of England's past: 'One aspect of order identified by Bhabha as a particular discourse which may function dynamically in the narrative is "the quality of justice, the common sense of injustice; the *langue* of the law and the *parole* of the people".'[18] The concern for law in the romances, manifested through the romance hero's judicial crises, represents the legal anxieties of the community. These anxieties can be seen to be representative of the changing interests of the romance audience. As Crane points out, the baronial concerns of the Anglo-Norman romances are gradually replaced by the more nationalistic tone of the later Middle English versions, appealing to what had by the later Middle Ages become a varied and heterogeneous audience.[19] By the time of the Middle English Matter of England romances the concerns regarding English law are likely to be varied indeed.

In the construction of the law within the romances, the role of the king is one of great importance. In medieval legal thought, the king was *rex infra et supra legem*, and as such occupied a crucial position with regard to both the creation and just enforcement of law.[20] It was the role of the king to govern, and be governed, by the laws of his realm, thus ensuring that the kingdom remained in a state of peace. This concept of the *rex pacificus* was an important ideal, used as a model both to criticize and to advise contemporary rulers.

Havelok the Dane begins with what is arguably the clearest explication of the importance of law to a king's peaceful rule that is to be found in the Matter of England romances. This image of Athelwold's peaceful reign establishes

---

16 Richard Firth Green, 'Medieval Literature and Law', *The Cambridge History of Medieval English Literature*, ed. David Wallace (Cambridge, 1999), pp. 407–31 (p. 426).

17 Ibid., p. 418.

18 Diane Speed, 'The Construction of the Nation in Medieval Romance', *Readings in Medieval Romance*, pp. 135–57 (p. 147). Speed cites Homi Bhabha, 'Introduction', in his *Nation and Narration* (New York, 1990), pp. 1–7 (p. 2).

19 For a recent discussion of the nature of the audience of 'popular' Middle English romance, see Jane Gilbert, 'A Theoretical Introduction', *The Spirit of Medieval English Popular Romance*, ed. Ad Putter and Jane Gilbert (Harlow, 2000), pp. 15–38 (pp. 20–6).

20 Ernst H. Kantorowicz, *The King's Two Bodies: A Study in Medieval Political Theology* (Princeton, 1957), p. 143.

an ideal state of rulership against which the audience can measure Godrich, and to which Havelok can return the kingdom:

> It was a king bi are-dawes
> That *in* his time were gode lawes
> He dede maken an ful wel holden.
> Hym louede yu*n*g, him louede holde –
> Erl and barun, dreng and þayn,
> Knict, bondema*n*, and swain,
> Wydues, maydnes, prestes, and clerkes,
> And al for hise gode werkes.
> He louede God with al his micth,
> And Holi Kirke, and soth and ricth.
> Ri*c*thwise men he louede alle,
> And oueral made hem for to calle.
> Wreieres and wrobberes made he falle,
> And hated he*m* so ma*n* doth galle;
> Vtlawes and theues made he bynde,
> Alle that he micthe fynde,
> And heye he*n*gen on galwe-tre –
> For hem ne yede gold ne fe.[21]
> Jn þat time a man þat bore
>
> . . .
>
> Of red gold upon hijs bac,
> Jn a male with or blac,
> Ne funde he non þat him misseyde
> N[e] with iuele on hond leyde.
> Þa*n*ne micthe chapme*n* fare
> Þuruth Englond wit here ware,
> And baldelike beye and selle*n*
> Oueral þer he wilen dwellen –
> Jn gode burwes and þer-fram
> Ne fu*n*den he non þat dede he*m* sham,
> Þat he ne were*n* sone to sorwe brouth
> An pouere maked, and browt to nouth.
> Þa*n*ne was Engelond at hayse –
> Michel was svich a king to preyse
> þat held so Englond in grith! . . .
>
> . . . Þe ki*n*g was hoten Aþelwold;
> Of word, of wepne he was bold.
> Jn Engeland was neure knicth
> Þat betere hel[d] þe lond to ricth.
>
> *(Havelok the Dane,* 27–61, 106–9)[22]

---

[21] Accusations of venality among the judiciary were common in the medieval period. See John A. Yunck, *The Lineage of Lady Meed* (Notre Dame, 1963), pp. 148–52, and Green, 'Medieval Literature and Law', pp. 416 ff.

[22] All quotations from *Havelok* are taken from *Havelok the Dane*, ed. G. V. Smithers (Oxford, 1987).

In many respects this description represents an ideal image of kingship not dissimilar from that found in other medieval texts. However, here it is specifically constructed as an image of Anglo-Saxon kingship, and as such offers a view of how this romance writer imagined the faultless rule of Havelok's royal Anglo-Saxon predecessor. Athelwold reigns 'bi are-dawes': the narrative is placed far in the past when this model of rule was not just an ideal, but also the practice of all rightful kings. The foundation of Athelwold's rule is established from the beginning of the passage – 'in his time were gode lawes/ He dede maken an ful wel holden'. The peace that the king establishes throughout England is born of a respect for law, and the equitable application of this law among all his subjects, regardless of age or status. 'Erl and barun, dreng and þayn, / Knict, bondeman, and swain,/ Wydues, maydnes, prestes and clerkes' – all the estates of Athelwold's England are subject to and protected by his laws. This harks back to a utopian age of the universal application of law, a far cry from the reality of the legal segregation of the clerical and secular courts.[23]

A similar demonstration of the peace created by lawful Anglo-Saxon rule is found in *Guy of Warwick*. *Guy* begins with a comparable, albeit much shorter, description of the peace that a wise and lawful ruler brings to a land:

> Speke we schull of the Stywarde:
> Well true he was, and highte Sywarde.
> This Syward was slighe and wise,
> Riche of kynde, and of grete prise:
> In his tyme no-on better was,
> For of grete worship was no-on in his caas . . .
>
> (Caius *Guy of Warwick*, 109–14).[24]

> . . . þei a man bar an hundred pounde,
> Opon him, of gold y-grounde,
> þe[r] nas man *in* al þis londe
> þat durst him do schame no schonde,
> þat bireft him worþ of a slo,
> So gode pais þer was þo.   (Auchinleck *Guy of Warwick*, 137–42)

Here the agent of the peace is the Earl of Warwick's steward, Syward. Fittingly for this romance, in which stewards are often more active than their lords, the agency is transferred from the earl to his chief official. These two accounts are linked by their use of the same motif to demonstrate the extent of

---

23 William I instituted the segregation of clerical and lay justice within English law. Doris Stenton writes of William that 'he separated lay and ecclesiastical justice in conformity with continental practice and substituted mutilation for the death penalty. He reshaped the murder fine for the protection of his followers, but added little to the procedure of the courts beyond trial by battle' (Doris M. Stenton, *English Justice: 1066–1215* (Philadelphia, 1964), p. 6).

24 While I make use primarily of the Auchinleck MS in this study, the initial 122 lines of the romance are missing in this MS and thus are supplemented here by the Caius MS 107/176 reading. Both the Caius MS and the Auchinleck MS versions are found in *Guy of Warwick, Edited from the Auchinleck MS in the Advocates' Library, Edinburgh, and from MS 107 in Caius College, Cambridge*, ed. J. Zupitza, EETS ES 42, 49, 59 (London, 1883–91).

the 'gode pais' that has been established in the land. The peace and stability of Anglo-Saxon England is expressed in terms of the security of the king's road (*via regia*).

That law creates and maintains peace is of course the underlying *raison d'être* of most legal systems, and it is no surprise that *Havelok* makes use of this notion. However, what is interesting is the use that *Havelok* makes of its construction of England as a realm characterized by the rule of lawful peace. Through the process of cultural comparison, *Havelok* presents an interesting construction of English legal space. The parallel construction of the narrative in *Havelok* invites a comparative analysis between the way in which law operates in England and Denmark. The doubling of the plot allows direct comparisons between the treatment of the two traitors, Godard and Godrich, and of the processes by which they are judged and punished.

An initial reading of the treatment of the two usurpers highlights one immediate difference: the punishments decreed for them. Godard is executed, in a particularly brutal manner, first by being flayed alive by a 'ladde with a knif' (2494), then by being drawn through the streets, and finally by being hung up as an example to the Danish people (2488–511). Godrich, rather more mercifully, is led through the streets on an ass and is then burnt at the stake, while his children are disinherited (2820–37). The shocking violence of Godard's death has been the cause of much debate, and has led to a number of varying interpretations. Some scholars have seen the pragmatic violence of the execution as an indicator of the intended audience of the poem, positioning it squarely within the realm of the tavern and the inn.[25] Others have viewed the violence differently, seeing it as an indication of an unrealistic narrative mode – the 'naive fantasy world' of the poem.[26] However, I would suggest that the representation of Godard's death may operate as an indicator of legal difference, real or imagined, between England and Denmark – a case of different legal remedies for similar crimes.

The nature of the execution aside, however, the trials of Godard and Godrich seem at a first reading to follow the same process – in both cases Havelok asks for the traitors to be judged by what seems to be some form of parliament, which then accordingly recounts their crimes and sentences them to death for their treachery. However, closer examination of the apparent similarities highlights a number of significant differences.

After returning to Denmark, Havelok, accompanied by Grim's three sons, wins over a number of followers, including the influential Ubbe, and is recognized as Birkabein's son and heir. He then receives oaths of fealty (through the ceremony of *manrede*) from the Danes and is crowned king (2319). Once Havelok's men have captured Godard, Havelok assembles a parliament and 'bad he sholden demen him rith' (2468). We might note Havelok's legal status

---

25 For a discussion of this see Robert Levine, 'Who Composed *Havelok* for Whom?', *Yearbook for English Studies* 22 (1992), pp. 95–104.
26 John M. Ganim, *Style and Consciousness in Middle English Literature* (Princeton, 1983), p. 30.

when he commands his subjects to judge Godard: by this point in the narrative he has received their fealty and has been crowned king. He is thus in a position of legal authority to impose the rule of law and order a trial for treason.

In contrast to Havelok's repossession of Denmark, the course of events upon his return to England is markedly different. The same set of events – military victory, receiving fealty, being crowned king, and judging the traitor – do occur, but in a different order. Havelok lands, leading a Danish army, and defeats Godrich in battle. He then asks the English to judge Godrich for his crimes: 'Lokes þat ye demen him rith' (2813). Significantly, at this point Havelok has not received the fealty of the English and is not yet the king. Lacking any legal authority to order Godrich's trial, he seems to be appealing to the innate sense of the rule and procedure of law present in England – in contrast to Denmark, where law needs to be imposed from above, or perhaps from without.

This contrast between England and Denmark is also reflected in the treatment of the two prisoners before their trials. After Godard is captured, he is bound hand and foot like a thief or a dog, and thrown on the back of a scabby mare to be brought before the king. In England the process is more lawful, or perhaps more civilized (or are these the same thing in *Havelok*?), and Godrich is bound in fetters of steel and brought before the rightful heir. Goldeboro reminds his captors that 'non ne sholde him bete / Ne shame do, for he was knith,/ Til knithes haueden demd him rith' (2764–66).[27]

As Diane Speed, among others, has previously pointed out, the rule of law does appear to be stronger in England than in Denmark.[28] Law seems to be inherent to England but needs to be imposed upon Denmark by Havelok, and this difference in the legal fabric of the two realms suggests an illuminating rereading of the initial descriptions of Denmark and England. As we have already seen, Athelwold's England is characterized by its reliance upon and maintenance of law. The description of Birkabein's Denmark, however, is conspicuous in lacking any reference to law or lawfulness:

> Jn þat time so it bifelle
> Was in þe lon[d] of Denemark
> A riche king and swyþe stark;
> Þ[e] name of him was Birkabeyn.
> He hauede mani knict and sueyn.
> He was fayr man and wicth:
> Of bodi he was þe beste knicth
> Þat euere micte leden uth here,
> Or stede on-ride or handlen spere.
> Þre children he hauede bi his wif –

---

27 Compare this with the treatment of Godard when he is captured – he is trussed up like an animal (ll. 2437–47).

28 Speed, p. 152.

He hem louede so his lif.
He hauede a sone, douhtres two,
Swiþe fayre, as fel it so.   (*Havelok the Dane*, 339–51)

In comparison to Athelwold's England, Denmark is constructed as a legal vacuum, ready to be colonized by English legal process through the body of its Anglicized king, Havelok. However, the nature of the punishment meted out to Godard by the Danes suggests that this process of acculturation is incomplete. Flaying a traitor alive was, according to the legal historian J. G. Bellamy, an example of continental rather than English punishment: 'In France they might be flayed alive or hanged and quartered, first being dragged, as they were in England, to execution at the horse's tail.'[29] The Danes' legal system, imagined in *Havelok* along continental lines in contrast with England, leads them to impose a particularly bloodthirsty doom upon Godard. It is evident that Denmark does not immediately become English when Havelok becomes king, rather it is in the process of becoming English – a process which, as would have been apparent to the audience of the romance, was never completed.

It is important to my argument to understand Havelok not as simply being Danish, nor as entirely English, but rather as a hybrid-figure who both manifests and facilitates the union of the two nations. This is, of course, not to deny Thorlac Turville-Petre's assertion that the romance integrates the Danish heritage of the northeast into the English mainstream, but rather to suggest that acculturation is by no means unidirectional.[30] While the narrative (and its protagonist) integrates the Danes into England, England simultaneously has a cultural, and legal, impact upon Havelok and Denmark. Through a comparison of legal process in Denmark and England, *Havelok* constructs England as a discrete legal space, subject to its own laws and punishments. Situating the narrative in the Anglo-Saxon past, the text makes use of the popular post-Conquest view of the Anglo-Saxon period as a Golden Age of law and order. This Golden Age is envisaged as being specifically English, and is explicitly linked to the rule of a rightful king who rules within the bounds of the law of the realm.

I have argued above that *Havelok the Dane* presents a construction of legal space that differentiates England and Denmark. In *Havelok* legal difference is an important element of the construction of Anglo-Saxon England. Or should that perhaps be 'of the Anglo-Saxon English'? Is legal affinity, as constructed in these texts, a quality of geography or of ethnicity? Robert Bartlett provides a possible answer to this when he quotes the ninth-century canonist Regino of Prüm, who defines ethnicity in terms of four categories: 'The various nations

---

[29] J. G. Bellamy, *The Law of Treason in England in the Later Middle Ages* (Cambridge, 1970), p. 13. See also W. R. J. Barron, 'The Penalties for Treason in Medieval Life and Literature', *Journal of Medieval History* 7 (1981), pp. 187–202.
[30] Turville-Petre, '*Havelok* and the History of the Nation', p. 132.

differ in descent, customs, language and law.'[31] Bartlett recounts the medieval principle of the 'personality of the law', which allocated each person their own ethnic law, regardless of where they lived or whom they served, and it is clear that during the Middle Ages 'distinctive legal status was one way of recognizing or constituting separate ethnicity'.[32] This was certainly the case within Britain. In certain border areas, those of Welsh origin were subject to Welsh law rather than English law: 'In 1356 the duke of Lancaster confirmed that the Welsh of Kidwelly should be tried and fined according to the law of Hywel Dda – that is, native Welsh law.'[33] This fourteenth-century legal relativism followed a long tradition of ethnically based English law: in the Anglo-Saxon period the laws of Wessex and Mercia operated alongside those of the Danelaw. Doris Stenton notes the different laws that pertained to the English and the French in the reign of William I:

> Englishmen appealed of a crime by Normans were allowed to choose either ordeal or the duel. A Frenchman appealed of crime by an Englishman who was unwilling to submit to proof by 'judgement or the duel, must purge himself by an unbroken oath.'[34]

Given the complicating factor of this ethnic legal relativism, how can England be constructed as a discrete legal space? This identity dilemma seems to be a concern addressed by the romances through their construction of English legal space.

We have seen in *Havelok* that English legal process exists most strongly within the geographical bounds of Athelwold's realm, and that while Havelok seems to carry some elements of English legal practice with him to Denmark, the foreign is constructed as essentially Other with regard to law. This attitude towards the distinctiveness of England and its laws can also be seen in *Horn Childe and Maiden Rimnild* in the account of Horn's exile from England:

> Houlac king wald nere wede,
> Þere he sat opon his seghe,
> & seyd, 'Traitour, fle!'
> Horn tok his leue & ȝede
>
> . . .
>
> Wiard rode souþe & Horn rode west;
> To Wales Horn com atte lest:
> Wel long er þai [t]o mete.   (*Horn Childe*, 589–92, 610–12)[35]

31 Robert Bartlett, *The Making of Europe* (London, 1993), p. 197: 'diversae nationes populorum inter se discrepant genere, moribus, lingua, legibus'.
32 Ibid., p. 204.
33 Ibid., p. 208. Cf. R. R. Davies, 'Law and Identity in Thirteenth-Century Wales', *Welsh Society and Nationhood: Historical Essays Presented to Glanmor Williams*, ed. R. R. Davies et al. (Cardiff, 1984), pp. 51–69.
34 Stenton, p. 6.
35 *Horn Childe and Maiden Rimnild*, ed. Maldwyn Mills (Heidelberg, 1988).

As Horn leaves England following his banishment by King Houlac, he adopts a new name, Godebounde. Secure within his new identity, Horn rides west towards Wales, a common destination of exiled Englishmen. Horn's first encounter in Wales is with a knight who bars the road and challenges him to either fight or yield his possessions. Horn, accustomed to the laws of England, attempts to assert his rights of free passage, claiming that 'Ful leue me were to ride' (621). The Welsh knight, either unwilling or unaccustomed to consider such claims, does not answer, but simply takes up his lance and charges. Denied his appeal to the rule of English law, Horn reluctantly enters into the lawless nature of this new realm and defeats the challenging knight. Following his victory, Horn interrogates the defeated knight as to the nature of his land. When he is asked about the Welsh king, the knight replies that 'Our kinges name is Elidan:/ In al Wales is þer nan/ So strong a man as he' (646–8). In contrast to the depictions of English royal rule that we have seen in *Havelok* and *Guy*, the Welsh King Elidan's rule is based solely upon martial and physical strength.[36] There is a clear opposition constructed here between Houlac's England, where Horn is taught 'þe lawes boþe eld & newe' (274),[37] and the demonstrably lawless Wales.[38]

Wales is constructed as a legal vacuum in *Horn Childe*, providing an environment in which Horn can enter into the martial world of the adventuring knight without being troubled by notions of legality. The process of proving oneself and gaining martial glory is by necessity one that is often problematic in terms of its relationship with the law, and this is reflected in the way in which the heroes of the Matter of England romances leave England, either by choice or necessity, in order to undertake the *aventures* that will win them fame.[39] England seems to be envisaged in these romances as a lawful realm where such *aventures* are rare. It is only once the protagonists have undertaken such deeds in foreign lands, and reached a state of chivalric maturity, that they can return to England to address more serious issues of national or patrimonial importance.

The nature of Horn's exile raises a number of further legal issues. While out hunting, King Houlac is informed by the treacherous Wikard and Wikel

---

36 The tradition of characterising the rule of Celtic kings as being based on violence rather than law was a well-established one. Gerald of Wales writes that the Irish kings 'obtained the monarchy only by force and arms' (Gerald of Wales, *The Topography of Ireland*, trans. by J. J. O'Meara (Harmondsworth, 1982), pp. 170–1, cited in Robert Bartlett, *Gerald of Wales: 1146–1223* (Oxford, 1982), p. 164). John Gillingham discusses William of Malmesbury's perception of the Welsh in 'The Beginnings of English Imperialism', in his *The English in the Twelfth Century: Imperialism, National Identity and Political Values* (Woodbridge, 2000), pp. 1–18 (pp. 10–11).

37 While *lawes* can sometimes carry the meaning of 'styles or modes' (*MED* sv. *laue* n. 9 (d)) rather than laws, Mills points out that in this case *riȝt* (273) supports a legal reading of *lawes* (p. 122).

38 Bartlett discusses Gerald of Wales's construction of Wales as a lawless and anarchic land (Bartlett, *Gerald of Wales*, pp. 162–4).

39 Of course, French writers construct England in a similar way, as can be seen in Chrétien de Troyes *Cligés* (*Arthurian Romances*, trans. William W. Kibler (London, 1991), pp. 123–206). This seems to be a case of a general principle by which 'abroad' is constructed as dangerous, while home is familiar, known and safe.

that Horn has been sleeping with the king's daughter Rimneld.[40] This *lesing* drives the king into a rage, and he draws his sword and cries that 'Horn schuld be slan' (506). However, his knights petition him, and when Horn comes before him he decides to exile him instead:

> 'Traitour, þou hast tresoun wrouȝt;
> Tomorwe ȝif Y þe finde,
> Bi mi croun þou schalt be slawe,
> Wiþ wilde hors al todrawe
> & seþþen on galwes hing.' (*Horn Childe*, 560–64)

Perhaps Houlac's decision to exile Horn rather than have him executed reflects the increasing reliance upon exile rather than execution as a punishment for treason during the later Middle Ages.[41] This practice seems to have grown in popularity as the *weregeld* system declined, and provided an alternative to execution that was of great utility, especially when dealing with noble traitors. Bruce O'Brien, commenting upon the laws in the *Leges Edwardi* that govern what was known as 'abjuration of the realm', notes that 'copious evidence attests to the fact that, under the Angevins, abjuration became a favoured mechanism for disposing of homicides and other felons'.[42]

Beues of Hamtoun is another English hero who is forced into such an exile by an English king. In Beues's case it is not a romantic tryst that is the cause of the king's displeasure, but rather the accidental death of King Edgar's son. Upon his return from the marvellous East, Beues brings with him his renowned horse, Arondel, a magnificent and, above all else, loyal steed. In fact, Arondel's loyalty is such that he will allow only Beues to ride him. The reputation of his steed is enhanced still further when Arondel carries Beues to victory in a summer race between the knights of Edgar's court. Unfortunately, and not for the first time in the romance, Arondel becomes the object of conflict. King Edgar's son, the prince, much taken by the magnificent steed, demands that Beues gives Arondel to him:

> Meche men preisede is stede þo,
> For he hadde so wel igo;
> Þe prince bad, a scholde it him heue:
> 'Nay', queþ Beues, 'so mot y leue,
> Þouȝ þow wost me take an honde
> Al þe hors of Ingelonde!'
>
> (Auchinleck *Beues of Hamtoun*, 3543–8)[43]

---

40 This crime, with its potential both to impinge upon the value of the woman in terms of marriage and dynastic succession, is defined as treason (Bellamy, pp. 226–8).

41 For a discussion of the process of 'abjuring the realm', see Jusserand, p. 83.

42 Bruce R. O'Brien, *God's Peace and King's Peace* (Philadelphia, 1999), p. 82. The *Leges Edwardi* state that: 'However, a murderer or a traitor, according to this law, will not in any way remain in the country if the king grants life and limb to them, but they will swear that they will travel to the sea in the time which the justice set for them and cross it as quickly as they can have ship and wind' (O'Brien, p. 177, cf. Naomi Hurnard, *The King's Pardon for Homicide before AD 1307* (Oxford, 1969), pp. 5–18).

43 *The Romance of Sir Beues of Hamtoun*, ed. Eugen Kölbing, EETS 46, 48, 65 (London, 1885–94).

The prince is not to be denied. He waits until later that evening, and while Beues is busy in hall carrying out his duties as the King's marshal, he attempts to steal the horse. Arondel, however, is not accustomed to allowing any man to handle him except for his master, and kicks out at the prince when he tries to untie him:

> And þo Arondel, fot hot
> Wiþ his hint fot he him smot
> And to-daschte al is brain.
> þus was þe kinges sone slain.
>
> (Auchinleck *Beues of Hamtoun*, 3561–4)

King Edgar, upon hearing of the death of his son and heir, descends into a fury and demands that Beues be punished, and 'swor, for þat wronge/ þat Beues scholde ben an-honge/ & to-drawe wiþ wilde fole' (3567–9). To be hung and drawn by wild horses is of course a fit end for a traitor, but, fortunately for Beues, his peers among the baronage decide that this punishment would not be legal.[44] In a similar manner to the knights in *Horn Childe*, Beues's peers 'it nolde nouȝt þole/ & seide, hii miȝte do him no wors,/ Boute lete hongen is hors' (3570–2).

This episode, expressing as it does baronial influence or moderation of the king's power, highlights a key tenet of English law as constructed in the romances – that the king does not have free reign to judge and to impose punishment entirely as he wishes.[45] As we have seen in *Havelok*, treason (and the killing of a royal heir is of course such) is properly a concern not only of the king but also of his parliament. As we have seen in *Horn Childe*, the king's initial rash judgment condemning the traitor to death is commuted through the advice of his nobles into a lesser punishment.

Complicating things still further here are the details of the case – after all, it is not Beues who is accused of the crime but his horse.[46] The vagaries of animal trials and the legal responsibility of owners were no less complex during the medieval period than they are today. Richard Firth Green, commenting upon the treatment of such animal trials in England, tells us that

---

[44] Hanging and drawing was a common punishment for treason in England during the later Middle Ages (Thomas S. R. Boase, *Death in the Middle Ages: Mortality, Judgment and Remembrance* (London, 1972), p. 16). Bellamy notes that: 'To draw a man to the gallows for execution had always been the hall-mark of treason . . .' (p. 18).

[45] Susan Crane argues that that this amelioration of royal power is a reflex of baronial concerns: 'Magna Carta sought not to re-establish freer relations between king and barons, but to incorporate the king into his own legal system, to restrain him, too, within the fine new net of law he had cast around his barons' (pp. 20–1). This is not a concern that is exclusive to the Matter of England romances, but it does seem to be one with which they are especially concerned.

[46] Richard Firth Green writes that 'such stories were not restricted to romance: Frederick II is reported to have had one of his falcons judicially condemned for killing a young eagle' (*A Crisis of Truth: Literature and Law in Ricardian England* (Philadelphia, 1999), p. 422). For a detailed discussion of this case, see Ernst H. Kantorowicz, *Frederick the Second, 1194–1250*, trans. E. O. Lorimor (London, 1931), p. 347.

'English legal sources offer no such evidence of the ascription of culpability to animals as the *Sachsenspiegel*'s provision (3.1.1; 195) that all living creatures present at a rape were to be beheaded (presumably they were felt to be at fault for not raising the alarm)'.[47] Green argues that, from medieval common law's treatment of animal owners, we can see something of the popular attitudes towards the issue: 'Early law seems generally to have assigned liability solely to the offending animal itself and held its owner free of any direct responsibility for its wrongs; we hear of animals punished by death, mutilation, or even banishment, while their owners enter the picture only where they have actively assisted in the crime or sought to protect the criminal.'[48] Edgar's parliament seems to uphold this legal principle, permitting the king to punish only the horse, not Beues himself. However, the king's judgment comes to be of little significance – Beues refuses to accept that Arondel should be hung and chooses to leave England as an exile to avoid the punishment. This alerts us once again to the geographical limitation of English law: that its jurisdiction is limited to England. The medieval practice of abjuring the realm, so popular in England during the thirteenth and fourteenth centuries, operates in *Beues* as an opportunity for the text to comment upon the abuse of royal power. Beues's self-imposed exile stands as the ultimate act of condemnation. By abandoning both England and its laws for the east, Beues demonstrates the medieval belief that a king must embody both the laws and customs of his realm: if he fails to do so, this makes not only the king, but also the kingdom, despicable.

Both Horn and Beues are exiled for crimes that can be described as treason, Beues by his own choice and Horn at the command of King Houlac. In their exile both Horn and Beues discover that law does not seem to operate in other realms as it does in England. As in *Havelok*, in both *Beues* and *Horn Childe* we can see a construction of the double-edged geographical jurisdiction of English law: outside England the romance hero is safe from legal sanction, but at the same time loses the protections that English law confers. In the romances English law is limited to England, unlike the situation in the historical Middle Ages where, as Robert Bartlett tells us, 'individuals had their own ethnic law . . . regardless of the territory they inhabited or the lord they served'.[49] This allows these narratives to construct an image of English law as being specific to England, and more particularly specific to Anglo-Saxon England. This marks out England, and the English, from the rest of the romance world. Endowed with a legal heritage of demonstrated provenance and virtue, law becomes a powerful element in the creation of an English Identity, standing as a point of differentiation for the Anglo-Saxon England of the romances and, vicariously, for the post-Conquest England of their audi-

---

47 *A Crisis of Truth*, pp. 303–4.
48 Ibid., p. 304.
49 Bartlett, *The Making of Europe*, p. 204.

ences. This thematic concern within the Matter of England romances reflects the wider cultural reputation of the Anglo-Saxon past as the temporal genesis of English law, and contributes to the idea of Anglo-Saxon England as an English legal Golden Age.

7

The True Romance of *Tristrem and Ysoude*

PHILLIPA HARDMAN

Middle English adaptations of French romances have often suffered from an assumption of inferiority: being seen primarily as cut down and coarsened versions of sophisticated French narratives made to suit an English cultural context very different from the French-speaking audience of the original text. No romance has fared worse in this respect than the text known as *Sir Tristrem*.[1] It used to be valued mainly for its witness to the content of the missing portions of *Tristran*, Thomas's twelfth-century Anglo-Norman poem – though not a very satisfactory witness, given the difference in scale of the two works: 3,297 lines of *Tristran* survive, representing merely an estimated one-sixth of the original poem, as against the English romance, which is almost complete at 3,328 lines.[2] The English poem was consistently denigrated in the comparison, as a garbled and incompetent reduction of the earlier masterpiece. Helaine Newstead's judgement in the standard bibliographical manual represents the general view: '*Sir Tristrem* is unfortunately a much coarsened version of its subtle and moving original, significant chiefly because it preserves, however inadequately, the lost episodes of its source.'[3]

However, in medieval poetics *abbreviatio* was as important a literary skill as the *amplificatio* that characterizes *Tristran*, an equally legitimate method of

---

[1] The romance survives in a unique copy in the Auchinleck MS, Edinburgh, National Library of Scotland, Advocates MS 19.2.1. See *Die englische Version der Tristan-Sage: Sir Tristrem*, ed. Eugen Kölbing (1882; repr. Hildesheim, 1985).

[2] Thomas's *Tristran*, ed. and trans. Stewart Gregory, *Early French Tristan Poems*, vol. 2, ed. Norris J. Lacy, Arthurian Archives (Cambridge, 1998).

[3] Helaine Newstead, 'Arthurian Legends', *A Manual of the Writings in Middle English 1050–1500*, vol. 1, *Romances*, ed. J. Burke Severs (New Haven, 1967), p. 179. Despite several decades of intense critical interest in medieval vernacular romance, few have turned their attention to *Sir Tristrem*. W. R. J. Barron, *English Medieval Romance* (London, 1987), castigates the romance as an inept derivative of *Tristran*, written in 'the "rym dogerel" of *Sir Thopas*', a form 'unworthy of such a subject' (pp. 154–5), while Maldwyn Mills, though less judgemental about its 'disruption . . . of the narrative', 'jumbled . . . detail' and metrical 'difficulties', still conveys a rather negative impression ('*Sir Tristrem*', *The Arthur of the English: The Arthurian Legend in Medieval English Life and Literature*, ed. W. R. J. Barron, *Arthurian Literature in the Middle Ages*, vol. 2 (Cardiff, 1999), pp. 141–6). It may be that accusations of incoherence and unintelligibility in the romance have sometimes resulted from misunderstandings of the text: scholars from Walter W. Skeat ('The Romance of *Sir Tristrem*', *Scottish Historical Review* 6 (1908), pp. 58–62) to Myra Stokes and Ad Putter ('*Sir Tristrem*, ll. 1343–75, *Notes and Queries* 244 (1999), pp. 435–42) have elucidated some of the poem's difficulties.

generating new texts, and the Middle English romance merits consideration as a poetic recasting of the material into a new short form. Two perceptive articles by T. C. Rumble (1959) and C. E. Pickford (1973)[4] began the work of reappraisal, arguing for the 'intrinsic worth' of the romance and declaring it 'a fresh retelling of a great story', but even so, bearing in mind that the Tristan material would have been already available to those capable of understanding it in French, both Rumble and Pickford present the English poem as a version specifically intended for a 'relatively uncultured audience', 'having perhaps only a slight awareness of the existence of French or other versions of the story'; and neither seriously challenges the prevailing view that the complicated stanza is, at the very least, unsuitable to the material. I shall argue instead that it makes more sense to see the laconic, allusive style of the narrative as aimed at an audience already acquainted with the Tristan legend, and that the sophisticated French-inspired stanza form is a medium well suited to the poem's particular concentration on dramatic and lyrical effects (and perhaps not as 'unusual' as has been claimed: both the Auchinleck MS and its near-contemporary compilation, British Library MS Harley 2253, contain numerous examples of comparable stanza patterns, variously used for lyric, satirical, and narrative verse).[5]

Even the title of the poem is in doubt; it was named *Sir Tristrem* by its first editor, Sir Walter Scott (perhaps after the work cited by Robert Mannyng of Brunne with which he identified this romance).[6] But Scott, relying on a tran-

---

4   Thomas C. Rumble, 'The Middle English *Sir Tristrem*: Toward a Reappraisal', *Comparative Literature* 11 (1959), pp. 221–8 (pp. 223, 228); Cedric E. Pickford, '*Sir Tristrem*, Sir Walter Scott and Thomas', *Studies in Medieval Literature and Languages in Memory of Frederick Whitehead*, ed. W. Rothwell et al. (Manchester, 1973), pp. 219–28 (p. 228).

5   Derek Pearsall notes the comparative sophistication of features such as the prologue, 'with its graceful comparison of past and present with summer and winter', and the choice of metre (although he considers it 'difficult' and not successful for narrative), in 'The Development of Middle English Romance', *Mediaeval Studies* 27 (1965), pp. 91–116, repr. in *Studies in Medieval English Romances: Some New Approaches*, ed. Derek Brewer (Cambridge, 1988), pp. 11–33 (p. 26). The poem is also treated briefly but sympathetically by Flora Alexander, 'Women as Lovers in Early English Romance', *Women and Literature in Britain, 1150–1500*, ed. Carol M. Meale, 2nd edn (Cambridge, 1996), pp. 24–40.

6   *Sir Tristrem: A Metrical Romance of the Thirteenth Century by Thomas of Erceldoune, Called the Rhymer*, ed. Walter Scott, 2nd edn (Edinburgh, 1806). In his *Chronicle* (1338), Mannyng refers to his four-stress couplets as 'light ryme', accessible to 'lewed men' (Robert Mannyng of Brunne, *Chronicle: The Story of England*, ed. Frederick J. Furnivall, Rolls Series 87, 2 vols (London, 1887), ll. 118, 84), in contrast with complicated, French-inspired rhyme schemes, too difficult for most reciters and listeners, citing as example a superlative work marred by incompetent delivery:

> Þat may þou here in sir Tristrem;
> ouer gestes it has þe steem,
> Ouer alle þat is or was,
> if men it sayd as made Thomas;
> But I here it no man so say,
> þat of som copple som is away. (97–102)

It is impossible to know if Mannyng alludes to *Sir Tristrem* here, but in the context of his remarks on 'strange ryme' (112), the stanza of *Sir Tristrem* (a3b3 a3b3 a3b3 a3b3 c1 b3c3) makes it not unlikely, as Dieter Mehl assumes in *The Middle English Romances of the Thirteenth and Fourteenth Centuries* (London, 1967), p. 173. The purpose of Mannyng's reference would be to support

script by an assistant, failed to see the remains of the original title in the Auchinleck MS: '. . . de', in the same hand, ink, and position as the final letters of the extant title 'Horn childe and maiden rimnild' a few folios later.[7] It is likely, therefore, that each title originally named both lovers, and the fragment 'de' represents the last two letters of the heroine's name. Further, Scott misread the name of the heroine as 'Ysond(e)', while acknowledging that 'every analogy goes to prove . . . it ought to have been written and printed *Ysoude*',[8] and later editors and critics have followed suit, calling Sir Tristrem's beloved 'Ysonde', and his unhappy wife 'Ysonde with the white hand'. Yet *Horn Childe and Maiden Rimnild*, copied by the same scribe, contains the lines: 'Loued neuer childer mare/ Bot tristrem or ysoud it ware' (310–11), where the lady's name, identical in graphic appearance to the name in the Tristrem romance, is read 'Ysoud' in both modern editions of this text.[9] Following the manuscript evidence, therefore, I propose to refer to the Auchinleck text as *Tristrem and Ysoude*.

Central to the assessment of *Tristrem and Ysoude* is consideration of its genre. It is usually classed as a chivalric romance with typical emphasis on knightly prowess;[10] but Maldwyn Mills additionally sees in its 'unusually wide chronological range . . . something of the aspect of a romance biography' (p. 142), and has suggested it is the best example of a Middle English romance as a 'life'.[11] This is a persuasive idea that fits very well with the outline of the narrative tradition given in the poem's first stanza:

> Þer herd y rede in roun,
> Who Tristrem gat *and* bare;

his choice of 'light ryme' by pointing out that even so excellent a romance as *Sir Tristrem* is denied a proper hearing by the very sophistication of its elaborate form. Its importance now is the evidence it provides for the high esteem afforded a metrical Tristan story, and for the association of complex rhyme schemes with an audience not too 'lewed' to appreciate them, at about the same time as the unique extant copy of *Sir Tristrem* was made (c.1340).

7 Maldwyn Mills notes the presence of these letters in his edition of *Horn Childe and Maiden Rimnild*, Middle English Texts 20 (Heidelberg, 1988), p. 13, n. 6.

8 Scott, p. lxxxv. Similarly, Tristrem's foster-father 'Ro(u)hand' should be read 'Ro(u)haud' in the light of the Italian 'Roaldo' and the Norse 'Roaldr'. Neither name occurs in a rhyme, but this in itself is significant, for the romance often rhymes on 'ond(e)' or 'and(e)', and the demands of the rhyme-scheme are such that the poet would surely have used these frequently occurring names in the rhyme if he could (as he used 'Yrlond'/'Irland' and 'Ynglond'/'Ingland'). Skeat also suggests that Scott's and Kölbing's 'Ganhardin' should be read 'Gauhardin' to correspond with Thomas's 'Kaherdin'.

9 See Mills, *Horn Childe and Maiden Rimnild*; *King Horn*, ed. J. Hall (Oxford, 1901), appendix.

10 Barron maintains it is not a love-story but a tale of male adventure thwarted by mishap, with Ysoude not even mentioned until one-third of the way through the poem (p. 154); in fact this proportion is very similar in both the Norse *Tristrams saga ok Ísöndar*, a 'workmanlike' translation of *Tristran* (ed. and trans. Peter Jorgensen, *Norse Romance*, vol. 1, *The Tristan Legend*, ed. Marianne E. Kalinke, Arthurian Archives (Cambridge, 1999), p. 26), and in what can be reconstructed of Gottfried von Strassburg's *Tristan*.

11 This suggestion was made in discussion following a paper given at the Seventh Biennial Conference on Romance in Medieval England; see 'Generic Titles in Bodleian Library MS Douce 261 and British Library MS Egerton 3132A', *The Matter of Identity in Medieval Romance*, ed. Phillipa Hardman (Cambridge, 2002), pp. 125–38.

> Who was king wiþ croun,
> *And* who him fosterd ȝare,   (3–6)

The implied promise to retell this narrative is redeemed as the romance proceeds and the story of Tristrem's parents is brought to a close with the lines: 'Geten *and* born was so/ Þe child, was fair *and* white'(243–4). Tristrem's early life unfolds in familiar romance stages: his education under his foster-father's care, his precocious success at the court of King Mark of England, the revelation of his true identity as Mark's sister's son, his mission to avenge his father's death and regain his inheritance, and the climactic battle in which he saves the English nation and is promised the kingdom. There are complete verse romances that tell a story of about the same length as this (around a thousand lines), but this is only the preliminary part of Tristrem's 'life'.

A romance 'life', like hagiographic 'lives', needs a conversion or similarly transformative experience to give it structure, and in *Tristrem and Ysoude* that conversion is effected by the drinking of the love-potion, with its irreversible binding together of the lovers' two lives until their shared death: 'Her loue miȝt no man tvin/ Til her endingday' (1671–2). This occurs at the mid-point of the poem; henceforth, Tristrem's life consists of nothing but dangerous enjoyment of Ysoude's presence, repeatedly having to outwit their enemies at court, or reckless adventure in her absence, forced into exile and living a life of desperate knight-errantry:

> Tristrem fareþ ay
> As man þat wald be slain,
> Boþe niȝt *and* day,
> Fiȝtes for to frain.   (2623–6)

Thus the poet exploits the 'diptych' structure so characteristic of Middle English romances to produce a two-part 'life' that hinges on the transforming force of love: whereas Tristrem in the first part acts in accord with standard chivalric ideals, taking knighthood in order to overthrow Duke Morgan, the treacherous and 'cruwel' (267) usurper, volunteering to save England from the unjust tribute of three hundred children in single fight – 'Tristrem seyd: "Ywis/ Y wil defende it as kniȝt" ' (989–90) – and loyally winning Ysoude for the king by slaying the dragon that no one else dare confront, in the second part, Tristrem's motivation is dictated entirely by his desire for Ysoude.

In his first exile, after Ysoude's ordeal of the hot iron, Tristrem goes to Wales deliberately seeking a fight as a reaction to his loss of Ysoude:

> Tristrem, wiþ outen wene,
> Into Wales he is;
> In bataile he haþ ben
> *And* fast he fraines þis,
> Riȝt þare:

For he ne may Ysoude kisse,
Fiȝt he souȝt ay where.   (2293–9)

The situation he finds there, where the giant Urgan is wrongfully oppressing King Triamour, plundering his land and attempting to seize his daughter Blauncheflour by force, has echoes of Tristrem's early encounters both with the usurper Duke Morgan who insulted Tristrem's mother, also called Blauncheflour, and with Moraunt – 'An eten in ich a fiȝt' (950) who personified the wrongful Irish oppression of England. Indeed, a kind of retributive logic emerges in the conflict when Urgan reveals that he is Morgan's brother, bent on revenge, and Tristrem promises to repeat his previous victory: 'A pliȝt/ So kepe y þe to slo' (2332). The last of Tristrem's reckless adventures explicitly recalls his earlier encounters, when he insists on challenging Beliagog the giant, disregarding all warnings that Beliagog is the vengeful brother of Morgan, Urgan, and Moraunt, and so especially hostile to him. Tristrem courts danger with what seems wilful carelessness: ' "Þat cuntre wil y se,/ What auentour so bitide!" '(2738–9). There is no hint of the lover-knight's traditional desire to win renown for his lady's sake in any of these adventures: Tristrem is more like a man in search of oblivion if he cannot be with his beloved.

The English poet greatly simplifies Tristrem's itinerary in the later stages of the story: once he has repudiated his wife Ysoude of Brittany for her disloyalty in speaking to Gauhardin, her brother, about their unconsummated marriage, Tristrem reveals his love for Ysoude the queen to Gauhardin and leaves Brittany, never to return; it is Gauhardin alone who voyages back and forth between England and Brittany thereafter. This change strengthens very considerably the impression of Tristrem's inseparability from Ysoude, as his life now consists of lurking in disguise, lying under the walls, hiding in trees, waiting for the summons to Ysoude's bower. It is a far cry from the courtly life enjoyed by Thomas's Tristran with Kaherdin in Brittany (*Tristran*, 2154–69).

This structure of a 'life' in two parts, before and after the love-drink, makes sense of some of the alleged 'garblings' of the original in the English poet's remaking, and there are other instances of his having made 'structural rearrangements'[12] in order to strengthen the continuity of his abbreviated poem. Besides the simplification of Tristrem's itinerary mentioned above, for example, the account of his slaying the dragon and the contest with the false steward is rearranged to produce a simpler narrative sequence (1442–639);[13] the story of the wonderful dog Peticru and Tristrem's battle with Urgan is reordered and revised to omit the magic element, with the dog now introduced into the story as a reward offered to Tristrem by King Triamour (2300–420);[14]

---

[12]   *Pace* Barron's denial (p. 154).
[13]   Cf. *Tristrams saga*, Chapters 36–8, 42, 39, 43–5.
[14]   Cf. ibid., Chapters 62, 61, 63.

and the material relating to Canados, which in *Tristran* occupies two separate episodes (Cariado's jealous revelation to Ysolt of Tristran's marriage, and the long sequence dealing with Kaherdin's relationship with Brengvein), is reordered to form a single episode, with additional incidents that construct new connecting links (3015–289).[15] Continuity is further aided by brief passages (not paralleled in *Tristran* or *Tristrams saga*) in which characters in the narrative recapitulate past events, such as Tristrem's telling his uncle the story of his abduction (672–82), or describing to Ysoude how he praised her to King Mark (1607–12).

There are other innovations that point to deliberate construction of meaning in *Tristrem and Ysoude*. The central episode of the love-drink is one such; it has often been criticized for its brevity, but the choice of words and telling details carry a great weight of significance. Brengwain's simple mistake in fetching the drink and Ysoude's innocent sharing of the cup with Tristrem lead directly to the consequence: 'Her loue miȝt no man tvin/ Til her endingday' (1671–2), and the echoes of the rite of matrimony,[16] with the idea of a divinely sanctioned, indissoluble and lifelong bond, counterpoint the conventional note of tragic foreboding in the narrator's comment: 'In iuel time, to sain,/ Þe drink was ywrouȝt!' (1682–3). This produces a profound ambivalence that colours the whole treatment of the love theme in this romance. The touching detail of the faithful hound, Hodain, licking the discarded cup and sharing in the love-bond, is not mere English sentiment: 'Þai loued wiþ al her miȝt,/ *And* Hodain dede al so' (1693–4). It symbolizes the fidelity of their love relationship exactly as do the dogs carved beneath the feet of married couples on medieval tombs,[17] and the poet maintains this significance throughout the romance.[18] Once Ysoude has been married to Mark and the bed-trick with Brengwain taking Ysoude's place has successfully passed off, the poem returns to the love-drink, which in this version Brengwain has carefully preserved. Ysoude plays an elaborate fiction, calling for the drink as expected, and when it is her turn putting the cup down unnoticed without drinking, for 'Þerof hadde sche no nede' (1722): the love-drink has already bound her to Tristrem with a love that is beyond the skill of clerks to describe (1726–7). But the narrator then reprises the note of foreboding:

> Þai wende haue ioie anouȝ:
> Certes, it nas nouȝt so!

---

[15] Cf. *Tristran*, 834–941, 1198–2093; *Tristrams saga*, Chapters 72, 87–93.

[16] Sarum *Ordo ad faciendum Sponsalia*, *Monumenta Ritualia Ecclesiae Anglicanae*, ed. William Maskell, 2 vols (London, 1846), vol. 1, pp. 41–64; see Matthew 19:6.

[17] See J. M. Steadman, 'Chaucer's "Whelp": A Symbol of Marital Fidelity', *Notes and Queries* 201 (1956), pp. 374–5.

[18] Hodain and the dog Peticru that Tristrem sent as a present to Ysoude are both named as the lovers' companions in their forest exile (2467–8); images of both are carved with Ysoude in Tristrem's secret hall (2840–1); both dogs accompany Ysoude in Tristrem's absence, and he instructs Gauhardin to pay attention to the dogs, as well as displaying the ring she gave him, in token of his return (3083–113).

> Her wening was al wouȝ,
> Vntroweand til hem to;
> Aiþer in langour drouȝ,
> *And* token rede to go;
> *And* seþþen Ysoude louȝ,
> When Tristrem was in wo,
> Wiþ wille. (1728–36)

The shadow cast over the lovers' joy, the forecast of unexpected pain and separations, the hints of unhappy future deceptions, create an effect of pathos, especially affecting to those already familiar with the story.

The motif of the faithful dogs fits into the larger theme of truth and fidelity that was popularly connected with the figure of Tristram,[19] and which the English poet establishes as a constant throughout the life of Tristrem, not confined to his virtue in love. 'Tristrem (þe) trewe' becomes almost a fixed epithet, first mentioned at his conception: '*And* seþþen men cleped him so:/ Tristrem þe trewe fere' (108–9). He is known to all at Mark's court: ' "His name is Tristrem trewe" ' (601), and the name is pointedly repeated when he undertakes his greatest feats.[20] However, Tristrem's loyalty sets him in ambivalent relation to Mark when he rescues Ysoude from the Irish earl: 'Tristrem trewe fere' (1886) restores the queen, but only after a week of bliss in the wood, and the whole incident casts doubt on the king, branded a 'fals man' (1836) unless he yield Ysoude. The epithet is used again and again in this way to highlight such ambivalences as the love story develops. In the orchard scene the dwarf, motivated by 'falsnesse' (2069), sets a trap for the lovers, but Mark, persuaded that they have been guiltlessly slandered, is joyfully reconciled to Tristrem:

> Al sori Mark gan go
> Til he miȝt Tristrem kisse,
> *And* dedely hated he þo
> Him, þat seyd amis.
> Al newe
> Þer was ioie *and* blis,
> *And* welcom Tristrem trewe. (2161–7)

In the episode of exile in the forest, when Mark is convinced of the lovers' innocence on finding them asleep with a sword between them, 'Tristrem, þe

---

19 See Chaucer's balade, 'To Rosemound', l. 20; Gower, *Cinkante Balades*, XLIII.20.

20 See lines 1124, 1275, 1303 (having saved England from Moraunt); 1435–6 (when he faces the dragon); 2400 (on liberating Wales from Urgan). The use of the word 'trewe' in relation to other figures in the poem is carefully limited: Rohaud is termed 'trewe so stan' (115, 270) and 'trewe' (223, 288) in connection with his faithful guardianship of the boy Tristrem and his father's lands; Brengwain is 'trewe' to Ysoude when she keeps the secret of the wedding-night (1793, 1803); Gauhardin and Tristrem plight their troths as 'trewe' to each other in all things, and especially in the matter of love (2938–41, 3004–11).

trewe,/ *And* swete Ysoude' (2553–4) are fetched back 'to ful riȝt' (2563) and reconciled again with the king:

> Mark kist Ysoude þo
> *And* Tristrem trewe fere.
> Forȝeuen hem was her wo,
> No were þai neuer so dere. (2566–9)

The ambiguity inherent in the phrase 'trewe fere', where *fere* can mean both 'comrade, fellow' and 'lover, spouse', is never discussed in the poem; the whole point is that it cannot be resolved. The poet uses it to indicate Tristrem as the site of irreconcileable loyalties, at one and the same time Ysoude's inseparable lover and Mark's best knight. Tristrem's heart-searching over Ysoude of Brittany is given a similarly ambiguous colour when, as he wrestles with the 'wrong' and 'riȝt' of his situation, the narrator states: 'And trewely þouȝt he ay' (2675).

The concern with 'riȝt' and 'wrong' that informs this episode is evident all through the poem. When Tristrem returns to England after regaining his heritage and finds the people weeping over the new and inhuman terms of the tribute to Ireland – three hundred noble children instead of the former demands for three hundred pounds of gold, silver, and brass – he undertakes to fight Moraunt instead, but only after Mark has repeatedly stressed that the tribute was exacted 'wiþ wrong' from the outset (972, 974, 982): 'No was it neuer his/ Wiþ riȝt' (987–8). Similarly, Urgan is said to hold Wales 'wiþ wrong' (2312) before Tristrem wins it from him, and in Brittany Tristrem wins back all the Duke's possessions for him 'wiþ riȝt' (2646). Like his reputation for truth, Tristrem's concern with right and wrong is presented as intrinsic to his standing both as knight and as lover throughout the romance.

Tristrem's last adventure is focused directly on the issue of his identity as 'trewe Tristrem'. A second Tristrem appeals to him for help in rescuing his lady, and whereas Thomas's hero is called 'Tristran l'Amerus' to distinguish him from 'Tristran le Naim',[21] the English poet uses the familiar epithet: 'Tristrem, þat trewe hiȝt' (3336). The other Tristrem has no nickname, but is presented as a young knight, referred to as 'Þe ȝong Tristrem', who has sought Tristrem far and wide and now falls at his feet to beg his help with great urgency, appealing in the name of Tristrem's own lady: 'For loue of Ysoude fre' (3308).[22] At the end of the ill-fated encounter, the action is subtly altered so that instead of revenging himself on the knight who has fatally wounded him (as in *Tristran*, 2314–19), Tristrem is wounded while avenging the death of his young namesake (3334–7) – and thus Tristrem proves himself in one

---

[21] In *Tristrams saga* the ironic name 'Dwarf' for the giant knight is spelled out; in *Tristrem and Ysoude* the poet characteristically chooses a naturalistic revision of the original.

[22] A new narrative device is added when young Tristrem is introduced as 'A kniȝt þat werd no schon' (3296), raising the false hope that under Tristrem's guidance he will win his spurs in the fight to regain his lady.

economical episode both true to his love for Ysoude and true to his fellow lover-knight, 'trewe fere' for once without ambiguity.

Both structurally and thematically, then, *Tristrem and Ysoude* gives evidence of careful construction, of sustained control of the material, which makes it unlikely that the laconic style is (as often claimed) a mere effect of incompetence. The frequency of stanza-linking and of continuity of thought between stanzas in the unique copy of the poem suggest that loss of original material is not a major problem. So, bearing in mind the familiarity with the Tristan legend that Gower and Chaucer were able to take for granted in their readers,[23] it can be argued that *Tristrem and Ysoude* addresses an audience already familiar with the story, who will take pleasure in this allusive English poem with its focus on moments of dramatic intensity and lyrical emotion in the narrative, and its fashionable, sophisticated stanzaic patterning.[24]

There is a great deal for such an audience to enjoy in *Tristrem and Ysoude*: small details can resonate with meaning, and brief hints can indicate a well-known episode to come. For example, when Mark's barons choose Ysoude as his bride, a vivid image epitomizes her traditional white and red beauty: 'A brid briȝt þai ches/ As blod opon snoweing' (1354–5). However, the two elements, snow and blood, also foreshadow the famous incidents in which Tristrem's presence with Ysoude is betrayed first by footsteps in the snow and later by blood upon the sheets. Or again, when we are told of the stratagem to conceal the infant Tristrem's identity by reversing the syllables of his name: 'In court men cleped him so:/ Þo "tram" bi for þe "trist" ' (252–3), the use of the two definite articles draws attention to the fact that both syllables are nouns in Middle English, *tram* ('cunning device') and *trist* ('sorrow'), so that the line can be read as commenting in word-play on the purpose of the changed name; indeed, to an audience familiar with the Tristan story, the combination of 'cunning device' and 'sorrow' might seem an accurate synopsis of Tristrem's later life. A particularly striking device is the way the last two lines in the stanza, already slightly detached from the first eight lines by the presence of the short 'bob' line, are often used to give a brief indication of the content of the following stanza(s), in the manner of a 'headline' summary before the full story, inviting an audience already familiar with the story-line to recognize and remember what is coming next.[25]

---

23 See Gower, *Confessio Amantis*, VI. 470–5, VIII. 2496–503, *The Complete Works of John Gower*, ed. G. C. Macaulay, 4 vols (Oxford, 1899–1902); Chaucer, *The House of Fame*, 1793–7, *The Riverside Chaucer*, ed. Larry D. Benson et al., 3rd edn (Boston, MA, 1987).

24 A parallel might be drawn with the function of narrative scenes in medieval programmes of stained glass, which is not to provide a 'bible of the illiterate' in the simple sense of telling the story in pictures, but rather to stimulate reflection on scriptural or hagiographic events by visual reminders of episodes in an already well-known story.

25 For a 'comparison with the handling of allusion in *Beowulf*, allowing modern critics to speculate that the original audience were familiar with what is too briefly alluded to', see Claire Fennell, *Sir Tristrem: La storia di Tristano in Inghilterra* (Milan, 2000), noted by E. G. Stanley, '*Sir Tristrem* in Italy', *Notes and Queries* 246 (2001), p. 2. Derek Brewer describes a similar 'archaic' story-telling technique in *Morte Darthur*, where references to later events require the reader to

Dramatic moments in the poem have often attracted praise for the sharp, sometimes witty dialogue,[26] and the telling use of significant detail; a good example is the episode of Ysoude's casuistical oath, when Tristrem in disguise, carrying the queen across the Thames, deliberately falls 'Next her naked side' (2251).

> In water þai wald him sink
> *And* wers, ȝif þai may.
> 'ȝe quite him iuel his swink!'
> Þe quene seyd to hem ay.
> 'It semeþ, mete no drink
> Hadde he nouȝt mani a day;
> For pouerte, me þenk,
> He fel, for soþe to say,
> *And* nede.
> ȝeueþ him gold, y pray,
> He may bidde god me spede!' (2256–66)

Ysoude's attributing the 'poor' man's fall to lack of food, her desire that he be paid for his labour, and her hope that he may pray for her all fit plausibly together in the circumstances to enhance the impression of her innocence and goodness. This passage also shows the resources of the elaborate stanza: each (ab) pair of lines expresses a single idea, so that in fact the first eight lines read like four alexandrines with internal as well as final rhymes; the short 'bob' sums up Ysoude's argument and also leads on to the thought in the last two lines, with which it is connected by rhyme.

The stanza is equally suited to lyrical expressions of emotion, as in the oft-quoted incident when Mark sees the lovers asleep with a sword between them, while a sunbeam plays through a chink on Ysoude's 'face so schene' (2540), and is moved by the sight.

> His gloue he put þer inne,
> Þe sonne to were oway,
> Wreþe Mark gan winne,
> Þan seyd he: 'Wel ay!
> ȝif þai weren in sinne,
> Nouȝt so þai no lay!
> Lo, hou þai liue atvinne,
> Þai no hede nouȝt of swiche play
> Ywis!'
> Þe kniȝtes seyden ay:
> 'For trewe loue it is!' (2542–52)

'hold the whole story . . . simultaneously in mind' ('Malory's "Proving" of Sir Lancelot', *The Changing Face of Arthurian Romance*, ed. Alison Adams et al. (Cambridge, 1986), p. 128).

26 The poet has an excellent ear for speech, and some of the most spirited episodes contain extended dialogues, such as Tristrem's exchanges with Mark and Moraunt about the tribute to Ireland (964–1010); or with Mark and the Irish harpist earl about Ysoude (1849–925), which Tristrem ends with a dry rebuke: 'Sir king, . . . ȝif minstrels oþer þing'.

Opportunities for other affecting expressions of emotion are made by rearranging the material. For example, Rohaud gives Mark a ring as proof of Tristrem's true parentage; in other versions, Mark recognizes the ring as a family heirloom and its history is then related, but the English poet has lifted this passage and placed it much earlier in the narrative, reworked to make a touchingly simple speech from Tristrem's dying mother, Blauncheflour, as she gives the ring to the faithful Rohaud for her little son, hoping to secure his future:

> 'Mi broþer wele it knewe,
> Mi fader ȝaf it me;
> King Markes may rewe,
> Þe ring, þan he it se,
> And moun:
> As Rouland loued þe,
> Þou kepe it to his sone!'   (225–31)

Direct speech is often used in this way to create a sense of immediacy, as in the extended episode of Rohaud's reunion with Tristrem at Mark's court (575–759), where there is an effective contrast between the porter and the usher rudely addressing Rohaud as 'Cherl!' (620, 633) and Tristrem's kneeling to ask his forgiveness as 'Fader' (661), and a further moment of pathos when Rohaud has to break off his tale for weeping (727–30); but the poet also seizes opportunities to heighten emotional impact by narratorial involvement, as, for instance, in the comment on Tristrem's mother: 'For hir me reweþ sare:/ On child bed, þer sche lay' (216–17), or, more obliquely, in the description of Rohaud's self-restraint as he hides the young Tristrem's identity from the cruel usurper:

> *And* euer he dede as þe sleiȝe
> *And* held his hert in an,
> Þat wise:
> It brast þurch blod *and* ban,
> Ȝif hope no ware to rise.   (271–5)

The short lines are also particularly effective in representing thought: instead of Thomas's lengthy, exhaustive discussions, a few lines can convey penetrating insights. For instance, Mark, listening to Tristrem and Ysoude acting their parts in the orchard, is given a sudden conviction of their innocence in the midst of their speeches:

> Markes hert was sare,
> Þer he sat in þe tre,
> *And* þouȝt:
> 'Vngilti er ȝe
> In swiche a sclaunder brouȝt!'   (2141–5)

Tristrem experiences a similarly sudden access of knowledge in the episode of his marriage to Ysoude of Brittany. The English poem introduces into Tristrem's quandary something entirely lacking from Thomas's sophistical dissection of Tristran's motives: an awareness of moral constraints outside himself as he recognizes that no matter how much he feels Mark to be in the wrong or how firmly he believes Ysoude's love that has caused him such sorrow to be justly his own, biblically authorized laws forbid it:

> 'Mark, mi nem, haþ sinne,
> Wrong he haþ ous wrouȝt;
> Icham in sorwe *and* pine,
> Þer to hye haþ me brouȝt.
> Hir loue, y say, is mine,
> Þe boke seyt, it is nouȝt
> Wiþ riȝt!'   (2665–71)

Marriage to Ysoude of Brittany, it is implied, represents Tristrem's acceptance of society's ban on his love for Ysoude the queen. But in the wedding-night scene there is an equally striking innovation where, by contrast with Thomas (whose self-absorbed Tristran reveals little understanding of Ysolt's heart), the English poet gives his Tristrem a sudden devastating certainty that Ysoude would never have renounced their love as he has done: ' "Oȝain me swiche a þing/ Dede neuer Ysoude so" ' (2687–8). He blames himself in terms that bitterly echo the marriage-like bond of the love-drink:

> 'Mine hert may no man bring
> For no þing hir fro,
> Þat fre.
> Ich haue tvinned ous to,
> Þe wrong is al in me!'   (2691–5)

The poet thus exploits the resources of his chosen stanza pattern to produce an effect of emotional directness that is especially striking in this radically abridged reworking of the tragic love story.

   Much of the effectiveness of *Tristrem and Ysoude* – its emotional directness, its narrative vigour – has to do with the aesthetics of *abbreviatio*. The predominance of 'action and movement' is noted by Mills as characteristic of this and other Middle English 'reductions' of French romances, such as *Ywain and Gawain* or *Sir Percyvell* (*Arthur of the English*, p. 146); meaning tends to be invested in actions and brief expressive speeches rather than in extensive analysis of emotion and motives, and narrative pace is usually brisk. However, it is also the case, as Pickford points out, that 'the author does not always shorten' the narrative in *Tristrem and Ysoude* (p. 226), and it is interesting to note which episodes are given more extended treatment. As one would expect in a chivalric romance, major knightly encounters tend to be full and detailed and, not surprisingly, the details are often expressed in stock phrases; though each of Tristrem's battles (against Morgan, Moraunt, the dragon, Urgan and Beliagog; the tournament to requite his enemies at court;

the final fight on behalf of young Tristrem) is dealt with in a different and appropriate way: they are not just excuses for formulaic violence.

Equally expansive episodes occur in the earlier part of the romance dealing with Tristrem's youth: his boyhood education under the care of his foster-father Rohaud, and his life as a young henchman at the court of King Mark. Tristrem's education follows the normal pattern for a boy of noble birth: a curriculum including reading and studying in the school-room (278–86), acquiring the skills and accomplishments necessary for courtly life (289–92), and becoming expert in hunting (293–7). This account leads naturally into the episode of Tristrem's abduction by Norwegian mariners (298–396), turning as it does on his desire for fine hawks and his expertise at chess; while his noble status is signalled on his approach to Mark's court both by the rich cloth of his robe (408–11, 450) and by his extraordinary knowledge of the art of hunting (445–539). The king is further convinced of Tristrem's coming of 'riche kinne' when he excels all others in playing the harp (551–72), and the youth is given a favoured position at court, 'ful dere' to King Mark (574), dressed in fine new clothes (568–9, 599–600), and chosen to carve for the king (602–3). It is significant that a large part of Tristrem's education is to do with correct terminology:

> He tauȝt him ich a lede
> Of ich maner of glewe
> *And* euerich play in þede,
> Old lawes *and* newe.   (289–92)

This accords with the type of instruction provided in medieval English manuals of hunting, largely concerned as they are with proper terms, the exclusive specialized language that signifies a gentle education. English manuals have been described as focusing on the peripheral, 'social details of language, ritual procedure, horn music and hunting cries', precisely the matters in which Tristrem instructs the huntsmen, and the means by which hunting is raised from a utilitarian activity to a noble sport.[27] Books of courtesy teaching the etiquette of court life in matters such as appropriate dress and correct manners at table and in serving are equally clear about their purpose, which is that gentle breeding should be displayed in fitting appearance and behaviour.[28]

The concerns thus marked by their extended treatment – the exercise of arms and the programme of noble education – may give an indication of the readership for which this romance was produced; and a further indication may be seen in the treatment of the love theme. Despite the centrality of *un*married

---

[27] Anne Rooney, *Hunting in Middle English Literature* (Cambridge, 1993), p. 7. William Twici's *Art of Venery*, contemporary with *Tristrem and Ysoude* and circulating in both AN and ME versions, covers the same topics as Tristrem's teaching.

[28] See Jonathan Nicholls, *The Matter of Courtesy: Medieval Courtesy Books and the Gawain-Poet* (Cambridge, 1985).

love in the story of *Tristrem and Ysoude*, it is notable how far the poet has
striven to associate the lovers' irrevocable and faithful union symbolically
with the bond of marriage; and this innovation is supported by a clear
emphasis on regular family relationships in other passages peculiar to this
version of the story, such as the invention of the dying mother's care for her
baby son, the representation of Gauhardin's liaison with Brengwain as a
formal betrothal before marriage,[29] and the comparatively extended treatment
of the wedding of Tristrem's parents (155–63). These concerns – martial
prowess, courtly accomplishments and family ties – fit well with the context
of *Tristrem and Ysoude* in the Auchinleck MS, a volume that appears to be a
family compendium produced for a wealthy knightly household.[30]

Tristrem and Ysoude is, I would maintain, a much more coherent narrative
than has usually been allowed, freely and deliberately adapted from Thomas's
Anglo-Norman *Tristran* for an audience already acquainted with the Tristan
story, able to appreciate the poet's skill in the use of *abbreviatio* and the virtu-
osity exhibited in his complicated stanza, and engaged with the values
projected onto the traditional material in this retelling.

My project in 'The True Romance of *Tristrem and Ysoude*', besides
restoring the proper name of the romance, has been to take seriously its claim
to a place in the Tristan tradition, to highlight the genuine centrality of the
love story in the narrative design, and to elicit the thematic significance of the
emphasis on 'Tristrem trewe'. However, there is yet one more aspect of the
poem as a 'true romance' that merits attention. The romance opens with the
narrator's assertion that he heard this story at a specific place from a particular
authority: 'I was a[t Erceldoun,]/ Wiþ Tomas spak y þare' (1–2), and 'Tomas'
is cited on a further four occasions in the poem (10, 397, 412, 2787). Perhaps
the explanation for this vexed reference,[31] whether or not the name Tomas
cited throughout the text also refers to the author of the Anglo-Norman
Tristran, is that it is a version of the conventional truth claim.[32] The poet

---

[29] 'Gauhardine treuþe pliȝt/ Brengwain to wiue weld' (3134–5). On this aspect of Middle English
romance, see Felicity Riddy, 'Middle English Romance: Family, Marriage, Intimacy', *The
Cambridge Companion to Medieval Romance*, ed. Roberta L. Krueger (Cambridge, 2000), pp.
235–52; Jennifer Fellows, 'Mothers in Middle English Romance', *Women and Literature in
Britain, 1150–1500*, pp. 41–60.

[30] See Thorlac Turville-Petre, *England the Nation: Language, Literature and National Identity,
1290–1340* (Oxford, 1996), pp. 108–41. *Tristrem and Ysoude* demonstrates the concern for
England that Turville-Petre finds exemplified in *Guy of Warwick*: like Guy, Tristrem is also shown
as an explicitly English champion: 'God help Tristrem, þe kniȝt!/ He fauȝt for Ingland' (1033–4).

[31] 'Erceldoune', 'sir Tristrem' and 'Thomas' are all mentioned within seven lines in Mannyng's
Chronicle (93–100); Scott attributed the poem to 'Thomas of Erceldoune, called the Rhymer, who
flourished in the thirteenth-century' (p. iii); a tantalizingly similar place name occurs in Béroul's
Tristran, where Arthur comes to Iseut's aid from 'Isneldone' (3373).

[32] James A. H. Murray endorses Wright's opinion that 'the person who translated the Auchinleck
version from the French original, finding a "Thomas" mentioned therein, and not knowing who he
was, "may have taken him for the Thomas whose name was then most famous, viz. Thomas of
Erceldoune, and thus put the name of the latter to his English edition" ' (*The Romance and Prophecies of Thomas of Erceldoune*, EETS OS 61 (1875), p. xxii). Given the emphasis on 'trewe' in

attaches his text to the name of Thomas of Erceldoune, celebrated author of prophecies, and the opening stanzas with their riddling introductory style, somewhat resembling that of the cryptic prophecies attributed to Thomas of Erceldoune,[33] are thus given the appearance of truth.

Tristrem and Ysoude, an association with 'True Thomas' the prophet-poet as a deliberate truth claim seems just as likely.

[33] See, for example, MS Harley 2253, fol. 127.

8

Did Knights Have Baths?
The Absence of Bathing in Middle English Romance

ELIZABETH ARCHIBALD

How frequently did knights, or indeed anyone else, have baths in the Middle Ages, in literature and in real life? Diametrically opposite answers are given by two distinguished nineteenth-century medieval scholars. According to the French historian J. Michelet, there were no baths for a thousand years: 'Soyez sûr que pas un de ces chevaliers, de ces belles si éthérées, les Perceval, les Tristan, les Iseult, ne se lavaient' ('Certainly not one of these knights and these ethereal ladies, the Percevals, the Tristans, the Iseults, washed themselves').[1] It is not difficult to think of a scene involving Tristan that proves Michelet wrong: when he returns to Ireland in disguise to be cured of his wound, he is having a bath when he is recognized by Iseut as the killer of her uncle.[2] This scene is very frequently illustrated in medieval art, in manuscripts and tapestries; the Tristan story seems to have been a much more popular topic for illustration than the Arthurian romances, and the bathing scene is often included.[3] But at the other extreme, the comments of critics who do believe that bathing was very much a part of medieval life are also problematic. In striking contrast to Michelet, Thomas Wright, that prolific editor of medieval texts, wrote a history of domestic life in which he assumes that bathing was the norm in the Middle Ages:

> The practice of warm-bathing prevailed very generally in all classes of society, and is frequently alluded to in the mediaeval romances and stories. For this purpose a large bathing-tub was used. . . . People sometimes bathed immediately after rising in the morning; and we find the bath used after dinner, and before going to bed. A bath was also often prepared for a visitor on his arrival from a journey; and, what seems still more singular, in the

[1] J. Michelet, quoted in Augustin Cabanès, *Moeurs intimes du passé (2e série): La vie aux bains* (Paris, 1900), p. 123.
[2] Gottfried von Strassburg, *Tristan*, 10147–10361, ed. Karl Marold, 3rd edn (Berlin, 1969); trans. A. T. Hatto (Harmondsworth, 1960), pp. 175–8. I cite verse texts by line number (given immediately after the title), and prose texts by page number; chapter numbers are given where appropriate.
[3] See R. S. Loomis, *The Arthurian Legends in Medieval Art* (London, 1938), pp. 19 and 42–69.

numerous stories of amorous intrigues, the two lovers usually begin their interviews by bathing together.[4]

Wright is not alone in this view. In *English Life in the Middle Ages*, the architectural historian L. F. Salzman writes:

... we read in innumerable romances that it was the first act of hospitality on the arrival of a visitor at a castle, to provide him with a bath, and the illustrations to these romances show that great houses often had a kind of bath-room, a curtained alcove containing a large tub.[5]

Margaret Wood, reiterating this point, adds that baths were offered to 'an important guest, travel weary, or to a knight returning from the joust'.[6]

These comments may come as a shock to literary critics, especially those who specialize in Middle English romance. When Wright refers to amorous intrigues begun in a shared bath, he is probably referring to French fabliaux and the *Decameron*, where such scenes do occur, though they are by no means standard; there are very few fabliaux in English, and they do not involve baths (the tubs in Chaucer's *Miller's Tale* are kneading tubs).[7] But what about baths in 'innumerable romances'? What texts do Salzman and Wood have in mind when they assert that baths are such a standard aspect of romance hospitality, offered to tired travellers and jousters as a matter of course?

The *Middle English Dictionary* gives examples of *bath* and *bathen* from a wide range of texts, but relatively few of them are romances. A striking number come from Layamon's *Brut*.[8] He describes the founding of Bath with its baths by Bladud (1421–4); he also tells how Cordelia orders a bath for Lear (1781), Vortigern does the same for Constans (6592), and Aurelius arranges baths for his troops after the defeat of Hengest (8278–80). Some of these baths are therapeutic, and this trend can be found in later writers too, though healing

---

4 Thomas Wright, *The Homes of Other Days; A History of Domestic Manners and Sentiments in England from the Earliest Known Period to Modern Times* (London, 1871), p. 271. See also Lawrence Wright, *Clean and Decent: The History of the Bath and Loo* (London, 1960 [4th imp. corr. 1963]), p. 31; this engaging book includes many striking illustrations, but very inadequate citations of their sources. There is much discussion of medieval baths, with many illustrations (again inadequately cited) in Hans Peter Duerr, *Nacktheit und Scham*, vol. 1 of *Der Mythos vom Zivilisationsprocess* (Frankfurt-am-Main, 1988); see especially pp. 25–72. See also the section on bathing in Philippe Braunstein, 'Toward Intimacy: The Fourteenth and Fifteenth Centuries', *A History of Private Life*, Vol. 2: *Revelations of the Medieval World*, ed. Georges Duby, trans. Arthur Goldhammer (Cambridge, MA, 1988), pp. 535–630 (see pp. 600–10). Both these scholars discuss attitudes to nudity, an important topic that is beyond the scope of the present essay, but which I hope to address in a larger study of medieval bathing.

5 L. F. Salzman, *English Life in the Middle Ages* (London, 1926), p. 106.

6 Margaret Wood, *The English Mediaeval House* (London, 1965; rpt 1994), p. 372.

7 For examples in fabliaux, see Jean Larmat, 'Les Bains dans la littérature française du moyen âge', *Les Soins de beauté*, ed. Denis Menjot (Nice, 1987), pp. 195–210 (pp. 206–8). L. Wright prints a comical manuscript illustration from *Les Trois Chanoinesses de Couloigne* showing the three canonesses sitting in bath-tubs while the man on whom they have designs eats at a table between them: see *Clean and Decent*, p. 45.

8 Layamon, *Brut*, ed. and trans. W. J. R. Barron and Carol Weinberg (Harlow, 1995).

baths seem relatively rare in romance given the number of battles and journeys undergone by the heroes. Baths often occur when heroes have gone temporarily mad. In *Ywain and Gawain,* Ywain is given a bath by the ladies who find and cure him.[9] In Malory's *Morte Darthur* Tristram is bathed and washed during his madness: 'And there they bathed hym and washyd hym, and gaff hym hote suppyngis, tylle they had brought hym well to hys remembraunce.'[10] Danielle Régnier-Bohler refers to 'the ritual of the bath' as 'an essential feature of any reintegration into society', but Malory makes no mention of baths when Lancelot recovers from his madness, perhaps because he is cured by the Grail.[11]

What about all the sane heroes who spend so much time out questing and fighting? The only instance of bathing in the Middle English metrical romances, according to the useful *Concordance to the Middle English Metrical Romances,* is in *Sir Orfeo,* where the hero is bathed and shaved after the recognition scene; no doubt this was very necessary after all those years in the wilderness.[12] Sir Eglamour is given a bath after hunting a boar (though it is not entirely clear whether it is to restore him after his exertions, or to prepare him for his fight with the giant next day).[13] His bath is filled with herbs, and we are told that he lay in it all night; does this mean that servants were up all night replenishing the hot water, or was it macho to spend the night in a cold bath? In *Beves of Hamtoun,* Beves is given a healing bath by Josiane at a very early stage in their relationship, when he has been wounded by Saracens:

> In to chaumber ȝhe gan him take
> And riche baþes ȝhe let him make,
> Þat wiþ inne a lite stonde
> He was boþe hol and sonde.[14]

---

9 *Ywain and Gawain,* 1864–6, ed. M. Mills, *Ywain and Gawain, Sir Percyvell of Gales, The Anturs of Arther* (London, 1992). This bath also occurs in the source, Chrétien's *Yvain,* 3127–30, ed. M. Roques, CFMA (Paris, 1978). Earlier in both versions of the story Yvain is given a bath by Lunete before his first meeting with Laudine (*Yvain,* 1881–4; *Ywain and Gawain,* 1101–4), but this seems to be cosmetic rather than medicinal.

10 Malory, *Works,* ed. E. Vinaver, 3rd edn, rev. P. J. C. Field, 3 vols (Oxford, 1990), 501/7–10 [IX.21] and 819/24–7 [XII.2]; references to Malory are given by page and line number (the pagination is continous through the three volumes); the numbers in square brackets refer to Caxton's chapter division. Malory recounts the recognition in the bath scene (pp. 389/15–390/25), and so does the thirteenth-century stanzaic *Sir Tristrem,* 1239–43, ed. Alan Lupack, *Lancelot of the Laik and Sir Tristrem,* TEAMS (Kalamazoo, 1994).

11 Danielle Régnier-Bohler, 'Imagining the Self: Exploring Literature', *A History of Private Life,* vol. 2, ed. Duby, trans. Goldhammer, pp. 311–94 (see p. 369). For Lancelot's recovery, see Malory 824/18–27 [XII.4].

12 *A Concordance to the Middle English Metrical Romances,* Vol. 1: *The Matter of England,* ed. T. Saiko and M. Imai (New York, 1988); there is no entry for *tub* or *stew. Sir Orfeo,* 585, ed. A. J. Bliss, 2nd edn (Oxford, 1966).

13 *Sir Eglamour of Artois,* 518–22, ed. F. Richardson, EETS OS 256 (London, 1965).

14 *The Romance of Sir Beues of Hamtoun,* 731–4 (Auchinleck version), ed. E. Kölbing, EETS ES 46, 48, 65 (London, 1885–94).

Here, as in the Tristan story, it is apparently quite acceptable for a princess to act as a bath attendant to a wounded visitor.

There are several references to baths in *Guy of Warwick*.[15] Guy bathes his wounded friend Heraud (Auch./Caius 1781), and Tirri is given a bath when he escapes from prison (Auch. 6377; not in Caius); these seem to be therapeutic baths. When Guy agrees to fight on behalf of the pagan king Triamour, the king orders a bath for him (Auch. st. 89/Caius 8073). But later when Guy is about to fight for Tirri against the emperor's steward, there is an interesting divergence between the texts. In the Auchinleck version the emperor's daughter gives him a bath, but he refuses the silk clothes she offers him (Auch. st. 180); in the Caius version, he refuses both bath and clothes (Caius 9570–3). The king and the princess seem to think that baths will strengthen the hero; does he think bathing enervating, or does he consider it too effete, along with the silk clothes?[16] The text gives us no clue. *Guy of Warwick* seems unusual in the number of baths it includes, but what is missing here, as in most other Middle English romances, is the bath as an agreeable form of hospitality when a knight arrives at a castle, as described by Salzman and Wood. The omission seems particularly striking in *Sir Gawain and the Green Knight*. Poor Gawain has been sleeping rough in his armour among the icicles, so one of the main comforts Hautdesert could have offered him would surely have been a bath. Bercilak's court is presented as the equal of Camelot in its splendour and hospitality, and other aspects of the luxurious living there are described in detail, but baths do not seem to be on offer (it should be said that they are not mentioned at Camelot either).

The writings of Chrétien de Troyes provide an interesting point of comparison. Again, baths are not particularly frequent.[17] Here as in the English romances, it seems to be quite normal for a protagonist to change into splendid clothes without any reference to bathing or washing. The baths Chrétien does mention can be divided into two categories: healing baths and baths before the knighting ceremony. Healing baths are not particularly common in Chrétien's works. Lancelot is given baths by Bademagus' daughter after she has rescued him from the tower; Régnier-Bohler mentions this passage and asks: 'Were these baths signs of hospitality, were they therapeutic, or were they erotic in intent?'[18] Perhaps the answer is all three. Yvain is bathed during his recovery from madness; Guivret arranges baths for Erec once the latter is no longer in pain, and in *Perceval* the proud knight's lady is

---

[15] *Guy of Warwick*, ed. J. Zupitza, EETS ES 42, 49, 59 (London, 1883–91). I cite both the Auchinleck and Caius versions; references to the tail-rhyme section of the Auchinleck version are by stanza number, abbreviated as st.

[16] I am grateful to Dr David Freemantle of Southampton University for the information that silk was used in various parts of the world to prevent wounds from becoming infected.

[17] I have not yet completed a broad survey of the incidence of bathing in French romances, but there is a brief discussion in Régnier-Bohler, 'Imagining the Self', pp. 363–6.

[18] *Le Chevalier de la Charrete*, 6658–65, ed. M. Roques, CFMA (Paris, 1978); Régnier-Bohler, 'Imagining the Self', p. 366.

sent to bathe and rest until she recovers from her mistreatment.[19] Baths associated with the knighting ceremony are more problematic; historically, manuals of chivalry mention the ritual bath before the overnight church vigil, but it is not clear whether this practice was in fact very widespread.[20] According to Keen, the title Knight of the Bath did not belong to a formal order, but was the term used for knights who had been knighted according to a specially complex ritual.[21] This might suggest that the bath was an optional extra not widely used. It must have been known in late twelfth-century France, for in Chrétien's *Erec* Arthur has a hundred squires bathed before they are knighted on the occasion of Erec's wedding; in *Cligés* Alexander and his friends do not bother to have tubs heated before being knighted, but bathe in the sea; and at the point where *Perceval* breaks off, the old queen orders that a startling five hundred tubs be heated for the squires who are going to be knighted by Gawain.[22] Can these numbers be plausible? Even if they are greatly exaggerated, they suggest that there might well be numerous tubs in a single castle. Bathing does seem to have been a part of the knighting ceremony in England, at least on some occasions; Robert Ackerman and Faith Lyons mention Geoffrey Plantagenet's knighting in 1129, and Froissart's account of 'bathing and robing for the mass investiture at Henry IV's coronation in 1399'.[23] But this ritual bath is strikingly absent from Middle English romances, as Ackerman points out.[24] He does not think this omission particularly significant, but, as will become apparent, I think it may be part of a larger trend in medieval England.

In Chrétien's romances, although they are not as frequently mentioned, bath facilities seem to be considered an important part of gracious living. In addition to the examples given above, there is the evidence of the lovers' refuge in *Cligés*. Jehan promises Cligés that the tower he has just built is very suitable for housing an 'amie', for it includes 'estuves/ Et l'eve chaude par les cuves/ Qui vient par conduit desoz la terre' ('baths and hot water for the tubs brought by a pipe under the earth'); in the fifteenth-century prose version the plumbing arrangements are much more complex in both design and decoration.[25] The popularity and familiarity of baths in Chrétien's time are also indi-

---

19 *Yvain*, 1900; *Erec*, ed. M. Roques, CFMA (Paris, 1981), 5180–1; *Perceval*, 3950–3, ed. William Roach, TLF (Geneva, 1959).

20 Maurice Keen, *Chivalry* (New Haven, 1984), pp. 7 and 65; Keen prints an image of the bath of knighthood opposite p. 84 (Plate 16), though the bather looks rather feminine. On accounts in romance, see Robert W. Ackerman, 'The Knighting Ceremonies in the Middle English Romances', *Speculum* 19 (1944), pp. 285–313 (see p. 309), and Faith Lyons, 'Aspects of the Knighting Ceremony', *The Medieval Alexander Legend and Romance Epic: Essays in Honour of David J. A. Ross*, ed. Peter Noble, Lucie Polak and Claire Isoz (New York and London, 1982), pp. 125–30.

21 Keen, *Chivalry*, p. 78.

22 *Erec*, 1963–5; *Cligés*, 1134–8; *Perceval*, 9171–82.

23 Ackerman, 'Knighting Ceremonies', pp. 307 and 309; Lyons, 'Aspects', p. 127.

24 Ackerman, 'Knighting Ceremonies', pp. 309 and 311–12.

25 Compare *Cligés*, 5561–3, and *Prose Cligés*, ed. W. Foerster, *Christian von Troyes, Sämtliche Werke*, vol. 1 (Halle, 1884), p. 327. I am indebted for the latter reference to a lecture by Prof. Jane

cated by a metaphorical allusion when Cligés' mother Soredamors falls in love: 'Amors li a chaufé un baing/ Qui molt l'eschaufe et molt li nuist' ('love has heated her a bath that scalds and hurts her very much').[26] Extremely hot baths also play a crucial part in a contemporary text, Marie de France's *Equitan*, which I discuss later.

I have not come across many references to Middle English romance heroines having baths, medicinal or pleasurable. When Trivet's Constance arrives in Northumberland, she is restored with food and baths and other comforts so that she regains her beauty, but neither Chaucer nor Gower allow their Constances the comfort of a bath, nor do other calumniated wives such as Emaré have them.[27] Percyvelle's mother is given a bath when she is restored to sanity at the very end of *Sir Percyvelle*.[28] In *Huon of Burdeux*, Lord Berners's early sixteenth-century translation of a Burgundian prose version of a twelfth-century French poem, Huon's wife Esclarmonde is given a reviving bath after she has been imprisoned: 'And the lady had iiii ladyes to serve her and she was bayned and stuyd and aparayled.'[29] Later Huon's granddaughter Ide, who is cross-dressing and has become a successful knight, is ordered by the angry Emperor of Rome to take a bath publicly in order to establish whether she is a man or a woman (this bath does not actually happen, as God intervenes to transform her into a man). She begs to be spared this ordeal on the grounds that ' "I haue not ben accustomed to be bayned" '.[30] Is she saying this in her role as a macho knight? Is the public bath here an indication that there was much less prudery about public bathing and nudity than one might have supposed, or is it intended to be shocking and humiliating? Female protagonists sometimes have baths before weddings – though not as often as one might expect. Gower's Hag in his Tale of Florent is given a bath and a rest 'as it was that time lawe'.[31] Does this suggest that baths are no longer common but are part of a legendary past? This seems unlikely. In Capgrave's fifteenth-century life of St Katherine, Jesus says that the saint must be washed clean in baptism as preparation for her mystic marriage.[32] The Virgin adds reassuringly:

H. M. Taylor on the Burgundian *Erec* and *Cligés*. It may be relevant that the setting of this romance is Constantinople, part of the Roman empire and a byword for sophistication.

[26] *Cligés*, 464–5. Régnier-Bohler quotes a similar use of metaphor from the *Roman de la Rose* ('Imagining the Self', p. 365).

[27] Trivet's text is printed in Margaret Schlauch's essay on the *Man of Law's Tale, Sources and Analogues of Chaucer's* Canterbury Tales, ed. W. Bryan and G. Dempster (London, 1941), pp. 165–81 (see p. 169).

[28] *Sir Percyvelle*, 2268–71, ed. Mills (see n. 9 above).

[29] Lord Berners, *Huon of Burdeux*, ch. cxlv, ed. S. L. Lee, 2 vols, EETS ES 40, 41, 43, 50 (London, 1882–7), II. 543.

[30] *Huon*, ch. clxxix, ed. Lee, II. 727. In the French verse and prose versions, the Emperor gets into the bath himself and orders Yde to join him, but she makes the same excuse; see *Esclarmonde, Clarisse et Florent, Yde et Olive*, ed. Max Schweigel (Marburg, 1889), pp. 81 and 162.

[31] Gower, *Confessio Amantis*, I. 1746, *English Works*, ed. G. C. Macaulay, 2 vols, EETS ES 81 and 82 (London, 1900–1).

[32] John Capgrave, *Life of St Katherine of Alexandria*, 3.1030–65, ed. Karen Winstead (Kalamazoo,

'It is a goodely usage, sothely to seye,
Who schal be weddyd onto duke or kynge
Befor hir weddyng to hafe a bathynge

For to make her swete, for to make her clene,
Else myght she renne in ful grete offens . . . [cause great offence]
Aftyr your waschyng ye schal be full mery!' (1069–73, 1078)

There is an interesting play here on two types of bathing. The baptismal bath ordered by Jesus is the equivalent of the ritual bath on the eve of the knighting ceremony, while the Virgin's comment evokes the world of aristocratic gracious living. Is the Virgin explaining an unusual and unfamiliar request, or is she merely endorsing the already standard practice of bathing? The latter seems to me more likely, though it would contradict the indication in Gower's tale that bathing before a wedding is no longer required.

Baths are also linked to magic and to Christian legends, in stories of healing wells and magical transformations. Limitations of space do not permit me to explore this theme here, but in relation to women in romance, and to the connection between baths and magic, it is worth noting a curious reference in Malory, one of his very few mentions of bathing. When Lancelot arrives at Corbenic for the first time, the people urge him to release 'a dolerous lady that hath bene there in paynes many wyntyrs and dayes, for ever she boyleth in scaldynge watir'; this lady is Elaine, the future mother of Galahad, and the enchantment is a punishment imposed on her by Morgan le Fay.[33] The doors are unbolted and he 'wente into the chambir that was as hote as ony styew [bath]. And there sir Launcelot toke the fayryst lady by the honde that ever he sawe, and she was naked as a nedyll.' But is she in a bathtub, or a bathroom, or both? In the source, the French Vulgate *Lancelot*, she is first seen in a marble bathtub ('une cuve de marbre') when Gawain tries unsuccessfully to release her; later on when Lancelot succeeds, she is in a basin of water.[34] In comparison, Malory's account seems very vague. Did he have difficulty in visualizing this scene, or did he think that his audience might be baffled? Is he trying to evoke the enchantment by being mysteriously imprecise, or would it have been quite obvious to his audience that Elaine was in a tub?

The connection between women and baths is central to several French romances that have no analogues in Middle English; they offer useful evidence of the popularity of both private and public bathing. Gerard de

---

1999). Braunstein discusses an early sixteenth-century German allegorical text by Thomas Murner called *Badenfuhrt* (Cleansing Journey), 'an allegory of conversion in whch Christ borrows the trumpet of a bathhouse attendant'; see 'Toward Intimacy', pp. 608–9 (n. 4 above).

33 Malory, 791/31–792/20 [XI.1].

34 The Gawain episode is ch. lxvi.5–8 in vol. 2 of *Lancelot*, ed. A. Micha (Geneva, 1978), pp. 373–4; the Lancelot episode is ch. lxxviii.45 in vol. 4 (Geneva, 1979), pp. 201–2. The Lancelot episode may be the scene represented in an engaging image of a knight in armour talking to a naked woman in a bath-tub, apparently out of doors, which is reproduced in L. Wright, *Clean and Decent*, p. 41; it also appears in T. Wright, *History of Domestic Manners*, p. 271, where it is said to come from a French Grail manuscript, BL Addit. MS 292, fol. 266.

Montreuil's *Roman de la Violette* (c. 1228) is an analogue of the *Cymbeline* plot in which a lady whose virtues have been greatly praised by her lover is spied on in her bath by another man who peeps through a hole in the door and sees the violet birthmark on her breast; he then claims to have slept with her.[35] *Flamenca*, an Occitan romance written in the later thirteenth century, is set in a famous French spa town, Bourbon-Archambault, and the plot hinges on the popularity of therapeutic bathing.[36] The hero falls in love with a young married woman whose jealous husband allows her out only to go to church and to the baths. In order to be able to meet her admirer, she feigns illness (explaining her symptoms in great detail to her husband), and is thus permitted to visit the baths regularly. The resourceful suitor takes a room in the inn next door to the baths and tunnels through so that they can consummate their passion. Régnier-Bohler comments that 'baths encouraged eroticism', and that *Flamenca* 'is unusually rich in its documentation of explicit eroticism and of the sociability of the baths'.[37] This link between baths and sex is lacking in Middle English romance, in spite of the comments of the social historians quoted at the beginning of this essay; of course, aristocrats and royalty would not be using public baths.

The evidence in Middle English romances for bathing in England seems rather thin, but there can be no doubt about the popularity of bathing in Western Europe in the later Middle Ages. Private bathing facilities certainly existed in the houses of the well-to-do, and there were public bathing facilities in many towns, though possibly fewer in English towns than on the continent. Evidence for bathing in England comes in various forms. Entries in the accounts for building work in royal palaces show that some features of medieval English bathrooms would be quite familiar to us today. In 1275 Robert the Goldsmith received payment for taps for the palace of Westminster in various shapes, including leopard heads, and also for waste pipes.[38] In 1324 Reigate stone was used to create a screen in front of the royal bathtub in Westminster Palace.[39] Edward II and Richard II both had tiled bathrooms, and Edward bought 24 mats at 2p each as protection against the cold floor.[40] Tubs often had canopies too; Princess Margaret of Flanders acquired some red ones in 1403, and also bought 64 ells of cloth to pad two bathtubs.[41] In 1351 Edward III paid for taps for the hot and cold water supply to his bathtub at Westminster, though this degree of sophisticated plumbing seems to have

---

35 Gerbert de Montreuil, *Roman de la Violette ou de Gerart de Nevers*, 618–74, ed. Douglas L. Buffum (Paris, 1928); the later prose version is edited by Lawrence F. H. Lowe as *Gérard de Nevers* (Princeton and Paris, 1928), pp. 13–15. Duerr reproduces an illustration of the heroine alone in her tub being spied on: see *Nacktheit*, p. 39.

36 *Flamenca*, ed. and trans. E. D. Blodgett (London, 1995).

37 Régnier-Bohler, 'Imagining the Self', pp. 364–5.

38 L. F. Salzman, *Building in England down to 1540* (Oxford, 1952; rpt 1967), p. 276.

39 Ibid., p. 130.

40 Wood, *English Mediaeval House*, p. 373.

41 Ibid., pp. 371–2.

been very rare; there are many references to the use of jugs and pots of hot water for filling baths.[42] Joseph and Mary Gies describe what must have been normal for most baths in private houses:

> Baths were taken in a wooden tub, protected by a tent or canopy and often padded with cloth. In warm weather, the tub was often placed in the garden; in cold weather, in the chamber near the fire. When the lord travelled, the tub accompanied him, along with a bathman who prepared the baths.[43]

King John took his own tub on his travels, along with a bathman called William.[44] Roger of the Chamber was responsible for the baths of Eleanor de Montford; apparently a noblewoman could be attended in her bath by a male servant (again this raises the question of attitudes to nudity).[45]

One might expect to find some discussion of bathing in the courtesy books, but I have found only one significant example. John Russell, sometime servant of Humfrey of Gloucester, gives detailed instructions on how to prepare a bath for a lord in his manual for superior servants, *The Book of Nurture*.

> ȝeff youre souerayne will to þe bathe, his body to wasche clene,
> hang shetis round about þe rooff; do thus as I meene;
> euery shete full of flowres & herbis soote and grene,
> and looke ye haue sponges .v. or vj. þeron to sytte or lene:
> looke þer be a gret sponge, þer-on youre souerayne to sytt:
> þeron a shete, & so he may bathe hym þer a fytte;
> undir his feete also a sponge, ȝiff þer be any to putt;
> and alwey be sure of þe dur, & se þat he be shutt.[46]

He goes on to describe medicinal baths and the properties of various herbs – a combination of aromatherapy and homeopathy.

The association of bathing with medicine was widespread, as can be seen in the allusions in romances discussed above. Many of the references to baths in the *Middle English Dictionary* are to medical tracts. According to the influential Constantine the African, regular bathing was an important aspect of good health, together with sexual intercourse, exercise, a good diet and adequate sleep.[47] There is a thirteenth-century Latin poem by Peter of Eboli

---

42 Ibid., p. 372.
43 Joseph and Frances Gies, *Life in a Medieval Castle* (London, 1974), p. 71.
44 W. L. Warren, *King John* (London, 1961), pp. 136–7, cited by Wood, *English Mediaeval House*, p. 372.
45 See C. M. Woolgar, *The Great Household in Later Medieval England* (New Haven, 1999), p. 167, cited by Sarah Salih in 'At Home; Out of the House', *The Cambridge Companion to Medieval Women's Writing*, ed. Carolyn Dinshaw and David Wallace (Cambridge, 2003), pp. 124–40 (see p. 131); I am indebted to Linda Gowans for this reference.
46 John Russell's *Book of Nurture*, 975–82, ed. F. J. Furnivall in *The Babees Book*, EETS OS 32 (London, 1868), pp. 182–5.
47 See James A. Brundage, *Law, Sex, and Christian Society in Medieval Europe* (Chicago, 1987), p. 187.

about the thirty-five different baths at Pozzuoli, outside Naples, each of which had a specific therapeutic value; this poem survives in at least twenty copies, some with wonderful full-page illustrations.[48] It is unclear whether this poem was read in England (all the known manuscripts come from Naples); but the very popular *Secreta Secretorum* certainly was, and many versions of it include a section on baths, with recommendations about the seasons in which they should and should not be taken.[49] Spring is a good time for blood-letting and for sweating and bathing (56/28–31), but in summer blood-letting, bathing, and women (i.e. sex) should be avoided as much as possible (57/18–20). In winter, moderate sexual activity is advised, and baths are good because of the cold weather. Excessively long baths lead to fatness and to feebleness (59/15–22); bathing in sulphurous water leads to thinness (60/3–4). There are detailed recommendations about what herbs to put in baths (59/22–5). Another fifteenth-century version of the *Secreta Secretorum* is *The Governance of Lordschipe*, which includes a chapter called 'Of ordinance of stuynge'; this describes the bath as 'on of þe merveylles of þys werld, ffor yt ys housyd after þe ffoure tymes of þe ʒeer', and recommends four different bathhouses so that the bather can move from cold through luke-warm to hot and then dry.[50] This sounds very Roman; one wonders whether any late medieval Englishmen actually had such bathing facilities. The same doubt applies to the detailed instructions for building a bathhouse in a fifteenth-century English version of the book on husbandry written in the fifth century AD by Palladius:[51]

> It is not strange, if water wol suffice,
> An husbonde on his baathe to be bethought;
> For therof may plesaunce and helthe aryse.   (1079–81)

It is impossible to know whether this Mediterranean handbook was actually used as a building guide for baths in England, though the translator apparently saw no reason to omit this section. Did the medieval Englishman's fancy often turn to thoughts of bathhouses? It seems more likely that portable tubs were the norm for most rich people apart from royalty.

As for public baths, in France at least, every town of any size had them. In twelfth-century Paris, according to Alexander Neckham, one was likely to be woken by streetcries such as 'li bain sont chaut' ('the baths are hot').[52] Big

---

48 Peter of Eboli, *De balneis puteolanis*. See C. N. Kauffmann, *The Baths of Pozzuoli* (Oxford, 1959), and Patricia Skinner, *Health and Medicine in Early Medieval Southern Italy* (Leiden, 1997), p. 34.

49 *Secreta Secretorum: Nine English Versions*, ed. M. Manzalaoui, vol. 1, EETS OS 276 (London, 1977). Baths are mentioned in many of the versions included. I cite the fifteenth-century Ashmole version (pp. 18–113); page references are given parenthetically.

50 *Three Prose Versions of the Secreta Secretorum*, ed. R. Steele, EETS ES 74 (London, 1898), p. 82 (ch. 63).

51 *Palladius on Husbondrie*, 1079–1141, ed. B. Lodge, EETS OS 52, 72 (London, 1873), p. 40.

52 Urban T. Holmes, *Daily Living in the Twelfth Century, based on the Observations of Alexander Neckham in London and Paris* (Madison, 1952), p. 133. See also the essays in *L'Eau au Moyen Age* [*Senefiance* 15] (Aix-en-Provence, 1985).

cities like Paris had many public baths; in the thirteenth century there were apparently thirty-two.[53] Public baths generally had a bad reputation, of the sort that bathhouses and massage parlours have in our own day.[54] *Estuves*, a word for baths and heated rooms derived from the stoves or furnaces that heated them, came into English as *stews*, with the alternative meaning of brothel. In later fifteenth-century London there was a notorious red-light district in Southwark known as Stewside, where there were eighteen brothels.[55] The earliest examples of all senses of *stew* in the *Middle English Dictionary* are from the late fourteenth century. Gower uses the word without apparent negative connotations in his retelling of the story of Apollonius of Tyre, to describe the baths in Tyre, which are closed when the people discover that their prince Apollonius has left them (fleeing the wrath of Antiochus).[56] In the late classical source, the *Historia Apollonii*, the closing of public baths as a sign of public mourning made perfect sense; it is interesting that Gower retains this detail, but adapts the later gymnasium scene so that Apollonius finds young men playing a 'commun game' in an open space in front of the king, naked 'As it was tho custome and use' (678 and 685). Bath culture apparently made sense to Gower, but gymnasium culture did not.[57] It is also interesting that he uses *stew* in a positive sense here. Later in the story, when Apollonius' virgin daughter is sold to a pimp, Gower reduces the brothel scene to a very brief interlude, and uses *bordel* rather than *stew* (e.g. 1411, 1415).

Chaucer and Langland both use *stew* in its negative sense.[58] In the *Pardoner's Tale* the three rioters haunt folly in the form of 'riot, hasard, stewes and tavernes' (465). Langland's Sloth marries 'Wanhope a wenche of the stuwes' (B. XX.159), Piers Plowman ploughs 'As wel for a wastour and wenches of the stewes/ As for hymself and hise servaunts' (XIX. 437–9), and

---

53 On the number of baths in Paris, see Jean Gimpel, *The Medieval Machine: The Industrial Revolution of the Middle Ages*, 2nd edn (London, 1988), p. 91; I am indebted to Dr David Freemantle for this reference. The craft guild regulations show that there were both male and female bathhouse keepers in Paris: the relevant passage from Etienne de Boileau's *Livre des Métiers: XIIIe siècle* is translated by Emilie Amt in *Women's Lives in Medieval Europe: A Sourcebook* (London, 1993), p. 197.

54 The proprietor of a new bathhouse opened in Avignon in 1446 took great pains to insist that it was really a bathhouse, not a brothel, and that there were respectable women available there to look after any ladies who wished to bathe; see Brundage, *Law*, p. 527.

55 See Brundage, *Law*, p. 523; Ruth Mazo Karras, 'The Regulation of Brothels in Later Medieval England', *Signs* 14.2 (1984), pp. 399–433, and *Common Women: Prostitution and Sexuality in Medieval England* (Oxford, 1996); Martha Carlin, *Medieval Southwark* (London, 1996), pp. 211ff. This part of Southwark was under the jurisdiction of the Bishop of Winchester, hence the use of the phrase 'Winchester geese' to refer to prostitutes (for instance in Pandarus' epilogue in Shakespeare's *Troilus and Cressida*, V.x.54).

56 Gower, *Confessio Amantis*, VIII. 484–5.

57 For further discussion of the treatment of the bath scene in medieval versions of the Apollonius story, see Elizabeth Archibald, *Apollonius of Tyre: Medieval and Renaissance Themes and Variations* (Cambridge, 1991), pp. 72–5.

58 References to Chaucer are taken from *The Riverside Chaucer*, ed. L. D. Benson et al. (Oxford, 1987). References to Langland are taken from *Piers Plowman: A Complete Edition of The B-Text*, ed. A. V. C. Schmidt (London, 1978).

Langland uses the idiom 'Jonette of the Stuwes' (B. VI.70), which also appears in the Wakefield Last Judgement play (350).[59] Public baths must already have been widespread and popular for some time for *stews* to have acquired this idiomatic meaning by the later fourteenth century. The brothel sense is probably intended in a reference to *stewes* in Lydgate's translation of Deguilevile's popular allegory, *The Pilgrimage of the Life of Man.* [60] When Grace Dieu is lecturing the pilgrim at length on how to reform his life and save his soul, she tells him that one of his servants has now inappropriately become his master, and is being shockingly indulged:

> 'Al hys desyrs thow pursues,
> Somwhyle to lede hym to the stewes,
> To wasshe and bathe hym tendyrly,
> And to leyn hym sofftely
> On ffether beddys, mad vul wel,
> ffor to slepe hys undermel . . .'   (9039–44)   [afternoon]

Then it turns out that this honoured guest on whom hospitality is lavished is the body, enemy of the soul. The juxtaposition of bath and bed recalls images of elaborately furnished brothels containing both, such as those in fifteenth-century Burgundian manuscripts of Valerius Maximus' *Dicta et facta memorabilia* (Book 9).[61] Hostile references to baths can also be found in the work of medieval preachers: G. R. Owst quotes a comparable allusion from a sermon by John Bromyard, stating that after death the rich will lie in a narrow pit instead of a scented bath.[62] Such passages offer further evidence for the popularity of baths in the later Middle Ages, not just among aristocrats and royalty but also among the bourgeoisie. Charles d'Orléans, who spent many years as a prisoner in England, wrote a rondeau on the pleasures of life in which the refrain is 'souper ou baing et disner ou bateau' (to sup in a bath and dine in a boat).[63]

Given all this evidence for the popularity of baths, as well as many images of both private and public bathing, the absence of references to bathing in Middle English romances is all the more puzzling. Perhaps it has to do not so much with romance as with England. I hesitate to suggest that the English washed less than their continental neighbours, but it does seem to be a possibility; after all, in modern times the spa and sauna culture has been much more popular in continental Europe than in England until very recently. Almost all the Middle English texts I have discussed in which baths are mentioned are

---

59 *Medieval Drama*, ed. David Bevington (Boston, MA, 1975), p. 649.
60 Lydgate, *Pilgrimage of the Life of Man*, ed. F. J. Furnival, EETS ES 77, 83, 92, 3 vols in 1 (London: 1899–1904).
61 Duerr reproduces two of them in black and white (and rather small) in *Nacktheit*, pp. 48 and 49 (illus. 25 and 26); there are good colour reproductions in F. de Bonneville, *The Book of the Bath*, trans. Jane Brenton (New York, 1998), pp. 34–5.
62 G. R. Owst, *Literature and Pulpit in Medieval England*, 2nd rev. edn (Oxford, 1961), pp. 293–4.
63 Rondeau 147, quoted by Larmat, 'Les Bains', pp. 204–5.

translations from French or Latin sources. The writer of an early thir-teenth-century chronicle, describing the Danish invasions, dwells on the fact that the Danes bathed on Saturdays (he mentions it twice in twelve lines), and attributes to this obsession with personal hygiene their great success with chaste and noble women.[64] This seems to suggest that in his own experience few people – or few fighting men – took frequent baths. Bath-tubs may have been available in many castles and large households in England, but in modern historical studies there is little reference to public bathhouses (other than brothels), though some must have existed, given the frequent references to *stews*. Where baths are used, the emphasis seems to be on either healing or pleasure. It may be that cleanliness was only considered to be important in relation to the visible parts of the body; there are quite a lot of references to washing hands and faces before meals, in courtesy books and in romances, and social historians note that basins were conveniently located close to banqueting halls.[65]

Perhaps it is unreasonable to expect to find many references to baths in Middle English chivalric literature, since they do not seem to be very frequent in other kinds of English non-medical writing. In Chaucer, for instance, the only direct references to baths refer back to classical times: Seneca's suicide in his bath (*Monk's Tale*, 2503–10), and the first stage of Cecilia's martyrdom in a boiling bath (*Second Nun's Tale*, 512–25). The only other character who has a bath is Pertelote the hen in the sand in her yard (*Nun's Priest's Tale*, 3267–8). Chaucer's other allusions to baths are all metaphorical: they include April showers bathing the plants (*General Prologue*, 1–4), a lover bathing in bliss (*Wife of Bath's Tale*, 1253), and tears bathing the face of Griselda when she is reunited with her children (*Clerk's Tale*, 1084–5). In view of Capgrave's reference to the aristocratic convention of bathing brides-to-be, one might have expected baths in some of Chaucer's wedding scenes, and one might also have expected them in the classical context of *Troilus*, but none are mentioned.

Baths do not seem to features very frequently in French romance either, except for medicinal purposes and for knighting ceremonies. Perhaps they were perceived as not macho; that might be the implication of Guy of Warwick's refusal of a bath before one of his battles, though it does seem worrying that chivalric heroes so often arrive at a castle and change into new and splendid clothes without apparently washing at all. Or perhaps they were thought to be debilitating; the *Secreta Secretorum* gives elaborate advice about seasons in which one should and should not bathe. Perhaps baths were also perceived as dangerous in a non-medical sense. In Marie de France's

64 *The Chronicle attributed to John of Wallingford*, ed. Richard Vaughan, Camden Miscellany 21 (London, 1958), p. 60.

65 On lavers and domestic piscinas, see Wood, *English Mediaeval House*, pp. 369–71. See also Georges Vigarello, *Concepts of Cleanliness: Changing Attitudes in France since the Middle Ages*, trans. Jean Birrell (Cambridge, 1988); I am indebted to the late Prof. Keith Hopkins for this reference.

Equitan, the adulterous wife suggests to the king that he and her husband should take baths together after being bled; the husband's will be so scaldingly hot that it will kill him.[66] Two tubs are put side by side in the bedroom. But the plan backfires: caught in flagrante, the king jumps into the wrong tub and dies, and the faithless wife is thrown in too by her wronged husband. Here is a rare literary example of what we see in many images, the tubs side by side.[67] Clearly it was an honour for the steward to be asked to bathe with his king. This macabre episode indicates that water for baths could be very hot, even if it is not true that it could be hot enough to kill someone.

Death in a bath-tub probably makes readers today think of Agamemnon, or else of the famous painting by David of the death of Marat. According to Marjorie Chibnall, it was a standard epic motif. It may be that there are interesting examples to be found in *chansons de geste.* Dr Elisabeth van Houts has kindly alerted me to some 'historical' examples in chronicles. In an interpolation in the *Gesta Normannorum Ducum* of William of Jumièges, Orderic Vitalis recounts how Harold had the king of Wales beheaded in his bath, and then married his wife.[68] In his *Ecclesiastical History,* Orderic Vitalis tells how the alarming Mabel of Belleme, wife of Robert Montgomery, was murdered in bed while relaxing after a bath.[69] Lydgate follows Boccaccio in telling how the Roman Emperor Constantine III was murdered in 'a preue stewe' by his own knights, a scene dramatically illustrated in some manuscripts.[70] And it was not just rulers and heroes who met their deaths in baths: according to Cabanès, 1,400 people were killed or badly wounded in the baths in Ghent in a period of ten months in 1479![71]

It may seem surprising to put medieval Europe on a par with ancient Rome or modern Japan in its enthusiasm for bathing, but there is a great deal of evidence, historical, literary and artistic, for the widespread popularity of baths, both for medical purposes and for pleasure, both private and public, at least on the Continent.[72] So was it fear that prevented Middle English romance heroes from having baths, whether based on their knowledge of literature or on contemporary events? Or was it a macho aversion to sybaritic pursuits? Is it really the case that baths are less frequently mentioned in English romances

---

66 Marie de France, *Equitan,* 241–306, *Lais,* ed. A. Ewert (Oxford, 1969), pp. 26–34; trans. Glyn S. Burgess and Keith Busby, *The Lais of Marie de France* (Harmondsworth, 1986), pp. 56–60 (see pp. 59–60).

67 There is a good example in Holmes, *Daily Living,* opposite p. 115.

68 *The* Gesta Normannorum Ducum *of William of Jumièges, Orderic Vitalis and Robert of Torigni,* VII.13 (31), ed. Elisabeth van Houts (Oxford, 1995), II. 160.

69 *The Ecclesiastical History of Orderic Vitalis,* V.ii.411, ed. and trans. Marjorie Chibnall (Oxford, 1969–80), III. 136–7.

70 Lydgate, *Fall of Princes,* IX. 589–616, ed. H. Bergen, 4 vols (Washington, DC, 1927), III. 935–6. For an illustration from a French manuscript of Boccaccio (MS Arsenal 5193) showing the emperor in his bath wearing only his crown as a soldier pierces his breast with a long spear, see Salzman, *English Life,* p. 107.

71 Cabanès, pp. 204–5 (see n. 1 above).

72 Cleansing and hygiene seem to have been much less significant factors; see Larmat, pp. 209–10 (n. 7 above). The evidence of ecclesiastical writers and architecture is beyond the scope of this essay.

than in French ones? Further research will be required to answer this last question. It seems that there is some truth in both the quotations that I contrasted at the beginning of this essay. Wright is correct in saying that medieval people were very keen on baths, and that bathing facilities were available, both in private houses and in public institutions; but Michelet is also right that the Percivals, Tristans and Isoudes of romance (at least, Middle English romance) did not do a lot of bathing.[73]

---

[73] I am grateful to the participants in the Durham conference on Middle English Romance, to my colleagues at Bristol, and to the medievalists at the University of Southampton for helpful comments on earlier versions of this essay.

9

Some Notes on 'Ennobling Love'
and its Successor in Medieval Romance

DEREK BREWER

The term 'ennobling love' is taken from Stephen Jaeger's stimulating book with that as the main title.[1] Jaeger's argument is that we have been misreading much of the history of love as recorded in medieval literature and culture. He believes that the crucial development has not been, as maintained for example by C. S. Lewis in a famous book, *The Allegory of Love*,[2] a new development of the structure of love, developing between the sexes in the late eleventh and twelfth centuries in Europe, but the collapse of the ancient pre-existent structure of love between highly élite males, going back to Cicero's *De Amicitia* and before. Such love between men built on, no doubt, the ancient loyalties and male-bonding of warrior-societies, but was more refined. One of Jaeger's prime examples is the love expressed by the great scholar and teacher Alcuin (d.804) for colleagues and pupils sometimes even before he met them. This virtuous love, shared by only a few of the most elevated and noble but not always learned men, was not sexual, or to put it more bluntly, was not sodomitical. Sexuality was either suppressed, sublimated or ignored, but the feeling and the elaboration of love was intensified. Relationships with women were irrelevant.

Jaeger's argument is effectively conducted, needs no detailed rehearsal here, and seems convincing. The historical threads go back to Cicero's *De Amicitia* but have also a more general literary ancestry in the references to, or literature of, masculine friendship 'passing the love of woman' (II Samuel 1: 26). James Brundage in his magisterial and encyclopaedic survey of law, sex and society in medieval Europe gives what we may call the background to such literature. At all medieval periods sodomy, together with all the other varieties of sexual practices as discussed by legal, ecclesiastical and civil documents, was known and doubtless practised. Though never approved, attitudes varied in the severity of condemnation. Roman law recognised but had

---

[1] C. Stephen Jaeger, *Ennobling Love: In Search of a Lost Sensibility* (Philadelphia, 1999). See my review, *Arthuriana* 2 (2001), pp. 124–9. All subsequent references to Jaeger will be cited by page number.

[2] C. S. Lewis, *The Allegory of Love* (London, 1936).

not been especially concerned with sodomy, though the passive partner in gay sex suffered various legal penalties, and was thought to have 'betrayed the masculine virtues proper to free male citizens; he was penalized primarily for treachery to the social order'.[3] This attitude of contempt was probably less severe in the case of boys, whom Roman law, like other legal systems, attempted, in the case of free citizens, to protect from the exploitation that was apparently the common lot of young slaves.[4] Medieval law seems to have become more severe during the centuries, especially after the drive towards the celibacy of the clergy in the twelfth century. The notion that sexual relations in general may involve 'ritual pollution' seems to be ancient, but the 'filthiness' of even what one may dare to call normal sexual relations within marriage came to be emphasised almost to an hysterical degree by, for example, St Jerome (d.420), who drew to some extent on earlier Stoic sources.[5] How much more so, therefore, was sodomy repudiated, though Jerome does not seem to have devoted much thought to this. Jaeger's point is that male ennobling love not only abstains from sexual expression in the form of sodomy, but that the abstinence from sex intensifies the emotion.

Some of this is related to the ancient literary tradition of passionate male friendship as exemplified in classical sources, as in the *Aeneid* (it was not possible for medieval men to go back to the example of Achilles and Patroclus), in the Biblical account of David and Jonathan, and in later stories, down to that exemplified by the medieval romance in Middle English, *Amis and Amiloun*.[6] Such stories are part of what may now usefully be termed the 'homosocial' bond between men.

Jaeger makes the further point that the expression of ennobling love was public, not private. What made the emotion 'real' was its external expression, as he well demonstrates through Alcuin's letters and with illustrations from chronicles. While accepting the argument for externality we must recall that there were many cases of treason and betrayal, in other words, of private inclination over public expression, where clearly the private, or secret, was more 'real' or 'true', when it eventually became public, than the previously asserted public 'truth'. There must have been some degree of what one can only call subjectivity in such cases.[7]

A crude summary of Jaeger's further argument is that the trouble with ennobling love, or rather, what had become a 'refined love', comes when ladies enter the scene in the twelfth century and love becomes associated with

---

3   James A. Brundage, *Law, Sex, and Christian Society in Medieval Europe* (Chicago, 1987), p. 49.
4   Ibid., p. 49.
5   Ibid., p. 90.
6   These are discussed with bibliographical references by Jill Mann, *Feminizing Chaucer* (Cambridge, 2002), pp. 152–73.
7   C. S. Lewis in *The Allegory of Love* notes the personal passion of loyalty, 'with an intensity which our tradition is loath to allow except in sexual love. . . . It rises more easily to heroic prodigality of service, and it also breaks more easily and turns into hatred: hence feudal history is full of great loyalties and great treacheries.'

heterosexuality. Such well-recognised developments in the twelfth century as recognition of the power of internal feeling, and of the significant place of women in courtly life, destroyed the structures of courtly masculine love, while to some extent taking them over to tragic effect. Jaeger comments that Gaston Paris set up

> Chrétien's most ironic and overdrawn work, *Lancelot*, as a paradigm of courtly love, and so directed medieval studies onto one of its oddest and longest detours. The minimum of explanatory power met with the maximum of scholarly consensus.
>
> Regarding love as a public experience of the nobility shows that the paradigm that frames courtly love has been – not recently established – but recently shattered, and the literature of courtly love represents, not a 'system' or a widely recognized and accepted social ethic, but rather fidgeting attempts at solutions to the problems that that shattering created.
> *(Ennobling Love,* p. 186).

I may have missed some of the subtlety of Jaeger's argument but it would seem that there is some risk here of conflating nineteenth-century scholarship and criticism with complex cultural developments in medieval Europe. There are also the complications created when we mingle 'real life', or at least what we can trace of it through historical records, with literature, especially when that literature is necessarily based on assumptions different from our own. It not quite clear to me whether 'the fidgeting attempts at solutions' of the shattering of the previous ethic of ennobling love are those of medieval authors or of nineteenth- and twentieth-century scholars and critics. What does seem clear is that certain great authors in Europe of the twelfth and thirteenth centuries were fascinated in some of their works by the problems of reconciling overmastering physical heterosexual desire with some social constraints, especially marriage. Two groups of these stories, those centring on Lancelot and Tristan, became very but not exclusively popular. Chrétien wrote only one *Lancelot*, while his *Cligés* has often been taken for an anti-*Tristan*. *Erec et Enide* and the *Perceval* (the latter, like *Lancelot*, unfinished) are each in various ways about marital love. In this respect it is nineteenth- and twentieth-century criticism that has exaggerated, or at least focused on, the systemisation of so-called 'courtly love', which was seen inevitably to involve adultery, which Jaeger condemns. The dramatisations of Arthurian stories in the late nineteenth century emphasised the story of Tristan,[8] and it would seem that adultery is a favourite twentieth-century topic. But again one must remember the multitude of love-stories and their changing focus.

The 'code of courtly love' became a favourite of twentieth-century criticism and was accepted as a new but familiar cultural and literary phenomenon by C. S. Lewis (he writes 'every one has heard of it'). He summarised the

---

[8]   Beverley Taylor and Elisabeth Brewer, *The Return of King Arthur* (Cambridge, 1983), pp. 214–39.

characteristics of the new sentiment with his usual clarity as 'Humility, Courtesy, Adultery, and the Religion of Love' as they appeared in Troubadour poetry, emphasising that it was a highly specialised form of love.[9] Most of this is now left behind by modern criticism but it is worth revisiting, for it still has some truth. Lewis was restating the work of the then leading modern critics and historians. Jaeger strongly contests 'C. S. Lewis's sense that what they [twelfth- and thirteenth-century European poets] depicted was "an entirely new way of feeling".'[10] Chrétien and Gottfried expressed not a discovery of the new but a sense of loss of traditional love and friendship. One may add that not all troubadour poets always expressed very notably the 'new' kind of love. The highly varied though tiny *oeuvre* of William IX of Poitiers, recognised as the first troubadour, has ribald and derisive poems as well. Several poets lamented at the same time the demise of chivalry, a lament that has been repeated by modern scholars. This supposed decline was a common *topos* in later centuries, despite the activities of such *preux chevaliers* as Edward Prince of Wales (1330–76), recognised as a chivalric hero throughout Europe, and Sir Philip Sidney (1554–86).[11] In the sentiment of love Jaeger posits a collapse of the former tradition, of highly wrought devotion. But that collapse might be described rather as a transfer or even development from male–male to male–female sentiment, with consequential adjustments. Jaeger sees the development of the earlier sentiment of élite ennobling love between males into the sentiment of a similar love by men for women, or rather, nobles for ladies, as a cultural blind end because of the intrusion of heterosexual desire. Jaeger's connection of the former homosocial sentiment of love to the latter heterosexual sentiment seems convincing. It is also convincing to find the new sentiment potentially in conflict with other aspects of medieval culture, notably the ecclesiastical view that all sexuality was at least to some degree tainted with sin, even within monogamous marriage, a view strongly expressed in Chaucer's *Parson's Tale*. Homosocial love, or to use an older and better if more general term, 'friendship', if accepted as superior to heterosexual love, might still not clash with it (cf. the lecherous King David) nor clash with marriage. An early celebrated statement of the inherent contradiction between heterosexual love and marriage is found in the *De Arte Honeste Amandi* of Andreas Capellanus of around 1200, whose first two books give dialogues for lovers of various kinds, presenting a variety of love-problems. A strong point is made that love of this courtly kind cannot exist between man

---

[9] Lewis, *Allegory of Love*, p. 2.
[10] Jaeger, p. 184; Lewis, *Allegory of Love*, pp. 4, 11.
[11] Some sentiments are, like Charles II, an unconscionably long time dying. The last hero of a novel who to my knowledge tried to adhere to the ideal of the *preux chevalier* was Bertie Wooster, for example in *Jeeves and the Feudal Spirit* (1954) and *Jeeves in the Offing* (1960). Granted that this is farcical, though highly literate comedy, there is still a recognisable basis of feeling and behaviour for readers of that now somewhat remote generation. See also Derek Brewer, 'Chivalry', *A Companion to Chaucer*, ed. Peter Brown (Oxford, 2000), pp. 58–74.

and wife.[12] The third book, as is well known, condemns love *paramours*, but as Jaeger points out, the paradigm of the earlier chaste love between men does leave its traces in the love that transcends sexuality between virtuous men and women. Jaeger develops this theme of love without physical expression in his discussion of the mutual love of Christina of Markyate and the Abbot (of St Albans) Geoffrey. The point here is that Christina and Geoffrey overcame carnal temptations. Jaeger asks 'But did the cure of carnality need to be so carnal?' (p. 181). I certainly do not know, but it seems unsympathetic, to say the least, so to seem to belittle the spiritual conquests of Christina and Geoffrey. One less desperate solution was at hand at least to the laity, or at least to lay-romanciers, that is, marriage. Again Jaeger illustrates this with an admirable and complex account of 'Love Domesticized' by Wolfram von Eschenbach in the *Parzival*. With whatever variations and qualifications, the conclusion of Wolfram's work has to be that sexual love and marriage can and should be combined, though Jaeger treats this conclusion with some irony (p. 190).

More to Jaeger's taste is the demonstrable incompatibility of sexual love and marriage in the stories of Tristan's love of Isolde and Lancelot's love of Guinevere. In the case of Tristan the exaltation of love and the incorporation, if that is the right word, of sexual passion with the idealism of love, is seen to involve contempt for the values of society. There is an irresolvable dilemma in reconciling ethical and sexual love (p. 191). This seems indisputable, but as we all know, it makes for a highly interesting narrative, which offers many interesting moments and many interesting reflections on life and love. Jaeger, like Lewis before him, makes many valuable comments, sometimes expressing a perhaps underlying scepticism about the passion of love: 'The ennobling force of passion is like a product that you can't afford if you have to ask the price' (p. 191). In other words, you have to be so rich that the price is irrelevant – though as the story shows, it will cost all that you possess. As a model of life that has its shortcomings, as a narrative of a certain kind of tragic obsession, and certain assumptions, such love is worth exploring. One of the advantages of literature is that we can participate by imagination in what we would prefer to miss in real life – though we should not make too absolute a divide between fantasy and 'real life'. Fantasy is part of real life, has its own reality, and can often influence real-life experience and assumptions.

As with the story of Tristan so with that of Lancelot, though they are obviously far different in structure, and different authors make somewhat different things of their love. Chrétien is far different from Malory. What is common to all accounts of Lancelot is the total devotion and loyalty of the lovers to each other expressed mainly through the man, the elevation of sentiment, the adultery, and the frustration. But there is no need to take it as an exclusive or

---

12 C.S. Lewis's account in *Allegory of Love*, pp. 32–43, is still very useful. See also Jaeger, pp. 114–16 and elsewhere.

didactic model of love. Lancelot's love is eventually seen, as in Malory, as destructive of a whole society and in Malory is deeply repented. But Chaucer, of a different temperament from Malory, mocks it (Sq T(5) 287; NPT(7) 3212).[13] There is also in the underlying structure of the story of Lancelot a certain infantilism involved in *fin amor*. Chaucer recognises this element delightfully derisively when he makes Absolom, the village dandy and hopeless lover of the carpenter's young wife, say of his love, 'I moorne as dooth a lamb after the tete' (*The Canterbury Tales*, I, 3704). It is Lancelot in Chrétien's *Le Chevalier de la Charrette* who shows the most abject devotion to his mistress, but most modern critics would see varying degrees of irony, even mockery, in Chrétien's portrayal.

'That men have died for love, and worms have eaten them' was surely not a new story in the twelfth century, yet we cannot but be aware of new formulations, new changes of direction, new stories, as well as new lyric poetry in European languages, from the twelfth century onwards. The causes of such developments must be multiple and we need deny neither continuity, fracture, nor novelty. The simple facts of literary history give us the constantly growing corpus of love-stories in Europe. We may also note, in the bewildering variety of such stories far beyond my knowledge, that most of the love-stories lead heroine and hero to marriage, and are based on heterosexual desire. In all this, the refinements of love may well not be of prime interest. For many, perhaps most romances, a strong element of folktale carries them through the familiar pattern of a love-story between a young man and young woman. Sometimes this may have a sad outcome (to call it tragic may be to exaggerate its effect), though the outcome of the stories of Tristan and of Lancelot may in the hands of great writers be called tragic.[14]

We may well ask where is the courtliness in this broad development. It lies partly in the environment of this literature, which could not be other than what we may roughly call upper class, despite the folktale basis. These are in a sense the folktales, or some of the folktales, of European courts, and as love-stories they express what seem to me to be the natural desires and ambitions of most young people, but especially of young men. In this respect the male-orientated nature of courtly society is obvious, and is equally obviously conditioned by many social and physical factors. Almost all societies at the stage of development at which we find the European Middle Ages seem to be warrior-based, religious (and hence 'priests' of whatever kind are important), hierarchical and agriculturally based even where there are cities. Women are at a twofold disadvantage: they lack male musculature, and child-bearing is burdensome and often mortal. Women are also usually the objects of male physical desire, which may pay little attention to women's own desires and

---

[13] All references to Chaucer's works will be from *The Riverside Chaucer*, 3rd edn, ed. Larry D. Benson et al. (Oxford, 1987) and will be cited by line number.

[14] On folktale, see Derek Brewer, 'The Interpretation of Folktales', *A Companion to the Folktale*, ed. H. E. Davidson and Anna Chaudhri (Cambridge, 2003).

needs. In such societies (and many still exist) women are treated as inferior however unjust that may be.[15] What is remarkable about European medieval society is the degree, limited as it was, to which it achieved some sort of status and respect for ladies, a part of 'the civilising process'. The causes are complex, but one factor, hard as it is to evaluate in its practical effect, must have been the love and respect accorded to women in the romances, once the male–male bond had been modified. This male–male social bond continued, and Professor Mann has illustrated the secondary importance accorded to wives in the romances of male friendship, which continued the ancient warrior-based ethos of masculine loyalty.[16] Yet although such romances were read, the romances of love and marriage outnumber them. Part of the respect accorded to women, inadequate as it must seem to a post-industrial, non-religious society, may well be attributed to the practical instructions of *frauendienst* conveyed by so widely popular a work as *Le Roman de la Rose*. When these instructions by Love are begun, we are told by the poet to attend, 'For now the romance bigynneth to amende'(*Romaunt*, 2154). Lewis rates this passage as of only historical, not poetical interest, but at least the historical interest is considerable, especially in the English version, which slightly sharpens the French. The reader is everywhere assumed to be a young gentleman. He is instructed to learn 'the craft of love' (2166), just as Chaucer makes his young lover tell, in *The Book of the Duchess*, how 'I ches love to my firste craft' (791) and Troilus took his purpose 'loves craft to suwe' (I, 379). Such purpose is immediately after the young gentleman has been stricken with desire for the lady, which is natural and involuntary, but needs to be 'educated'. In *The Legend of Good Women* the lover is taught 'al the craft of fyn lovynge' (F.544). Craft has no pejorative association here, but denotes a learned skill, as of a trade. It is morally neutral, and like other skills it may be turned to bad ends in other contexts, as with the cunning seducer Diomed (*Troilus*, V, 90ff.). The meaning of 'craft' sometimes overlaps with 'art' in Chaucer's works, as, for example, 'And coude of love al craft and art' (*LGW* 1607). The God of Love in *The Romaunt* (and of course in *Le Roman de la Rose*) goes on to say that the lover must avoid all 'vilanye'. Here is that demand for conscious, willed virtue that is part of the general tradition of love going back to Cicero and Plato, not to mention other more general sources of morality and religion. That the lover is in every sense a gentleman (that now abandoned ideal) is insisted on in the *Romaunt* with the further qualification, occasionally noticed in other medieval literature, and in Chaucer's *Wife of Bath's Tale* (*The Canterbury Tales*, III, 1113–70):

> Though he be not gentill born,
> Thou maist well seyn, this is in soth,

---

[15] On this wide topic, see for reference and criticism Corinne Saunders, *Rape and Ravishment in the Literature of Medieval England* (Cambridge, 2001).

[16] Mann, *Feminizing Chaucer*, pp. 152–73.

> That he is gentil by cause he doth
> As longeth to a gentilman . . .   (*Romaunt of the Rose*, 2194–7)

In practice there is no evidence that any men other than gentlemen read *Le Roman de la Rose*, though that women did read it is evidenced by such as Christine de Pisan and the whole 'Querelle de la Rose', which need not detain us here. The emphasis on being 'a gentleman' echoes throughout the English metrical romances.[17] In the *Romaunt* we see how this requirement is put into action in behaviour, coming down to matters of careful dress.

Care for fine dress is a form of ennoblement though one in some ways alien to that modern sensibility, which consciously cultivates the dirty, slovenly clothing that implicitly claims, 'I am above mere appearances and am other, and better, than my poor appearance'. We have here yet another variation on the relations between appearance and reality. On the whole, in the Middle Ages and Renaissance, clothes were of great significance as direct witness to the true inner man and woman, and often related to a person's normal activities. A courtier's chief expenses might be his clothes. So a lover should be clean and smart. At the same time he will suffer physically as well as mentally, becoming painfully thin, 'Who loveth trewe hath no fatnesse' (*Romaunt*, 2686). Such appearances in relation to the inner life may be both voluntary and involuntary and could be pursued on a wider scale throughout romances, especially in matters of love. Stories of disguise and deceit, even of wild adventure, must inevitably play with themes of appearance and reality. Throughout so many variations the theme of ennoblement may take many forms. Jaeger comments on the hopeless dilemmas faced by Lancelot and Tristan when noble love comes into conflict with social compulsions and current moralities and creates deplorable results. To this extent, he argues, heterosexual desire and particularly the culmination in marriage spells the death of ennobling love. Yet the narration of this deplorable tragedy in the stories of Lancelot and Tristan is obviously not in itself deplorable. It points to one characteristic of a certain kind of love and its inevitably temporary nature.

In this respect we should note the powerful, if in literary terms rather neglected, tradition of love-sickness, touched on in *Le Roman de la Rose* and the *Romaunt* as just referred to. The famous Biblical precedent is Amnon who fell sick with love of his sister Tamar and raped her (II Samuel 13: 1–21). Love-melancholy,[18] its causes and cures, was well recognised in the Ancient World and extensively discussed in medical treatises up to the eighteenth century. It was the passion of heterosexual love and might lead to madness and death. There was much discussion about its cure. One cure was coition, preferably with the loved one but if she was not available, as normally by

---

17 Derek Brewer, 'The English Metrical Romances', *A Companion to Romance*, ed. Corinne Saunders (Oxford, 2004), pp. 45–64.

18 Love-melancholy as an historical phenomenon is extensively discussed in Jacques Ferrand, *A Treatise on Lovesickness*, ed. and trans. Donald A. Beecher and Massima Ciavolella (Syracuse, 1990). Ferrand's original *Traité de l'essence et guérison de l'amour* was first published in 1610.

definition she was not, then an alternative partner might do. The cure at its most drastic is illustrated in the earliest story, that of Amnon. Once he had raped Tamar he hated her exceedingly, more than he had loved her. Chaucer notices 'the loveris maladye/ Of Hereos' and briefly discusses the relation to 'mania' in *The Knight's Tale* ((1) 1373–74), where Arcite suffers so badly that he is quite unrecognisable. Both he and Palamon are faithful chaste lovers of Emily. Troilus suffers 'a double sorrow' for love. The first episode though acute does not involve actual illness, though he takes to his bed at times and feigns illness in the house of Deiphebus at the suggestion of Pandarus in order to obtain a private interview with Criseyde. He achieves a cure when he becomes Criseyde's accepted though secret lover, and sleeps with her. At this point Chaucer presents him not exactly as ennobled, because he was noble before and did not need love to make him so, but as even more noble, a good man made even better by successful love (*Troilus*, III, 1771–806). There is surely much psychological truth in this. Happiness and sexual satisfaction in a faithful relationship may often be morally improving, making us less selfish, kinder even to the smaller animals – kindness to animals being a quite remarkable trait in the medieval period, in which Chaucer here follows Boccaccio literally. Troilus' fighting ability is improved, his speech is all of love and virtue, and – a rich touch of Chaucer's own invention – even though he came of royal blood he was rude to no one. Here is 'ennobling love', produced by sexual fulfilment, although on a base of established nobility of rank and temperament. (This is true of all the heroes of English romance. Even Havelok, who had to serve as a kitchen-porter, was royally born and had the sign of it as a light emanating from him as he slept. Royal status is a characteristic folktale manner of indicating high self-esteem even if the hero or heroine, like a Cinderella, is for a time poor and oppressed.) To this degree success in sexual love has in no way impeded the ennobling process. But of course Troilus's love is secret. In the poem there is no obvious reason why he should not be married to Criseyde. Although it is implicit that there is some sort of social barrier preventing the marriage of Troilus and Criseyde it never becomes plain. It seems clearer in Boccaccio's *Filostrato* where Troilo is clearly a young prince having an affair with a young middle-class widow. Why should he marry her? Princes and noblemen had a steady stream of mistresses, often kept quite openly, as John of Gaunt kept Chaucer's sister-in-law as his mistress for years. When he eventually married her courtly opinion was shocked, not at the preceding arrangement, but that a man should marry his mistress. This is in fact perhaps the nub of Troilus' problem. He cannot marry his mistress.[19] Boccaccio takes this for granted. Chaucer inserts an obsession with her honour as a chaste widow, and it is her honour and the

---

19 Montaigne, who had rather easy-going views on these matters, like most aristocrats in most societies, encapsulates what seems to have been the common wisdom: 'Few men have married their mistresses without repenting it': *Montaigne: The Complete Essays*, trans. M. Screech (London, 1991), Essay III, 5, 'On some lines in Virgil', p. 563.

consequent need to keep her love secret, which prevent either marriage or, as Troilus suggests, elopement.[20] All this is despite the fact in the poem that Paris keeps Helen as his mistress quite openly without any social exclusion of any kind, though this is the very cause of Troy's disastrous war with the Greeks. A medieval romance does not seek the naturalistic mimesis of a novel to convey its images and truths. It is fruitless to consider whether Troilus' sterile passion for Criseyde could have continued for a lifetime if they could have married or even eloped. Its prolongation for the rest of Troilus' presumably short life is brought about by the frustration of her absence and then her rejection of Troilus for another or other lovers, an almost infallible recipe for the prolongation of love, which may be either ennobling or degrading. At his final loss of Criseyde Troilus becomes subject to a second, much more serious bout of love-melancholy, which reduces him even to the need for a walking-stick (*Troilus*, V, 1222). He is cured of the sickness by suicidal rage at Diomed and the Greeks, albeit that, as he says, he cannot find it in his heart 'To vnlouen yow a quarter of a day!' (V, 1698). Frustrated sexual love may survive, be sublimated and ennoble, as Jaeger traces it in admirable chapters on Heloise and Abelard, Christina of Markyate and Abbot Geoffrey. Throughout *Troilus* the poet emphasises Troilus' 'grete trouthe and servise' in Criseyde's words (III, 992), which characterise noble love, but sexual jealousy destroys the effects of ennoblement here. Yet to equate sexual love and its potentially ennobling effects with inevitable frustration from social or personal causes is too sweeping, certainly in regard to English medieval romances.

Concluding a fascinating analysis of the story of Tristan and Isolde, Jaeger writes that following ennobling love 'increasingly privatised and fictionalised, led us to the insight that in *Tristan* ennobling love makes its peace with sexual passion. I am very aware how much the wealth of courtly literature is diminished by the reduction to that perspective' (p. 196). Here one must pause over the word *fictionalised*. This must mean that it is not a true account of true love, that the story is inadequately or falsely worked out. We may concede that their love is in some way deplorable, or we may believe that the respect and even adulation accorded by some to this kind of romantic passion is an error of judgment, but it would be hard to deny its intrinsic and continuing interest. Even if we belittle it by describing it as infatuation, or even deny that it has a necessarily tragic end, such infatuation is a feature of some, by no means everybody's, lives. The Tristan story may, as literature often does, present an extreme case. It is indeed possible to argue, as in effect Jaeger does, that other people have interpreted it wrongly, taken it too seriously. Chaucer, again, is one who at least has a joke at its expense, in the amusing poem 'To Rosemounde':

20 Derek Brewer, 'Honour in Chaucer' in *Tradition and Innovation in Chaucer* (London, 1982), pp. 89–109, esp. p. 105.

Nas never pyk walwed in galauntyne
As I in love am walwed and ywounde,
For which ful ofte I of myself devyne
That I am trewe Tristam the secounde.   (17–20)

The younger Chaucer had listed Tristan with other famous lovers portrayed on the temple wall in *The Parliament of Fowls* (290), as unhappy, along with Troilus. Various attitudes are possible to the stories of such heroes.

A *tour d'horizon* of English medieval romances offers an interesting test of Jaeger's thesis, not to disprove it but to note where it is less applicable, and where more.[21] The three earliest romances in English are *Horn, Havelok* and *Floris and Blanchefleur*. In *Horn* the lady makes the first advances, and though the lovers are long separated both are faithful and true. In *Havelok*, as already noted, the hero and heroine are intrinsically royal, again faithful and true, but with no love-service, no special refinement of manners. They marry and have fifteen children, but that is another story. (There are indeed English romances of family love, for example *Sir Isumbras* and *Sir Amadas*, and it is an issue in many others, but they do not affect the current argument.) In the slightly later *Guy of Warwick* the eponymous hero is too shy at first to 'tell his love' for the beautiful heroine of slightly higher status (as an old joke, not without some general truth, has it that all men marry above themselves – itself a fragment of the old 'courtly love' tradition). Eventually Guy goes off to earn his lady's love by fighting various enemies including dragons, and to this extent is improved or perhaps 'ennobled', but manners and highly wrought feelings are not the poet's concern. More to the point is the hero's piety and faithful sexual love, where marriage is the expected end. As soon as he has married and begotten a son Guy has a religious revelation and goes off for years fighting various foes, sometimes 'for England's sake'. It would be possible to interpret this twofold structure of departure, found for example in Chrétien's *Yvain* and some folktales, as a subconscious reluctance to undertake the burdens of marriage and domesticity, but the reluctance is always worked out and overcome. It does not concern 'ennobling love' and does not show the incompatibility of love with faithful marriage. One might view it as not only the maturation of the hero but as the maturation of heterosexual marital love into friendship.

Chaucer is the poet who shows some consciousness of the kind of problem that Jaeger indicates. Chaucer illustrates how sexual love may break down friendships between men in *The Knight's Tale*. As soon as the two cousins, sworn bloodbrothers, Palamon and Arcite, see the beautiful young Emily from their prison, love-rivalry makes them passionate enemies. Only when Arcite is dying from wounds can he marry Emily and with his dying breath become reconciled to Palamon, and so to speak bequeath Emily as bride to Palamon. The structure of this story emphasises marriage as the natural

---

[21] See further Brewer, 'The English Metrical Romances'.

127

climax to love. Frustration is a significant element in heterosexual love but is properly resolved in faithful marriage.

Chaucer, two centuries after Chrétien, explores the development of love in relation to marriage, very much in the light of *Le Roman de la Rose*. In the early *Book of the Duchess* the lover recalls that it was Love who was the Lord to whom he did homage, who instructed him, and prepared him so that he might honour his lady, for many a year, 'Or that myn herte was set owher' (776). This is, as often pointed out, the 'feudalisation' of love and despite Jaeger's objections does seem to be a new direction for heterosexual desire, originating in the homage to the lady in some of the troubadour songs, as Lewis and others long ago argued. The homage is to Love, not immediately to the lady, and traces can be found as early as such classical sources as Ovid, where it is a commonplace that Venus and Cupid are powerful deities. So it is important not to exaggerate the change, but equally important to note the new intensity and seriousness, which yet does not seem to be built on the fragments of male friendship. A notable point is the inferiority that the lover feels towards his lady. He could only ask her for 'Mercy' (*BD* 1219), which she eventually granted (*BD* 1270), taking the lover in her 'governaunce' (*BD* 1286), and they were always true to each other until her lamented death. The inequality of the relationship, and the fact that the lover is 'educated' by the lady, depend also on a certain fundamental social equality, which is taken for granted. It is not irrelevant to recall that the known background of the poem, clearly if punningly signalled near the end (*BD* 1315–20), is the marriage of John of Gaunt to Blanche of Lancaster and her lamented, untimely death after bearing five children.

Here death has frustrated love. The slightly later *Parliament of Fowls* better illustrates Jaeger's thesis. The birds of the core narrative clearly represent human suitors for a lady. Various attempts, which need not concern us here, have been made to identify the persons in real life. The suitors, represented as eagles, are already of noble birth and habit. Each expresses himself in suitably humble terms, summed up in the speech of the noblest of them, 'Unto my soverayn lady, and not my fere' (*PF* 416). He expresses above all his everlasting 'trouthe'. The other suitors of lower rank express the equal greatness of their love, the intensity of their 'service'[22] and its undying persistence. Here the dilemma arises not primarily from the constrictions of social morality but from the possessiveness of love itself. Legal requirements apart, no male here wants to share his woman with others. This seems to be a fairly general characteristic and was certainly widespread in medieval times. It was also closely connected with honour, and the wish of fathers that true sons

---

[22] The force of this expression is as far as I know nowhere found in the records of male friendship where equality of feeling ultimately becomes significant, even if the relationship began as between master and pupil, as with Abelard and Heloise. The meaning of 'service' is variable, of course, becoming both honourable and degrading according to context and, later, political attitudes, but it retains its sexual implications in modern farming where it refers to the breeding of cattle and horses.

should inherit property. Even in naturally promiscuous societies sexual jealousy is known. In Chaucer's works only the low-class Miller in *The Canterbury Tales* is not jealous of possible lovers of his wife provided she satisfies him first.

The dilemma in *The Parliament of Fowls* is that each suitor has to put in the highest possible bid for the lady, and that must include life-long devotion. That means that once her choice is made two suitors, if they keep their word, must remain celibate for life, and this suppression of feeling would be highly unwelcome. Whether it would 'ennoble' the suitor, on the assumption that he could by definition have no significant relationship with the beloved, must be doubtful. The dilemma here might, as Jaeger argues, be seen to arise because sex has entered the equation. It could have been avoided if the sentiment of sexual love had not been exaggerated, as one may say, by the infusion of the moral sentiment of everlasting loyalty in love. This is the sentiment that connects the suitors' expressions of love with those of Lancelot and Tristan. Another connection is the feudal concept of absolute loyalty to one's lord. Though that was in essence without sexual content it evidently became part of the sentiment of love as expressed in the extensive medieval literature of secular love. The question of adultery does not enter the equation here because an enormous amount of love-literature, especially in English, is concerned with pre-marital love. Lancelot and Tristan each became obsessed with another man's wife, complicating the situation further by the man being the lover's feudal lord. Moreover, each lover is the outstanding knight of his day, the most highly gifted in almost all respects. Not every knight was gifted enough to complain if his wife was seduced by Tristan, as the case of Segwarides in Malory's *Le Morte Darthur* seems to illustrate.[23] To this extent Jaeger is surely right in denying representative quality to Lancelot and Tristan. Yet we may also invoke the paradox that the extreme example of a given set of feelings may also be the most illuminating. The suitors in *The Parliament of Fowls* are not contemplating either adultery or treachery – quite the reverse – yet may witness how the sentiment of overmastering love may be doomed in some cases to everlasting frustration, and may be infertile. That is, unless we invoke another paradox not explored here by Chaucer, that if the rejected suitors then went off and 'married' someone else they would thereby prove false to their word and so unworthy anyway to have been accepted as a lover. By a further paradox still, if we extend the story altogether beyond the bird-actors, we may say what a good thing it was that only 'love' was the issue, since if it was a question of marriage, rather a different matter, we may paraphrase the cuckoo's sensible remark, 'But she wol love hym, lat hym love another!' (*PF* 567). The comments of the vulgar birds well, and comically, illustrate the commonsense solutions to the highly courtly sentiment of love,

---

[23] See Sir Thomas Malory, *Works*, ed. E. Vinaver, rev. edn P. J. C. Field (Oxford, 1990), pp. 402, 442.

but only by knowing nothing of it, and ignoring its entirely natural base in the kind of obsessive passion felt by some people, which most cultures recognise, whatever degree of importance they give to it.

Chaucer himself pursued the problem as already noted in *Troilus*, where he stripped its conflict of the social structure of marriage to concentrate on the obsession. The conclusion here seems to be that Troilus' love could only be sterile *because* it could not issue in marriage. There is a sort of inner block, as well as the external causes of Criseyde's banishment to the Greeks and her own unfaithfulness.

Chaucer does not leave this intriguing question here. Two of *The Canterbury Tales* treat it in very different ways. One is *The Wife of Bath's Tale*, and perhaps we may include her *Prologue*. *The Wife of Bath's Prologue* does not include love *paramours*, but we may note that after all the sexual promiscuity and the domestic battles she finds marriage offers a reasonable contract, when each side is true to the other, provided she has mastery. Her tale offers a similar moral, except that the wife is completely obedient to her husband (*CT* III, *WBT* 1255). Here we have moved far from ennobling love, except that the rapist knight has been tamed into 'gentillesse'. He gladly accepts marriage.

The Franklin's Tale explores love within marriage and, as every one knows, the problem of mastery. This is another version of the problem of irreconcilability that Jaeger sees between medieval love and marriage. In *The Franklin's Tale* the apparent solution is expressed in the arrangement whereby the knight Arveragus and Dorigen his wife agree that she shall have mastery and he will be 'Servant in love, and lord in marriage' (*Frankl T* (V) 793). Each must practise patience with the other:

> That freendes everych oother moot obeye,
> If they wol longe holden compaignye.
> Love wol nat been constreyned by maistrye.   (*Frankl T* (V) 762–3)

The mutual obligation of love is here a significant development beyond the 'feudalisation' of love. Self-control and restraint ('Pacience' (*Frankl T* (V) 773)) involve a certain suppression of the feelings not *of* love, but *by* love. Here the keyword is 'freendes'. This is not the place to follow the turns of the well-known plot, only to notice that mutual forbearance and the ultimate allegiance of all the persons to 'gentillesse', which includes 'trouthe', that is, loyalty both to person and to promise. These are the qualities that sum up love that is not only heartfelt but goes beyond passion to a willed deliberateness that incurs the risk of deep pain if loyally followed. This story has a happy ending, yet it could be that in order to test the greatness of love it should be tested to destruction, as many stories of love and loyalty testify: 'Greater love hath no man than this, that a man lay down his life for his friends' (John 15: 13). Death is the endorsement as it is the greatest test of love, and perhaps the greatest love stories bear this out. But that is not because of the intrusion of sexual love, despite nineteenth-century retellings.

A different medieval English example of the interplay between sexual desire and its control or suppression in the name of a great love is offered by the alliterative poem *Sir Gawain and the Green Knight*, contemporary with Chaucer's works. Here there is test, suppression, nobility, but Sir Gawain is not ennobled by love, though virtuous in the proper suppression of sexual desire. At the beginning of the poem he is already noble, the first of Arthur's knights, chaste, young. The poem is about his testing, not of his love for his friends, but of his own integrity reflected in his devotion to the Virgin Mary, which is expressed in his chastity. Yet while the suppression of physical desire on moral grounds (specifically not to betray his host's trust and not to commit adultery) preserves Gawain's own life, the concern is not to achieve a higher level of relationship with another person. The control of his own desire paradoxically 'makes for life', in the old Leavisian phrase, and has wider implications for any civilised life. It has a lonely integrity, part of which is Gawain's own sense of having failed to achieve his own highest ideal, though his host, the Green Knight himself, and all Arthur's court, forgive him any shortcoming and recognise his full moral worth. Any number of modern critics regard Gawain as a 'failure', as he does himself, but this is surely absurd. Not only has he preserved his integrity but he has behaved with exemplary courtesy in the treacherous world of high society. As to the bizarre attempt by Carolyn Dinshaw to force a sodomitical interpretation, which she admits is not within the poem's meaning, one can only point out that this is literally a perversion of the ideals of friendship traced by Jaeger, to what different effect, in earlier centuries.[24]

The ideal of passionate friendship between men as exemplified in *Amis and Amiloun* was not lost. It is reiterated for example in Lydgate's *Fabula Duorum Mercatorum* where the two friends, middle-aged merchants, 'fall in love' at a distance. It recurs in Shakespeare in those sonnets directed to a young man, which are quite different in tone from those concerned with a woman. It is seen in the friendship of Antonio and Bassanio in *The Merchant of Venice*. It can be traced in later centuries. In the First World War there was a number of 'Pals' Battalions', mainly from the North of England, recruited on the basis of friendship – not a good idea, militarily speaking, as friends are inclined to rescue each other when wounded, which leads to heavier casualties. None of this means that sodomy was not known, though it was always repudiated. In the sixteenth century the most notable treatment of ennobling love in English, related to but very different from Jaeger's early examples, is given by Spenser. In *The Faerie Queene* Spenser creates an eclectic mixture of medieval English and Italian romance, Florentine Neoplatonism and a fully Puritan emphasis on chastity outside marriage and full sexuality within it. Love, based on 'chaste virtue', is most highly praised as friendship between man and wife.[25]

---

[24] See also Jane Gilbert, 'Gender and Sexual Transgression' *A Companion to the* Gawain-*Poet*, ed. Derek Brewer and Jonathan Gibson (Cambridge: D. S. Brewer, 1997), pp. 53–70.

[25] For a general survey of medieval English romances with summaries, see *A Manual of Writings in Middle English 1050–1500*, vol. 1, ed. J. Burke Severs, *Romances* (New Haven, 1967).

Postscript

The concluding paragraphs of this essay were written before the publication of Alan Bray's study, *The Friend*.[26] Bray takes up the theme of devoted love between men, which relates to the topic of love discussed by Jaeger, though Bray disregards literary evidence. Similarly modern literary criticism of medieval literature, with the exception of Mann (see note 13 above), largely disregards love between men. It is, however, discussed by Michel Foucault in relation to fourth-century BC Greek thought.[27] Foucault discusses friendship between men, in Greek *philia*, as distinguished from the erotic love felt by grown men for beautiful boys, which is Foucault's main interest. (It is symptomatic that 'friendship' has been missed in the index to Foucault's volume, though the subject of several pages.) According to Foucault the erotic love of men for boys '(doomed to disappear)' could be converted 'into a relation of friendship, of *philia*', which ideally was lifelong and based on equality of the individuals. *Philia* was 'an affinity of character and mode of life, a sharing of thoughts and existence, mutual benevolence' – 'indestructible friendship' enjoyed 'down to old age'.[28] The love of boys might graduate into 'a stable relationship where physical relations would no longer be important and where the two partners would be able to share the same feelings and the same possessions'. Foucault invokes notions of 'anxiety' and 'problematisation' as intrinsic to the erotic relationship, not to *philia*.[29]

The interest of Bray's book is in the historical evidence provided primarily by those instances, relatively few but more conspicuous than previously realised, of the graves of devoted men friends who were buried together. These are men of equivalent status, and even if differing in age have no pupil–teacher relationships. They are not examples of ennobling love, but nor are they examples of physical sexual love between men, or at least they are not recognised as such. To this extent they illustrate another development of love, or rather, the continuity of a sentiment, as suggested by Jaeger, of a kind no longer recognised in the current attempt, particularly by feminists such as Dinshaw, to sexualise all human relationships. Male friendship has become a delicate area both socially and in literary terms, which there is no space to explore here. It is not the concern of those heterosexual relationships that are mainly the subject of medieval English romance (always with the exceptions already noted of such romances as *Amis and Amiloun* and Lydgate's *Fabula* with their European analogues). The delicacy arises from some fuzziness in the line between male friendship, as it may best be called, and male

---

[26] Alan Bray, *The Friend* (Chicago, 2003).
[27] Michel Foucault, *The History of Sexuality*, vol. 2, *The Use of Pleasure*, trans. Robert Hurley (Harmondsworth, 1992: French original 1984).
[28] Ibid., p. 201.
[29] Ibid., p. 225.

homosexual, i.e. sodomitical, love. The word 'sodomy' is in itself a difficulty in that it always implies physical repulsion and moral condemnation (neither Foucault nor Bray use the word, though Foucault allows 'penetration'). The modern moral climate has changed to such an extent that nowadays newspapers print requests by men for men lovers, women for women. Before we read such love into earlier stages of our own culture we have to recognise the much greater degree of physical expressiveness in such periods, as Foucault and Bray do, compared with what was, at any rate until recently, usual in modern Western culture. Even here there are national differences. Who is there grown up before 1990 who has not seen on television fat elderly Communist leaders kissing each other in greeting, admittedly in a very gingerly fashion?

It is time to reinstate friendship, especially non-sexual friendship between men, of which there are myriad examples in social history, as a recognisable, uncontentious area of love. It will then be important similarly to recognise female friendship. These are not cases of 'ennobling love' and they have many gradations from friendly acquaintance to deep feeling. They presuppose standards of integrity and constancy. For Chaucer, as already quoted above, 'friendship' seems the highest expression of marital love. With an interesting similarity and profound difference, Criseyde when she is finally breaking off her relationship with Troilus says, 'And frendes love, that shal ye han of me' (*Troilus* V, 1080) (like the modern cliché, 'just friends'), a term that here specifically excludes sexual relations. But Troilus is committed to the earlier model of sexual love when the lover is 'servant', the lady 'sovereign'. A different model of equality in friendship was available throughout the ages, independent of sexuality, of which marriage might also be the analogue:

> Let me not to the marriage of true minds
> Admit impediments . . .
> Love's not Time's fool, though rosy lips and cheeks
> Within his bending sickle's compass come . . .
> [Love] bears it out even to the edge of doom . . .
>
> (Shakespeare, *Sonnet 116*)

10

'Therof seyus clerkus':
Slander, Rape and *Sir Gowther*

NEIL CARTLIDGE

*S*ir *Gowther* is one of the most self-consciously shocking of all Middle English romances, a lurid version of a tale about a woman who is in effect raped by the Devil, and about the child born from this unnatural union.[1] The Devil's child duly expresses his evil proclivities – even as a tiny infant he kills no fewer than nine of his wetnurses by suckling them to death; and he later goes on to a career of violence in which the highlight is probably the rape and incineration of a whole convent of nuns. Such extravagantly scandalous matter is all too readily refigured by literary critics into psychological, anthropological or folkloric motifs – translated, that is, into a play of symbols reflecting tensions or uncertainties deep in medieval society or in the medieval psyche. Yet such approaches as these risk giving the impression that medieval romances can only be analyzed in terms of superstition or neurosis; and they are often at odds with the way in which medieval writers themselves recognized and dramatized the dangers of representation. *Sir Gowther* is in fact explicitly furnished with a warning about the nature of its contents in the first twenty-one lines of the text; and although most critics pass over them without comment (perhaps taking them as a merely rhetorical or playful apology for 'rehercing a cherles tale'), these lines are actually more complex and provocative than they at first appear:

> [God that art of myghtis most,
> Fader and Sone and Holy Gost,
>   That bought man on Rode so dere;
> Shilde us from the fowle fende
> 5   That is about mannys sowle to shende
>   All tymes of the yere!
> Sumtyme the fende hadde postee
> Forto dele with ladies free

---

[1]   *Sir Gowther* [Edinburgh, National Library of Scotland, Advocates' MS 19.3.1 and British Library, MS Royal 17.B.43], ed. Maldwyn Mills, *Six Middle English Romances* (London, 1973), pp. 148–68; also by Karl Breul (Jena, 1885); and by Anne Laskaya and Eve Salisbury, *The Middle English Breton Lays*, TEAMS (Kalamazoo, 1995).

In liknesse of here fere;
10   So that he bigat Merlyng and mo,
     And wrought ladies so mikil wo
         That ferly it is to here.

     A selcowgh thyng that is to here:
     A fende to nye]ght wemen nere,
15   And makyd hom with chyld,
     Tho kynde of men wher thei hit tane
     (For of homselfe had thei never nan,
     For they themselves had no form;
         Be meydon Maré mylde).
     Therof seyus clerkus, Y wotte how,
20   That schall not be rehersyd now,
         As Cryst fro schame me schyld.
     Bot Y schall tell yow of a warlocke greytt,
     What sorow at his modur hart he seyt,
         With his warcus wylde.[2]

The poem begins with a prayer for protection against the Devil, a textual gesture that explicitly locates the threat of demonic intervention here in *this* world – the world shared by author and audience – and not just in the *other* world of fiction. What makes the prayer immediately and urgently necessary, the text suggests, is the very process of hearing about it. The conception of such men as Merlin and Sir Gowther by demons is said to be not just a 'marvelous' and 'strange' event (a 'ferly' and 'a selcowgh thyng', ll. 12–13), but in particular a 'ferly' and 'a selcowgh thyng . . . *to here*'.[3] That is, to hear a story about demonic sexual assault – to entertain it as a possibility even in the imagination – is to risk a certain complicity in the crime, providing the Devil with form and substance in a way that comes perilously close to invoking him. At one level, this suggestion clearly works to command attention to the text – as a source of arcane marvels, but also as something glamorously, and perhaps hazardously, uncensored. At another level, it problematizes the whole business of tale-telling by implicitly raising the question of discursive responsibility: for if it is accepted that describing the Devil's activities in any sense invites them, then the author's decision to tell the story of *Sir Gowther* has to be morally questionable.

From this perspective, it can only be significant that the text introduces the theme of the Devil's manifestations in this world along with a pious request for the Trinity to 'shield *us* from the foul fiend' ('shilde us from the fowle fende', l. 4), but then goes on to foreclose any further analysis of demonic

---

2   *Sir Gowther*, ll. 1–24, ed. Mills. The base-text of this edition is the Advocates' MS, but lines 1–14 are missing from Advocates' and are supplied from the Royal MS.

3   Cf. G. V. Smithers's remark that, 'the peculiar point of this story of Robert the Devil [to which *Sir Gowther* is related] would have been that it was a salutary warning against the dangers of entering into such liaisons, *or at any rate of attending to stories about them*' ('Story-Patterns in Some Breton Lays', *Medium Ævum* 22 (1953), pp. 61–92 (p. 77), my italics).

miscegenation in terms of a prayer for Christ to 'shield *me* from shame' ('Cryst fro schame me schyld', l. 21) – a subtle shift of perspective from humanity's fear of the Devil's works to an individual speaker's concern for the consequences of speaking about them. What is not immediately clear is why exactly the tale-teller's anxiety about his role modulates from fear in line 4 to shame in line 21, since even if we accept the text's suggestion that describing the Devil's activities in some sense substantiates them, it still seems strange that the romancier chooses to think of this risk in terms of shame – rather than, say, folly or pride. It might be tempting to identify this idea of shame with a conscious reaction against primitive or popular superstition, but in fact the text makes it quite clear that what is shameful here originates with learned, *clerical* discourse. The author of *Sir Gowther* states explicitly in l. 19 that it is clerks, educated men, who characteristically talk about the sexual activities of demons ('Therof seyus clerkus, Y wotte how'). He refuses to elaborate on that discourse ('That schall not be rehersyd now'), but what he has already said and what he implies he could have said effectively constitute a claim to initiation in this distinctively academic understanding of the supernatural.[4] It is perhaps significant that he chooses an essentially clerical figure, Merlin, as an example of the Devil's progeny. In the Middle Ages, Merlin was not just the wise man or wizard in the legend of King Arthur (as he tends to be in popular consciousness today), but was also the supposed author of an influential tradition of Latin prophecies – and as such the very type of the clerk privileged by his status to hidden, and perhaps forbidden, knowledge.[5] There is perhaps at least a hint here that, just as Merlin's knowledge was in some sense derived from – or at least authorized by – the legend of his diabolical descent, then so also clerical knowledge more generally might have some 'shameful' affinity with the Devil's powers. It is perhaps therefore as a clerk, or as a representative of clerks, that our author anticipates the possibility of shame – and with perhaps more than a suggestion

---

4   The author of *Sir Gowther* emphasizes that it is itself a written text ('wreton in parchemeyn', l. 745) in its final lines. Here he also acknowledges its origins in the Breton lay ('owt off a lay of Breytyn', l. 747), a genre whose nature is much contested by scholars, but which – even if it was at some stage in its development distinctively oral – can by no means by seen as an unelaborated or primitive form. See, for example, the usefully cautious consideration by Elizabeth Archibald, 'The Breton Lay in Middle English: Genre, Transmission and the Franklin's Tale', *Medieval Insular Romance: Translation and Innovation*, ed. Judith Weiss, Jennifer Fellows and Morgan Dickson (Cambridge, 2000), pp. 55–70.

5   In Geoffrey of Monmouth's *History of the Kings of Britain* the story of Merlin's conception by an *incubus* is the occasion for a distinctively bookish disquisition on demonology: ' "In the books written by our sages," he [Maugantius, apparently Vortigern's counsellor] said to Vortigern, "and in many historical narratives, I have discovered that quite a number of men have been born in this way. As Apuleius asserts in the *De deo socratis*, between the moon and the earth live spirits which we call incubus demons. These have partly the nature of men and partly that of angels, and when they wish assume mortal shapes and have intercourse with women. It is possible that one of these appeared to this woman and begot the lad in her" ' (Geoffrey of Monmouth, *The History of the Kings of Britain*, trans. Lewis Thorpe (Harmondsworth, 1966), vi. 18, p. 168).

that it is in clerical discourse, rather than vernacular storytelling, that the dangers of admitting the Devil's influence in the world really lie.

The romancer's decision to place on clerks the burden of moral responsibility for talking about the 'shameful' circumstances of his protagonist's birth is justified by the fact that medieval 'clerks' did indeed extensively discuss the physical possibility of diabolic miscegenation – and Merlin was often the paradigm that they chose. Many of these writers are frankly sceptical about the capability of otherworldly beings to 'dele with ladies free', but the sheer obsessiveness with which they debated the matter – an obsessiveness that only grew as the Middle Ages progressed – makes it quite clear that they found it a subject difficult to treat lightly.[6] After all, there was a patristic precedent for the serious consideration of such questions in St Augustine of Hippo's discussion of the origin of the giants described in Genesis 6: 4. *Sir Gowther* apparently makes specific reference to the Augustinian formulation of the 'problem' of demonic miscegenation in lines 15–17 – the problem that if demons are essentially incorporeal, then they can hardly father children themselves, unless they can temporarily borrow or possess bodily material.[7] This was a possibility that even scholastics as eminent as St Bonaventure and St Thomas Aquinas were prepared to endorse. Both men imagined an economy of exchange in which demons first adopted a female form (the *succubus*) in order to steal human semen and then metamorphosed into a male form (the *incubus)* in order to distribute it.[8] Such fantastic speculation about the supernatural biology of otherworldly beings is perhaps just what is evoked – and then conspicuously elided – in lines 18–19 of *Sir Gowther* ('That schall not be rehersyd now'). After all, the 'exchange' theory implicitly naturalizes both the sexual commerce of demons with human beings and demonic transcendence of gender in ways that are almost implicitly disturbing.[9] Yet what

---

6   See especially Dyan Elliott, *Fallen Bodies: Pollution, Sexuality and Demonology in the Middle Ages* (Philadelphia, 1999); also Corinne Saunders, *Rape and Ravishment in the Literature of Medieval England* (Cambridge, 2001), pp. 218–24; Barbara Newman, 'Possessed by the Spirit: Devout Women, Demoniacs, and the Apostolic Life in the Thirteenth Century', *Speculum* 73 (1998), pp. 733–70; Andrea Hopkins, *The Sinful Knights: A Study of Middle English Penitential Romance* (Oxford, 1990), pp. 163–6; Nicolas Kiessling, *The Incubus in English Literature: Provenance and Progeny* ([Pullman], 1977), esp. chapters 4 and 5.

7   St Augustine of Hippo, *Concerning the City of God against the Pagans*, trans. Henry Bettenson (Harmondsworth, 1972) III, 5, pp. 92–3 and XV, 23, pp. 637–42; also *Quaestionum in Heptateuchum libri VII*, ed. I. Fraipont, Corpus Christianorum, Series Latina 33 (Turnhout, 1958), I, q. 3, pp. 2–3; and see E. Mangenot, 'Démon d'après les pères', *Dictionnaire de théologie catholique [DTC]*, ed. A. Vacant et al., 13 vols (Paris, 1930–50), vol. 4, cols 339–84, esp. 370–2.

8   St Thomas Aquinas, *Summa Theologia*, ed. Fathers of the English Dominican Province, 61 vols (London, 1964–81), vol. 9 (ed. Kenelm Foster), I, q. 51, art. 6 (pp. 42–3); St Bonaventure, *Commentaria in quatuor libris sententiarum,* II, dist. 8, part 1, art. 3, q. 1, 5–6, *Opera omnia*, ed. Fathers of the College of St Bonaventure ad Claras Aquas, 10 vols (Florence, 1882–1902), vol. 2, p. 219. (St Bonaventure is also one of the writers who was prepared to discuss this question with reference to the ancestry of Merlin.) See also T. Ortolan, 'Démon d'après les scolastiques et les théologiens postérieurs', *DTC*, vol. 4, cols 384–407 and G. Bareille, 'Angélologie d'après les Pères', *DTC*, vol. 1, cols 1192–1222, esp. 1197–8.

9   Cf. Elliott, p. 153.

makes such academic speculation so very provocative is not so much the field of enquiry itself as the rigorous explicitness with which it is addressed. The self- consciously rationalistic approach adopted by Bonaventure and Aquinas necessarily involves the definition and systematization of horrifying possibilities that most people prefer to think about only vaguely, or not at all. This is perhaps why the *Sir Gowther*-poet chooses to insist on the risk of 'shame' in retailing clerkly discourse too openly to an audience that was likely to be vernacular, non-clerical and unused to the frankness of intellectual theology. In the face of such an audience, the poet's claim to familiarity with contemporary demonology could only be safely presented in terms of a gesture of conspicuous self-censorship.

At the same time, the sheer cumbrousness of the medium in which Aquinas and Bonaventure reported their demonological views – the scholastic *summa*, with all its apparatus of parts, distinctions, *questiones*, *articuli* and so on – served almost automatically to forestall any allegations of impropriety or salaciousness. The posture of 'clerkliness' adopted at the beginning of *Sir Gowther* might be read as the poet's attempt to clothe himself in a similarly 'scientific', Hippocratic aura. Learned Latin discourse on demons itself often insists on its own 'clerkliness' in this context – its own indebtedness to a distinctively bookish tradition of intellectual investigation – in very much the same way that *Sir Gowther* does, and for much the same reasons. The encyclopedist Vincent of Beauvais, for example, justifies his decision to tell two of the more baroque medieval tales about human–devil miscegenation with a display of informed and judicious scepticism in which both the authority of a vague magisterial tradition and an Augustinian aversion to the idea of diabolic corporeality are prominent:

> Sed nunc dicunt magistri, daemones non posse generare, licet possint, & nouerint femina commiscere: ad generationem hominis exiguntur non solum femina sed etiam operationes vtriusque, scilicet maris & fœminæ: vnde si dæmon semen viri proijceret in matricem mulieris nunquam per hoc tamen fieret hominis generatio. Itaque per commixtionem feminum quam faciunt dæmones illa sola animalia fieri possunt quæ fiunt per putrefactionem, vt ranae, muscæ, & quidam serpentes. Ea vero quæ fiunt per generationem non possunt per rationem prædictam. Dicunt ergo falsum fuisse, quod Merlinus dictus fit a dæmone progenitus, sed forte mater eius passa est illusionem in somnis a diabolo, ita quod videbatur sibi viro succumbere, vel aliquid tale. Et in ipsa illusione putabat se tunc concepisse, licet non concepit. . . .[10]

---

10 Vincent of Beauvais [Vincentius Bellovacensis], *Speculum Quadruplex sive Speculum Maius: Naturale/ Doctrinale/ Morale/ Historiale* (Douai, 1624; rpt. Graz, 1964), I, caps 126–8, cols 156–8, here cap. 128, col. 157: 'But yet the [academic] Masters say that demons cannot produce offspring, although they can and know how to have intercourse with a woman. For the generation of a human being it is necessary to have not just a woman alone, but the involvement of both sexes – that is, both a male and a female. Therefore even if a demon could project a man's seed into a woman's womb, it would still not result in the conception of a human being. So it is that out of the intercourse with women perpetrated by demons only creatures that come about through putrefac-

There are some striking parallels here with *Sir Gowther*. Just as the romancier seeks refuge in the assertion that 'Therof seyus clerkus', so Vincent appeals to the authority of academic masters – 'nunc dicunt magistri'; and just as the romancier expresses scruples about the nature of his story only in the course of telling it, so Vincent's expression of scepticism about cases of human–demon intercourse comes only after he has given over two chapters to reporting them. This passage suggests that typically 'scientific' writers such as Vincent could have directly provided the *Sir Gowther*-poet not just with the precedent for imagining the supernatural that he claims to exist in clerical discourse, but also with strategies for diffusing the moral responsibility for doing so. Even so, there is no trace in the romance of the two suggestions that Vincent tries to develop – that demons are capable only of conceiving vermin and that men thought to have been conceived by demons are in fact only phantasms ('non fuisse veros homines, sed phantasticos'). These ideas are hardly compatible either with each other or with Augustinian theology, and neither really explains the 'facts' of supernatural ancestry as Vincent himself states them in the tales that he tells. Indeed, it might be said that while his interest in the possibility of demonic miscegenation is palpable, his attempt to refute it by rational argument is, in comparison, remarkably lame.

What lies behind such learned discussion of the sexual powers of demons, it could be argued, is a certain unease (on the part of an almost exclusively masculine social group) about the very efficacy of the male seed in conception – an unease that might, in its suppression, also be read as a matter of shame. The precise nature of the masculine role in the biological mechanism of conception was impossible to demonstrate scientifically; and the possibility that women could conceive with supernatural rather than human assistance was impossible to dismiss unequivocally when viewed in the context of the Incarnation – the one fundamentally undeniable theological proof that women were physically capable of conceiving without any help from a human partner.[11] In this context, the author of *Sir Gowther*'s decision to swear by the Virgin Mary in line 18 has at the very least an ironic resonance and it may be that he is gently hinting at how much is at stake in the veracity of his tale. The allusion is not necessarily a mischievous one: since Mary is the one example of a woman who became pregnant to a more-than-human partner to purposes and ends that were wholly and absolutely good, it is only natural to evoke her

---

tion, such as frogs, flies and certain snakes come into being. These things truly cannot come about through [sexual] generation, for the reason stated. They say therefore that it is wrong to believe that the said Merlin was fathered by a demon, but perhaps an illusion produced by the devil befell his mother in her dreams, so that it seemed to her she slept with a man, or something like that; and in this illusion she thought that she had conceived, even though she had not. . . .'

11   The intellectual problems caused by the Virgin Birth are clearly registered elsewhere in medieval culture. In canon law, for example, it was impossible for lawyers to define consummation as an essential condition of marriage, since to do so would have been to have denied the validity of Mary's marriage with Joseph. See Gratian, *Decretum Magistri Gratiani [Concordia discordantium canonum]*, ed. Emil Friedberg, *Corpus Iuris Canonici*, 2nd edn, vol. 1 (Leipzig, 1879; Graz, 1959), II, C. 27, Q. 2, c. 45.

as a protective intercessor in the face of demonic activities that are the grotesque and terrifying antithesis of the divine grace that she received. It is significant, perhaps, that at the very moment when Sir Gowther turns to repentance, having heard his mother's confession of the true circumstance of his birth, the text recalls Mary once again, this time as the natural agent of his reconciliation with God – ' "Lorde mercy," con he cry/ To God that Maré bare' (ll. 236–7). Yet the evocation of the Virgin Mary in the context of Sir Gowther's conception remains disturbing – a reminder that Christian miracles and demonic marvels are intellectually parallel (even if eschatologically opposed) phenomena. Indeed, the lie that Sir Gowther's mother chooses to tell her husband – that her pregnancy was announced to her by ' "an angel down from bright heaven . . . who I hope was God's ambassador" ' (' "an angell com fro hevon bryght/ . . . I hope was Godus sond" ', ll. 82, 84) – clearly reads like a blasphemous attempt at appropriating the Annunciation as a gloss on her encounter with the Devil.[12] Although it might be argued that it is precisely as an anti-type to Mary – as a woman subjected not to divine grace but to demonic coercion and deceit – that the horror of her predicament is most emphatically expressed, there is also some justification for a contradictory interpretation: that, by inventing this story, the duchess in effect accepts liability for her own all too susceptible sexuality – and perhaps also for her own all too unconditional wish for a child ('On what maner scho ne roghth', l. 63). This more hostile assessment of Sir Gowther's mother's moral responsibility is perhaps more in tune with the logic of clerical discourse on *incubi*, in which masculine anxieties about the disruption of the paternal order by otherworldly visitants naturally tended to be translated into misogynistic assumptions about women's sexual – and moral – susceptibility.

The *Sir Gowther*-poet's palpable unease about the Devil's role in his story may reflect an awareness that the clerical tradition of speculation about the possibility of supernatural impregnation is almost inevitably discreditable to women – the victims, both physically and metaphorically, of any story of human/demon intercourse. It is in this sense also that his use of clerical demonology as a source of authority for his story might also be said to be a matter of shame. As he acknowledges, the begetting of figures like Merlin only brought great sorrow ('mikil wo', l. 11) to the ladies themselves; and there is perhaps at least a suggestion here that, just as the Devil's activities are in some way underwritten by an intrusive discourse about them, so his victims' sorrows are at least exacerbated – if not actually created – by being publicly discussed. The author of *Sir Gowther* is notably coy or apologetic at the moment in which his protagonist's mother meets the Devil in the flesh. 'Ho meyt a mon, *tho sothe to say*,/ That hur of luffe besoghth' (ll. 65–6), he says, using the parenthetical tag here ('tho sothe to say') in such a way as to

---

make it look less like a metrical filler than an apology. One obvious explanation for this unclerkly, unprofessional squeamishness about the indecorous-
ness of the theme is that the audience for vernacular romance was very much
more likely to include women than was that of a learned lecture. By claiming
academic authority for his tale in the way that he does, the *Sir Gowther*-poet
in effect presents himself as a representative of clerical culture in a deliberately staged confrontation with the sensibilities of an audience that is
imagined to be considerably less uniform in its education or expectations than
a clerical audience would have been. It is a means of creating dramatic
momentum in the performance of the narrative, but it is also a way of provoc-
atively highlighting some of the tensions that are undoubtedly inherent in the
material of the tale itself.

Even within academic contexts – and in the Middle Ages these were almost
exclusively masculine – the essentially scandalous nature of such stories
about women's impregnation by otherworldly beings is never entirely
forgotten. It is expressed not just in the uncharacteristic hesitancy of such
writers as Augustine and Aquinas, but also more deliberately even by clerical
writers with a more satirical turn of mind – and specifically in the context of
classical Latin literature's abundant repertoire of stories about divine paterni-
ties. For example, in Walter Map's *Dissuasio Valerii* ('Valerius's Argument
Against [Taking a Wife]') – an ostensibly virulent antifeminist tract that
should probably be read as a sardonic exercise in rhetorical display – the
legend of Plato's divine origins is translated into a misogynistic argument
with a rapidity that is deliberately and reductively ludicrous. The philoso-
pher's mother, Perictione, was supposed to have been visited in a dream by
the god Apollo and conceived her child by him – a story that was clearly
invented as an aetiology of Plato's 'superhuman' wisdom. Map, however,
chooses to interpret it only as an example of how utterly untrustworthy and
essentially lecherous women must be, if even in their sleep they manage to get
themselves knocked up:

> 'Perictio, uirgo uergens in senium et fama castitatis priuilegiata constanter,
> tandem Apollinis oppressa fantasmate concepit peperitque Platonem.
> Amice, ecce quam illabatam seruauerunt vigilie, deflorauit illusio per
> sompnium,'[13]

13 Walter Map, 'Dissuasio Valerii' in *De nugis curialium*, ed. and trans. M. R. James, C. N. L. Brook
and R. A. B. Mynors (Oxford, 1983), pp. 306–7: 'Perictione, a virgin verging on old age and
constantly eminent in her reputation for her chastity, eventually succumbed in a vision of Apollo,
conceiving and giving birth to Plato. Friend, take note that she preserved her chastity when awake,
but was deflowered by an illusion while she slept.' I have adapted and updated James's translation.
There is also a more recent edition of the 'Dissuasio' by Ralph Hanna III and Traugott Lawler, in
Jankyn's Book of Wikked Wyves, vol. 1 (Athens, GA, 1997), pp. 122–47. As it happens, one of the
medieval commentaries on the 'Dissuasio' also suggests (as I think *Sir Gowther* does) that the
threat of sexual assault by demons is heightened by consciousness of it: 'Imo vadens dormitum
non debet respicere dicta sanctorum circa illam materiam, quia facient in eo memoriam illius rei'
('Indeed, when going to bed, no one should look over the words of the saints on this matter, since
that will leave a memory of it there'). See Neil Cartlidge, 'Misogyny in a Medieval University?

This is surely the ultimate *reductio ad absurdum* of the conclusion towards which much of scholastic thinking on demonic miscegenation was tending – the idea that women are by nature more susceptible than men to sexual corruption of this kind. Similarly, the medieval Latin comedy *Geta* casts an interesting light on the method by which the Devil seduces (and in effect rapes) Sir Gowther's mother – that is, by impersonating her husband.[14] This same means of sexual conquest is used in *Geta* by another supernatural being, the god Jupiter. Yet what makes this play so revealing about the gendered dimension of such stories is the way in which much of the humour devolves on the multiple 'unmanning' of Geta, the cuckolded husband's servant. Geta is turned away from his own house by Jupiter's accomplice Mercury, who has been detailed to impersonate Geta himself – and the result of this for Geta is a stressful crisis of identity.[15] This crisis is compounded by the fact that while his master has been studying in Paris, Geta himself has learned more dialectic than is good for him, so that he is all too ready to assume (as an unsophisticated philosophical realist) that if he has no name then he cannot exist – and is therefore a figment of his own imagination. Not only is he not quite the man he thought he was, or even a person at all, but it also turns out that Mercury has unmanned him in a different sense, laying claim (along with the rest of Geta's person and personality) to the only physical advantage in which he can take pride of any kind – that is, his enormous phallus.[16] From this point of view, the play perhaps testifies to the threat of emasculation that medieval scholars increasingly tended to detect in such legends about the supplantation of earthly lovers by unearthly ones.[17] At the very least, the explicitness with which Mercury dwells on Geta's phallic accomplishments places the gods' seduction of human women in a context that is discreditably grotesque.

Yet, while there are medieval Latin texts that clearly recognize, and sometimes even deliberately exaggerate, the provocative aspects of such tales about superhuman lovers, reducing them in some cases to absurdity, they themselves are self-conscious products of a clerical milieu, and as a result

The "Hoc contra malos" Commentary on Walter Map's *Dissuasio Valerii'*, *Journal of Medieval Latin* 8 (1998), pp. 156–91 (p. 190).

[14] *Geta*, ed. Keith Bate, *Three Latin Comedies* (Toronto, 1976), pp. 15–34; and also Gustave Cohen, *La 'Comédie' latine en France au XIIe siècle* (Paris, 1931), pp. 34–57.

[15] Rape by impersonation is also the means by which Uther Pendragon begets the future King Arthur on the Duchess Ygerna (as in the 'history' told by Geoffrey of Monmouth, for example: see n. 5 above). Mercury plays the same role in *Geta* as Uther's henchman, Ulfinus, who is detailed (by Merlin) to impersonate the Duke of Tintagel's henchman, Jordan.

[16] *Geta*, ed. Bate, ll. 351–8.

[17] Here, of course, the context is consciously Ovidian: the supernatural lovers in this case are the gods (rather than the demons) whose encounters with humanity drive so many of the *Metamorphoses*. Even so, *Geta* still seems to me to illustrate a sense of the scandalousness of the idea of sexual encounters with supernatural beings. This is also an aspect of the anxieties that Arthur Golding sought to neutralize in the preface to his famous translation: see *Ovid's Metamorphoses: translated by Arthur Golding*, ed. Madeleine Forey (Harmondsworth: Penguin, 2002), Preface to the Reader, pp. 23–9, e.g. ll. 33–4, 42: 'Who, seeing Jove, whom heathen folk do arm with triple fire,/ In shape of eagle, bull or swan to win his foul desire/ [. . .] would take him for a god?'

generate irony more often than they acknowledge 'shame'. It is in vernacular texts that the friction between masculine, clerical culture and the values of society more largely is more likely to be expressed in such terms. The prologue to *Sir Gowther*, as it happens, contains a verbal resonance with a text that addresses illicit pregnancy – in somewhat less than supernatural circumstances – from what is purportedly a distinctly female and non-clerkly point of view. Line 21 of *Sir Gowther* ('As Cryst fro shame me schyld') is disconcertingly reminiscent of the final stanza of what is now one of the best-known of all medieval lyrics, 'As I went on Yol Day in owre prosessyon' or 'Kyrie Aleyson'. The relevant strophe is:

> Benedicamus Domino: Cryst fro schame me schylde;
> Deo gracias therto: alas, I go with chylde![18]

This coincidentally similar phrasing is hardly substantial enough to carry much weight in itself – even if there is no reason to think that medieval romanciers were insusceptible to absorbing phrases from texts of other generic types.[19] Yet it seems to me at least interesting that it also occurs in a text that is (like *Sir Gowther*) structured around a fundamental opposition between a powerful masculine culture supported by the resources of learning and a disempowered feminine experience in some ways victimized by it. Not only does the speaker in 'Kyrie Aleyson' fall victim to the seductions of the parish clerk in large part *because* of her perception of his educational accomplishments, but even when she is lamenting the consequences of her infatuation, she does so by incompetently misappropriating some of the terms of that literate culture in a way that implicitly mocks and undermines her. To her it seems that *Deo gracias* is no more than a pious but incomprehensible formula – perhaps one that she hopes will have some sort of talismanic power to deter evil consequences – for it is ironically clear that she is in a predicament for which 'thanks' are hardly appropriate. Indeed, the whole poem is structured by the incongruous imposition of the order of the Mass on the girl's lament for her seduction and consequent pregnancy out of wedlock. In this poem the sexual victim is also the butt of the joke, for we are clearly invited to identify with the clerical perspective of literate worldliness – despite the apparently female voice of the speaker – and to share and enjoy the callousness with

---

[18] 'Kyrie Eleison' [BL Sloane MS 2593, fol. 34r]: *IMEV* 377; ed. R. L. Greene, *The Early English Carols*, 2nd edn (Oxford, 1977), pp. 278–9. See also Neil Cartlidge, ' "Alas I Go with Chylde": Representations of Extra-Marital Pregnancy in the Middle English Lyric', *English Studies* 79 (1998), pp. 395–414, esp. 405–7; and for a very different interpretation, J. D. W. Crowther, 'The Middle English Lyric "Joly Jankyn" ', *Annuale Mediævale* 12 (1971), pp. 123–5.

[19] The Paston family were certainly capable of absorbing and deploying phrases identifiably drawn from medieval lyrics: see e.g. *Paston Letters and Papers of the Fifteenth Century*, ed. Norman Davis, 2 vols (Oxford, 1971, 1976), vol. 2, p. 379: Thomas Daverse to John Paston II (29 January 1467): 'But me thenketh Ouide *De Remedio* were more mete for you, but yef ye purposed to falle hastely in my lady Anne P. lappe, as white as whales bon, &c'. Cf. 'A wayle whyt ase whalles bon', *The Harley Lyrics: The Middle English Lyrics of MS. Harley 2253*, ed. G.L. Brook (Manchester, 1948), pp. 40–1.

which it regards the girl concerned. Yet, even though both the lyric and *Sir Gowther* choose to depict encounters between two oppositely gendered cultures in essentially hostile terms, the lyric differs from the romance in that there is no acknowledgment here, or perhaps only a deliberate failure to acknowledge, any responsibility on the part of 'masculine' culture for creating the shame that the 'female' speaker laments. The prologue to *Sir Gowther*, by contrast, explicitly accepts the responsibility for the scandal that it creates, acknowledging at least tacitly that to reveal what is shameful is itself a shameful act. The difference is perhaps most clearly signalled by the fact that in *Sir Gowther* it is the explicitly male and clerical speaker who prays 'Cryst fro schame me schylde' and not the pregnant woman herself.

What seems to be implicit here at the beginning of *Sir Gowther* is the idea that sexual transgressions and the naming of sexual transgressions are morally equivalent and perhaps even mutually constitutive crimes. This is perhaps the same logic that powers both Chaucer's 'Manciple's Tale' and Malory's depiction of Agravain's exposure of Guinevere's adultery at the end of the *Morte Darthur*. Criminality, in other words, exists in the eye of the beholder – 'Honi soit qui mal y pense' – and to that extent the beholder is infected by it, and all the more so if the crime is made into a social reality by its enactment in speech. This curiously 'solid' conception of the relationship between name and shame is perhaps what underlies the elaborate concern for verbal hygiene expressed by authors in both the rhetorical and the pastoral traditions; and why misogynistic texts in medieval literature, no matter how strident, have a tendency to betray a furtive sense of their own illicitness.[20] These are points that could be developed at length, but it is sufficient here to point out that the medieval law of slander, insofar as it existed at all, was based on Roman law: and Roman law defined *slander* exclusively as a form of injury – in such a way as to make it secondary or even irrelevant whether or not the slander might also be *true*.[21] The only clear criterion for slander was that it should cause damage – and in defining the nature of this damage Justinian, for example, aligns slander directly with physical (rather than verbal) outrages

---

[20] For a study of the pastoral tradition, see Edwin D. Craun, *Lies, Slander, and Obscenity in Medieval English Literature: Pastoral Rhetoric and the Deviant Speaker* (Cambridge, 1997); and for a representative of the rhetorical tradition, see Albertano of Brescia, *Liber de doctrina dicendi et tacendi: la parola del cittadino nell'Italia del duecento*, ed. Paola Navone (Florence, 1998). On misogynistic literature, see the useful anthology edited by Alcuin Blamires, with Karen Pratt and C. W. Marx, *Woman Defamed and Woman Defended: An Anthology of Medieval Texts* (Oxford, 1992), and also Blamires's study of the counter-tradition, *The Case for Women in Medieval Culture* (Oxford, 1997). Walter Map's *Dissuasio Valerii* is one example of a misogynistic text that seems thoroughly aware of its own transgressiveness; another is Jehan le Fèvre's *Les Lamentations de Matheolus et le Livre de Leesce de Jehan Le Fèvre de Ressons*, ed. A.-G. van Hamel, 2 vols (Paris, 1892, 1905).

[21] See *The Institutes of Justinian*, trans. J. B. Moyle, 5th edn (Oxford, 1913), IV. iv, pp. 169–70; *The Theodosian Code*, trans. Clyde Pharr (1952; rpt New York, 1969), IX, 34, 1, p. 249. For slander in medieval law, see R. H. Helmholz, *Select Cases on Defamation to 1600*, Selden Society 101 (London, 1985); and also M. Lindsay Kaplan, *The Culture of Slander in Early Modern England* (Cambridge, 1997), pp. 13–33.

against the dignity of the person, such as stalking, sexual assault and rape. In short, the tendency to see slander in such substantive terms was certainly an ancient one – and I suspect that, both in Roman and in medieval thinking, a true slander, as it were, was regarded as being no less, and perhaps even more, damaging than a false one, precisely because it could be substantiated.[22] So it is that the prologue to *Sir Gowther* can insist on the impartial truth of the Devil's sexual attacks on women, while at the same time admitting that to articulate that truth is something intrinsically shameful – a slander against the women concerned, if not also against all women generally.

From this perspective, it is perhaps significant that the penitence subsequently imposed on Sir Gowther is directed so much at his mouth – not only is he forbidden to speak, but the only food he is allowed to eat is what he can snatch from the mouths of dogs (ll. 292–7). His anonymous self-abasement in the Emperor's hall, sitting under the high table ('hye bord', l. 329), with the dogs from whom he steals his food, and sleeping in a little curtained cubby-hole ('a lytell chambur . . . hyllyd undur teld', ll. 365–6), is not just a secular and more melodramatic equivalent of the domestic asceticism expressed by such figures as St Alexis (who takes up residence under the stairs of his father's house):[23] it is also a means of marking the unspeakability of his crimes, in such a way as to implicate the romancier who does indeed speak about them in the process of his repentance. Similarly, just as Sir Gowther achieves redemption by becoming 'the dumb man' ('tho domp mon', l. 348), so the romance's figure of grace is the dumb princess ('soo dompe as hee', l. 372); and it is only when she discovers the power to speak that Sir Gowther's rehabilitation is complete. Sexually threatened by the Sultan who fights her father in order to possess her, she effectively provides the protagonist with an opportunity to use chivalric action as a means of reversing the crime of sexual coercion in which the Devil's wickedness was first embodied in the text; and it is only through her recovery of both consciousness and speech that the romancier is able to provide a penitential gloss for Sir Gowther's actions on the field of battle. Her dumbness, in other words, is a figure of the violence done to women, not just by the Devil's assault in Sir Gowther's mother, but also by the romancier's act of recording it. Her discovery of the power of speech is a marker, both of God's forgiveness of Sir Gowther, and of the romancier's absolution for telling the tale of his life.

It might seem paradoxical, if not downright self-contradictory, that a text that begins by so emphatically marking the potentially dangerous offensiveness of its own subject-matter, invoking God's protection against the demonic activities that it goes on to describe, should finish by making Sir Gowther

---

22 As Juan Ruiz advises in *Il Libro de Buen Amor*, 'nunca mal rretrayas a furto nin en conçejo/ desque tu poridat yase en tu pellejo;/ que commo el verdadero non ay tan mal trebejo' ('never speak ill either in secret or in public, keep your secrets under your own skin, there is no worse trick than a truthful one'): ed. and trans. Elizabeth Drayson MacDonald, *The Book of Good Love* (London, 1999), str. 923, p. 226.

23 *La Vie de Saint Alexis*, ed. Maurizio Perugi, Textes littéraires français (Geneva, 2000).

(who is the product of those activities) into a saintly figure. Words about Sir Gowther are no longer scandalous, we are told, but impossible to waste:

> Whoso sechys hym with hart fre,
> Of hor bale bote mey bee:
>> For so God has hym hyght.
> Thes wordus of hym thar no mon wast,
> For he is inspyryd with tho Holy Gost,
>> That was tho cursod knyght.   (ll. 727–32, ed. Mills)

As a saintly intercessor, Sir Gowther now has the power to cure the blind, the dumb and the crippled (ll. 733–8), and his power seems to inhere precisely in the fact that he was once 'that cursed knight' ('tho cursod knyght'). In other words, it is as if the Devil's magic so fearfully alluded to in the opening lines of the text has not been in any way cancelled or dissolved, but merely redirected 'Thoro tho grace of God allmyght' (l. 738). From this point of view the tale's happy ending by no means invalidates the anxiety about speaking of the Devil's works that is expressed so urgently at its beginning. Similarly, the absolving grace for the scandal of Sir Gowther's conception represented in the text by the figure of the dumb princess marks only a provisional reconciliation between the clerkly culture of scientific speculation, in which the idea of demonic miscegenation was sustained and refined, and the less socially and culturally specific principle that the moral liability for shameful discourse actually belongs to those who employ it. The confrontation temporarily suspended here is in practice a gendered one, for while demonological enquiry was an exclusive prerogative of men, the particular vulnerability of women to injury by slander is one of the common assumptions of late medieval social practice, since women's social status tended to be defined much more decisively by their sexual status. In short, *Sir Gowther* is a text that clearly walks along the boundaries of outrage, but its motives for doing so are neither unthinking nor subconscious. Rather, it is founded upon a clear awareness of what might be called the economy of scandal in medieval culture. It is on this that its dramatic momentum depends, for its discovery of sanctity in *Sir Gowther* is the direct effect of its miraculous recuperation of a tale that is essentially a slander against the natural order – and against the integrity of women.

11

Beyond the Kick: Women's Agency in *Athelston*

NANCY MASON BRADBURY

As one of its main themes, the useful new *Cambridge Companion to Medieval Romance* argues that medieval romances speak for the traditional values and ideals of an elite society, but also raise compelling questions about those values.[1] For the most part, medieval romance represents gender roles in highly traditional ways. The male clerics who shaped the genre were educated to take a dim view of women's social agency, the definitive negative example being Eve's show of initiative in the Garden of Eden. Yet we can also find within our corpus noteworthy moments in which romance writers imagine women acting constructively in the public sphere. Nearly a century ago, Edith Rickert wrote of the Middle English *Athelston,* 'the two women are the most vivid characters', a somewhat surprising observation about a tale of sworn brotherhood between two earls, the Archbishop of Canterbury, and the king.[2] This essay examines the anonymous poet's portrayal of Athelston's queen, whom Rickert called 'noble-spirited', and his equally resolute sister; it argues that *Athelston* opens an intriguing fictional space for imagined alternatives to firmly established female roles. Even more strikingly, *Athelston* explores the prospect of women's social agency in relation to some of the most urgent historical issues facing England between 1370 and 1400, the probable period of the tale's composition.[3]

At first glance, *Athelston* might seem an unexpected, even bizarre, choice for an inquiry into the prospect of women's agency in Middle English romance. Its most notorious incident is the kick that the enraged king delivers to the belly of his pregnant wife, a blow so violent that it not only silences her attempt to influence his judgment, but also kills their unborn child. Any

---

[1] Roberta L. Krueger, ed., *The Cambridge Companion to Medieval Romance* (Cambridge, 2000), pp. 1–9.

[2] Edith Rickert, *Early English Romances: Romances of Friendship* (London, 1908), p. xviii. All quotations from *Athelston* are by line number from the edition by A. McI. Trounce, EETS OS 224 (London, 1951). The four male characters are originally described as 'messengers' (13); Athelston inherits his cousin's throne (he is the son of the uncle of the old king, 29), and then raises his sworn brothers to the earldoms and archbishopric.

[3] No compelling evidence narrows the date of the tale; its single manuscript, Cambridge University Gonville and Caius 175, is usually dated to around 1410–20. See Trounce, pp. 60–1 and George Taylor, 'Notes on *Athelston*', *Leeds Studies in English* 3 (1934), pp. 24–5.

reading that regards the poet as at all sympathetic toward the king's actions will find the tale deeply hostile to the prospect of women's counsel or social agency. A substantial article by Elizabeth Ashman Rowe takes this line: Rowe reads *Athelston* as 'a political fable that uses the metaphor of society as family to justify the dual patriarchal power structures of the monarchy and the church at a specific moment in English history'. Noting that a medieval husband was legally entitled to chastise his wife, Rowe writes that 'the poet justifies a near-absolutist royal authority by means of his underlying metaphor, that of society as family'.[4] In contrast, I read the tale as a harsh critique of England's ruling classes and the kick as one among many calamitous actions that manifest the rapacity and *untrouthe* of king and barons alike.[5] In the absence of credible leadership from the king and his barons, the poet's imagination turns toward less conventional sources of good counsel and judicious governance. *Athelston* imagines for the queen and the king's sister more political wisdom and more social agency than we find granted to women in many a Middle English romance untainted by sensational incidents such as the king's savage kick.

Athelston explores at least three ideas related to women's role in public life: the problematic nature of women's movement from private to public space, the possibility of access to power through queenly intercession, and the beneficial use of that power to promote the 'common profit'. To begin with the question of gendered space, the *Athelston*-poet is unusual among romance writers in his attention to real physical places and their potential for political meanings. He distinguishes, for example, between London as city and Westminster as the seat of the king (237–8); he rivals Chaucer in mentioning well-known landmarks on the pilgrimage route between London and Canterbury (335–56); he sets a confrontation between king and archbishop in the choir ('qweer', 430) of a church. Felicity Riddy has argued that the early romance *King Horn* serves as a paradigm for the genre in a number of ways, including the meaningful contrast it draws between a castle's public 'hall' and the privacy of a 'chamber' or 'bower'. Horn passes freely in and out of his lady Rymenhild's bower, a feminine place conducive to refined emotions and poetic speeches. He must also negotiate the hall, site of the public challenges of male adulthood. Rymenhild, in contrast, scarcely exists outside her bower;

---

4   Elizabeth Ashman Rowe, 'The Female Body Politic and the Miscarriage of Justice in *Athelston*', *Studies in the Age of Chaucer* 17 (1995), pp. 79–98 (pp. 79 and 80).
5   In this interpretive vein, Susan Crane offers a brief but pointed historical reading of *Athelston* as a dark tale of the breakdown of law and language in *Insular Romance: Politics, Faith and Culture in Anglo-Norman and Middle English Literature* (Berkeley, 1986), pp. 71–3. Daniel F. Pigg also notes the atmosphere of moral and political crisis, 'The Implications of Realist Poetics in the Middle English *Athelston*', *English Language Notes* 32 (1994), pp. 1–8. Mary Housum Ellzey connects the value of the counsel offered by Athelston's queen with the 'presence of subversive or political undercurrents in the romance' in 'The Advice of Wives in Three Middle English Romances: *The King of Tars*, *Sir Cleges*, and *Athelston*', *Medieval Perspectives* 7 (1992), pp. 44–51. Also in this vein is my article 'The Erosion of Oath-Based Relationships: A Cultural Context for *Athelston*', *Medium Ævum* 73 (2004), pp. 189–204.

in Riddy's words, she belongs not to the hall, the ' "rational" realm of the exercise of law and justice', but rather to her private chamber, 'the realm of fantasy and feeling'.[6] Exceptionally, the women characters in *Athelston* abandon their chambers and assert themselves in the public sphere, allying themselves with the values of justice and the rule of law.

As the tale's main action begins, the king's sister, Edith, and his unnamed queen are both pregnant, and thus they are both found initially in their chambers, from which they can emerge only with conscious effort and in the face of male resistance. After inheriting the throne and raising his three sworn brothers to positions of great influence, King Athelston responds with irrational fury to the false accusation of one of his sworn brothers against another. Motivated by envy (79, 800), Earl Wymound has falsely accused the king's brother-in-law and favorite, Egelond, of plotting to poison the king and usurp his throne. The king's sister is specifically implicated in the charge against her husband (163–4). In response, Athelston orders the execution of Egelond's entire family. Egelond himself is a curiously passive male character who never attempts to defend himself or his family from the false charge. In fact, in a tale that proceeds largely by dialogue, he speaks only once. His lone speech mildly states his assumption that, despite an invitation from her brother, his pregnant wife will remain in her chamber until her confinement is over (218–22). Unlike Rymenhild, who patiently awaits Horn in her bower, Egelond's wife announces her intention to abandon her chamber and travel to London immediately, despite her pregnancy.

The countess Edith's motivation for her move to the public space of the court is normative and maternal – she believes a lying message from the king inviting the family to London for the knighting of her two sons. Nevertheless, by including her husband's assumption that she is unavailable even to her relatives until her delivery,[7] the poet acknowledges the problematic nature of her movement from private to public space. When her husband is 'feteryd faste' immediately upon arrival at court (242), she is quickly disabused of the pretext that they have been summoned to a joyful ceremony. In the vacuum created by her husband's silence, she cries 'ful lowde' in the defense of her innocent family (244–9). Although 'in herte he was ful woo' as he orders that his sister be led to prison, Athelston continues on his chosen course like one

---

6   Felicity Riddy, 'Middle English Romance: Family, Marriage, Intimacy', in Krueger, ed., *The Cambridge Companion to Medieval Romance*, pp. 235–52 (p. 240). For a discussion of *chambyr, boure, and halle* in English romance, see Geraldine Barnes, *Counsel and Strategy in Middle English Romance* (Cambridge, 1993), pp. 53–4. For male and female space in medieval texts and archival records, see Barbara A. Hanawalt, 'At the Margin of Women's Space in Medieval Europe', *Matrons and Marginal Women in Medieval Society*, ed. Robert R. Edwards and Vickie Ziegler (Woodbridge, 1995), pp. 1–17.

7   Egelond speaks 'with herte mylde' (217); his words are, 'My wyff goþ ry3t gret with chylde . . . Sche may nou3t out off chaumbyr wyn,/ To speke with non ende of here kyn,/ Tyl sche delyueryd be' (218–22). For the expression 'non ende off here kyn', i.e. 'no part of her family', see Trounce's note on line 221 and C. T. Onions, 'The Phrase *End of One's Kin*', *Medium Ævum* 1 (1938), pp. 118–19.

who is mad (250–2). His intransigent behavior calls to mind Chaucer's description of Walter in his version of the Griselda story: 'Somwhat this lord hadde routhe in his manere,/ But natheless his purpos heeld he stille,/ As lordes doon, whan they wol han hir wille' (IV.579–81).[8] The authorial judgment that the king 'as wood ferde' (250) and the truth of his sister's professions of innocence direct the audience's sympathies away from the king and toward the countess, despite her unwillingness to remain in the sequestered setting doubly appropriate to her gender and her condition.

While less protracted, the queen's exit from her chamber is also marked as a problematic but ultimately positive movement to the 'realm of the exercise of law and justice'. A squire friendly to the countess seeks help from the queen for the condemned family. In an appealing symbolic gesture, 'Gerlondes off chyryes off sche caste,/ Into the halle sche come at þe laste' (256–7). The garlands of cherries, or perhaps cherry blossoms, with which the queen diverts herself in private connect her chamber to Rymenhild's pretty bower of 'fantasy and feeling'.[9] Athelston's queen casts off the marks of her pleasant but inconsequential feminine pastime and moves purposefully into public space. She volunteers to stand surety for her husband's relatives until the issue can be debated openly and in accordance with the law:

'Sere kyng, I am before þe come
Wiþ a chyld, douȝtyr or a sone;
  Graunte me my bone,
My broþir and sustyr þat I may borwe,
Tyl þe nexte day at morwe,
  Out off here paynys stronge;

'Þat we mowe wete be comoun sent
In þe playne parlement
  [Who is wurþy be schent.]' (259–66, 449)[10]

When she evokes the value of 'comoun [as]sent' and advocates deliberation in 'playne parlement', the queen employs powerfully resonant terms that occur frequently in state records of the day.[11] The poet affirms the queen's counsel

---

8 I cite Chaucer's *Canterbury Tales* by fragment and line number from *The Riverside Chaucer*, ed. Larry D. Benson et. al. (Boston, MA, 1987).
9 Riddy, p. 240.
10 Trounce supplies ellipsis marks after *parlement* in lines 266 and 448, in the belief that the tail-rhyme stanzas are incomplete at these points. Kevin Kiernan argues persuasively that what is missing after 266 in the quoted passage is four lines resembling or identical to the end of the archbishop's closely parallel speech in 449–52. Thus I supply line 449 as a clarification of the queen's thought, though my point does not depend on this slight addition to her plea for parliamentary debate. Kiernan also argues that Trounce's stanzas 41 and 42, lines 441–52 of the archbishop's speech, should be printed as a single stanza, and that the supposed lacuna after 448 is created by Trounce, who, driven by an overly rigid standard of stanza regularity, sees textual corruption in what is actually allowable variation in the stanza form. Kevin S. Kiernan, '*Athelston* and the Rhyme of the English Romances', *MLQ* 36 (1975), pp. 339–53.
11 Barnes, *Counsel and Strategy*, pp. 55–9. Regarding the latter term, Barnes cites Helen Cam, who writes that *playne parlement* 'emphasizes a distinction between the formal or plenary session and

by replicating it in a later appeal from the Archbishop of Canterbury, who also urges the king to wait until they can 'enquere,/ And weten alle be comoun asent/ In þe playne parlement . . ./ Who is wurþy be shent' (446–9). Although the queen appeals to her husband on the basis of her pregnancy and the claims of family, her counsel arises from the ' "rational" realm of the exercise of law and justice' that Riddy opposes to Rymenhild's bower. Rather than pleading for outright pardon, the queen advocates open deliberation, a value with which the poet consistently allies himself. Egelond's privileged access to the king's private space excites the envy on which the whole plot hinges (73–9), and Wymound's evil scheme can only prosper under the conditions of privacy and secrecy (121–32). When the king denies his wife's plea, his first words are 'goo fro me' (267), a banishment from the public hall. Perceiving her plea as a challenge to his authority, Athelston fulminates that the accused baron will be drawn and hanged '3yff I be kyng off lande' (272). When his wife continues to plead, he delivers the infamous kick. Now in labor, the queen must be carried by her 'ladyys and maydenys' (285) back to the feminine space of her chamber. The queen's intervention is even less successful than her sister-in-law's, but their failure, to which that of the archbishop will soon be added, can only be construed as a further indictment of the king's tyranny.

While it is very difficult to judge the extent to which women's counsel actually affected decision-making by historical monarchs, the idea of queenly intercession before an intransigent king figures prominently in chronicle accounts of national politics as well as in the literature of late fourteenth-century England. In Chaucer's fiction alone, Theseus's wife and sister-in-law intercede for the lives of Palamon and Arcite in the *Knight's Tale*, Arthur's queen intercedes for the rapist knight in the *Wife of Bath's Tale*, and Alceste intercedes for the hapless persona of the poet himself in the Prologue to the *Legend of Good Women*. Literary depictions of queenly intercession had vivid models in national events, as Paul Strohm, John Carmi Parsons, and David Wallace have shown.[12] In a scene that shares details with the fictional inter-cession in *Athelston*, Froissart represents a pregnant queen, Philippa of Hainaut, interceding with Edward III for the burghers of Calais in 1347.[13]

---

the less formal and less public proceedings of smaller groups. . . . The connotation is of a court where the most solemn proceedings must be done in the sight of all men', 'From Witness of the Shire to Full Parliament' in Helen Cam, *Law-Finders and Law-Makers in Medieval England. Collected Studies in Legal and Constitutional History* (London, 1962), pp. 111, 126.

12 Paul Strohm, 'Queens as Intercessors', *Hochon's Arrow* (Princeton, 1992), pp. 95–119; John Carmi Parsons, 'Ritual and Symbol in the English Medieval Queenship to 1500', *Women and Sovereignty,* ed. Louise Olga Fradenburg (Edinburgh, 1992), pp. 60–77; 'The Queen's Interces-sion in Thirteenth-Century England', *Power of the Weak*, ed. Jennifer Carpenter and Sally-Beth MacLean (Urbana, 1995), pp. 147–77; 'The Pregnant Queen as Counsellor and the Medieval Construction of Motherhood' in *Medieval Mothering*, ed. John Carmi Parsons and Bonnie Wheeler (New York, 1996) pp. 39–61. Parsons's 'The Pregnant Queen' includes consideration of stanzas 24–7 of *Athelston*. David Wallace discusses Anne of Bohemia's role as queenly intercessor in *Chaucerian Polity* (Stanford, 1997), pp. 363–70.

13 Froissart's account is discussed in detail by Strohm (pp. 99–102); Parsons, 'The Pregnant Queen' (pp. 40–1) compares it with the depiction of queenly intercession in *Athelston*.

Interceding with the king had been a queenly role for centuries, but Richard II's reign would have provided the *Athelston*-poet with a particularly striking model for an autocratic king whose queen pleaded before him on numerous highly significant occasions. Contemporary accounts describe Anne of Bohemia interceding with varying success for the rebels of 1381, for John Northampton in 1384, and for the life of Simon Burley in 1388. In 1392, according to the *Westminster Chronicle*, 'more than once, indeed on many occasions' she 'prostrated herself at the king's feet in earnest and tireless entreaty' for the citizens of London.[14] The only surviving manuscript depiction of Anne shows her in an intercessory pose, kneeling before Richard to receive the charter of the city of Shrewsbury.[15]

A contemporary account with particularly interesting parallels to *Athelston* is the *Westminster Chronicle*'s narrative of Anne of Bohemia's intercession for former London mayor John Northampton at the council of Reading in 1384. Northampton's former secretary, Thomas Usk, had accused his employer of a long list of misdeeds.[16] According to the monastic chronicler, Northampton rashly informed Richard that he could not exercise jurisdiction in the absence of his uncle, the Duke of Lancaster. The king 'flared up' [ira totus incaluit] and asserted his authority to sit in judgment not only on Northampton but on the Duke of Lancaster as well. By this account, the furious king condemned Northampton on the spot to death by drawing and hanging. This was an unusually severe penalty, given that this particular hearing was apparently for misprision, not treason, and the present council was not empowered to pronounce death sentences.[17] According to the chronicler,

> Northampton would thus have brought his life to an ignominious close, as a result of his three blunders and his undisciplined behaviour, but for the chance presence of the queen, who in a plea for his life threw herself at the king's feet and humbly begged that Northampton should not die. Through her intercession the king granted him his life but ordered that he should be committed to lifelong imprisonment. So eventually Northampton, snatched

---

[14] See Strohm, pp. 105–11; Parsons, 'English Medieval Queenship', p. 64 n. 19; *The Westminster Chronicle 1381–1394*, ed. and trans. L. C. Hector and Barbara F. Harvey (Oxford, 1982), pp. 92, 330 and, for the quotation, pp. 502–3: 'Demum mediantibus amicis pro eis et precipue domina regina Anglie, que iteratis vicibus, immo multociens, prostravit se ad pedes domini regis tam ibi quam aput Notyngham, obnixe et sedule deprecando pro dicta civitate London' et pro statu civium ejusdem quatinus ut ipse suam indignacionem ab eis averteret.'

[15] The borough charter, Shrewsbury Museum MS I.24, depicts the royal couple within an elegantly decorated initial R (for Ricardus). It is reproduced in Nigel Saul's biography, *Richard II* (New Haven, 1997), plate 15, discussion on p. 455, and in Wallace, *Chaucerian Polity*, plate 11.

[16] *Westminster Chronicle*, p. 92. This act of queenly intercession is not among those explored by Parsons and is mentioned only briefly by Strohm, p. 106. He notes the chronicler's mention that Anne is present by chance, *casualiter*, a feature of contemporary accounts of queenly intercession that Strohm takes to indicate that the interceding woman has no formal role in the process of deliberation (p. 101). For the background to Thomas Usk's accusations against John Northampton, see Strohm's 'The Textual Vicissitudes of Usk's "Appeal" ', *Hochon's Arrow*, pp. 145–60.

[17] J. G. Bellamy, *The Law of Treason in England in the Later Middle Ages* (Cambridge, 1970), pp. 151–2, 223–4, cited by Hector and Harvey, eds, pp. 90–1, 93.

from doom by an act of grace, was expeditiously conveyed to Corfe castle, where he had been lodged in prison before.[18]

As the monastic chronicler narrates this account of Anne's intervention, Northampton's defiance causes the situation to flare up unexpectedly – there is no suggestion that Anne's actions were instigated by Northampton in advance. Indeed she is only present *casualiter*, by chance. These circumstances distinguish this instance from historical cases of intercession in which the queen simply carried a petition from a magnate or group of subjects to the king. In such transactions, the queen might serve as scarcely more than a messenger, her motivation for intercession depicted as a highly gendered instance of feminine identification with the powerless.[19] Here, as in *Athelston*, the queen is depicted as an agent in national politics rather than as a pawn in a transaction essentially between subject and king.

The Westminster chronicler seems to understand Anne's intercession for Northampton as a spontaneous response to the dangerous situation created by a monarch whose authority has been threatened. The chronicler gives no indication that her act is motivated by feminine compassion for Northampton himself. Richard's rash sentencing of Northampton recalls the imperious death sentence pronounced by Athelston on his sister's family, 'Þey schole be drawen and hangyd tomorn,/ Ʒyff I be kyng of lande' (271–2). Both acts are presented as impassioned, illegal, and tyrannical attempts to quell a perceived threat to royal power. Given the tale's uncertain dating, however, I do not argue that the poet patterns Athelston's behavior after this or any specific event of Richard's reign.[20] Rather, I suggest that the *Athelston*'s depiction of an absolutist ruler infuriated by limitations on his power would surely have had topical relevance for the subjects of a late medieval king, and for the subjects of Richard II in particular. In such an atmosphere, queenly intercession takes on a special importance, especially when it pleads not only for the interests of particular individuals, but also for judicious action, open consultation, and the rule of law.

Scholars are divided in their assessment of the politics of women's intercession. Certainly there are reasonable causes for skepticism about the agency it offered to medieval queens. One would not wish to overestimate the power

---

[18] Hector and Harvey, eds, pp. 92–4: 'Sicque J. Northampton' propter tria premissa ac propter incompositos mores vitam suam turpi morte finaliter termin[a]sset nisi domina regina ibi casualiter extitisset ac pro ejus vita ne moreretur domino regi provoluta humiliter supplicasset; cujus interventu rex concessit sibi vitam set jussit eum tamen perpetuo carceri mancipari. Demum J. Northampton' sic a mortis interitu graciose ereptus ad castrum de Corf' celeriter est adductus, ubi prius erat carcerali custodie deputatus.'

[19] Parsons, 'The Queen's Intercession', p. 160; 'The Pregnant Queen', pp. 47–8.

[20] As further reason for caution, little is known of Richard's marriage to Anne of Bohemia, but the two things that seem most certain are that he was very attached to her and that she never became pregnant. See Saul's biography, pp. 455–7. For an effort to identify the characters and actions of *Athelston* closely with the historical events and figures of Richard's reign, see the article by Rowe mentioned above.

wielded by a queen, either historical or literary, who abased herself before her husband to further the interests of some magnate or pressure group. The image of a compassionate woman pleading before a stern, justice-minded man reflects conventional ideas about feminine nature. Caroline Walker Bynum has shown how medieval male authority sought to complete and reinforce itself by annexing not just the conventionally male poles of dichotomies such as strong/weak, authority/nurture, and law/mercy, but also the female poles as well.[21] It is not always easy in medieval texts to distinguish ahistorical typologies from concrete reactions to particular historical moments. A powerful underlying model for queenly intercession is the humble, compassionate Virgin who intercedes with God. Both Strohm and Parsons observe that, rather than according power to historical women, queenly intercession could serve an almost allegorical function: the king marries 'mercy' and unites it with his own 'justice', thus enhancing his own kingship.[22] David Wallace, however, argues for a more positive view of the agency possible to queenly intercessors,[23] and both Strohm and Parsons acknowledge significant exceptions to their skeptical assessment of the efficacy of intercession. The *Westminster Chronicle* account of Anne's intercession for Northampton and the fictional intercession by Athelston's queen demonstrate that contemporary writers could conceive of acts of intercession as potentially effective interventions into national politics.

By holding out the possibility that a woman could indeed act as wisely and judiciously 'in hall' as her male counterparts, *Athelston* provides an important alternative to the many bower-bound Rymenhilds in Middle English romance. The queen espouses values with which the poet is in deep sympathy, she grasps the urgency of a crisis at once familial and national, and she takes practical steps toward resolution. Her clear-sighted acceptance of the severe limitations on her power contrasts pointedly with Athelston's self- aggrandizement. She recognizes that the king places sworn brotherhood above whatever authority accrues to queenship, and thus she sends for the archbishop on the grounds that the king 'wole doo more for hym, I wene/ þanne for me, þou3 I be qwene' (306–7). The poet represents in surprisingly concrete terms the queen's marshalling of her personal financial resources to meet this crisis. She holds lands in Spain as her *moregeue* (309–15), either as a gift from the king or as part of her dowry,[24] and she offers to 'sese' (310), or legally convey the property to a messenger if he will quickly summon the archbishop. The messenger's stated preference for gold coins in hand over

21 Caroline Walker Bynum, *Holy Feast and Holy Fast* (Berkeley 1987), pp. 282–8.
22 See the discussion by Strohm, 'Queens as Intercessors', pp. 96–105, where he suggests that 'the system of relations involved in queenly intercession may actually be seen to support, rather than contradict, the foundations of patriarchal authority' (p. 104) and that by Parsons, 'The Queen's Intercession', pp. 147–54.
23 *Chaucerian Polity*, pp. 363–4.
24 Trounce notes that the term is properly used of a 'morning gift' from the king to his bride, but is also used of a dowry.

promised lands in Spain (315–20) may represent a realistic doubt about whether the wife of an autocratic king can indeed dispose of her lands as she wishes.[25] When the summoned archbishop also fails to move Athelston, he threatens to seek military aid abroad to oppose the king, and he puts the whole kingdom under interdict, forbidding even the baptism of infants (468–81). Eventually, the barons (the 'lordys off Yngelond') threaten to tear the kingdom apart (499–530).

Taken on her own, Athelston's fictional queen succeeds only in summoning the archbishop, who initiates the events that finally bring the king to heel. There is no denying that the poet is much more interested in the principles she espouses than in the queen herself, who disappears from the tale as soon as she dispatches the messenger to Canterbury. In place of the queen, however, the poet returns to the king's sister who was so prominent in the early stanzas of the poem and who drops from sight while the queen holds center stage. The queen and her sister-in-law could almost be said to share one role since it is Edith, not the unnamed queen, who bears the child whom Athelston designates as his heir at the end of the tale. With one name between them, the two are doubles of the kind found frequently in romance. This very tale employs a second character named Athelston, also a messenger, just as the king was before his accession. Repetition and doubling are a crucial means of emphasis in this genre, and the second Athelston parodies the self-absorption of the first, just as the two women amplify one another's unconventional move from lying-in chamber to hall. The queen and her sister-in-law both leave their chambers in order to act in the national arena, and they both speak eloquently in public – only the archbishop is given lengthier and more resounding speeches. Edith dominates the final scenes of the tale, where the poet abandons history for an anachronistic trial by ordeal that proves the innocence of the falsely accused family. Her courage in facing the ordeal echoes the queen's courage in facing Athelston. It is not the figure of the queen that lies at the heart of the tale, however, but rather the sound advice that she and the archbishop vainly offer the king: do not precipitate a national crisis by rashly sentencing your subjects to death before their guilt or innocence can be deliberated openly in accordance with the law.

In stark, binary terms, *Athelston* reveals the cultural anxiety that accompanies the idea that women might leave bower for hall to intervene constructively in public affairs, an idea that would eventually restructure every existing social relation. Athelston's queen values the 'comoun [as]sent' just as Griselda promotes the 'commune profit' in Chaucer's *Clerk's Tale*. Both the queen and Griselda are contrasted with male authority figures of extreme intransigence. Very much like Walter, the king has 'a certain purpos take' and

---

25 I owe my suggestion to Janet L. Nelson's remark that a true test of a medieval women's 'ownership' of property is whether she could give it away, 'Medieval Women: Givers and Gifts', lecture presented at Smith College, Northampton, MA, 10 March, 2003. The messenger professes to pass up the queen's lands on the grounds that he has no right to her *moregeue* (317).

'kan nat stynte of [his] entencion'.[26] Also like Walter, Athelston puts his wife 'in angwyssh and in drede' (*CT* IV. 462). It is a somber thought that the fictions of this period that accord most respect to the possibility of women's social agency also subject those women to the most extraordinary cruelty. But this veering from extreme to extreme – from affirmation of women's intervention in public affairs to violent retaliation against them – shows how fraught with tension was the issue itself, and indicates how much was at stake for the authors and audiences of these fictions.

---

[26] *Clerk's Tale*, IV.431 and 701–7.

12

Torrent of Portyngale and the Literary Giants

ROGER DALRYMPLE

'Here begynneth a good tale/ Of Torrente of Portyngale': the contemporary *incipit* introduces one of the longest of the English tail-rhyme romances.[1] Traditionally dated to around 1400,[2] *Torrent* survives in full only in the late fifteenth-century manuscript Chetham 8009, where it appears in company with *Ipomadon* and *Beues of Hamtoun*.[3] Only the rougher edges of this 'good tale' remain perceptible: the Chetham witness to the poem is rife with textual corruption and *Torrent* still awaits a modern edition, being available to readers only in the EETS edition of 1887. Yet the poem's outline is an ambitious one, telling of a social climber of singular zest. Inheritor of an earldom, the aspirant Torrent passes through an arduous series of suitor's tests to secure domains and a king's daughter – 'Both the Erth and the woman' (1323) in the poem's unceremonious parlance.[4] The hero is ultimately elected Emperor of Rome at the close of a story that centres on one of the classic encounters of the romance tradition – that between man and monster, between knight and giant.[5]

The romance shows many debts to the literary giants of the insular tradition: story motifs are borrowed from *Guy of Warwick* and *Beues of Hamtoun* as well as from the shorter tail-rhyme romances *Octavian*, *Sir Ysumbras* and

---

[1] I am grateful to audiences at the Durham *Romance in Medieval England* Conference and at the Oxford Early Tudor Reading Group for valuable comments and observations on this essay. My particular thanks to Elizabeth Archibald, Helen Cooper, Katherine Duncan-Jones, Linda Gowans, Paul Strohm and David Watt.

[2] The romance is dated c.1400 by *A Manual of the Writings in Middle English 1050–1500*, vol. 1, ed. J. Burke Severs (New Haven, 1967), p. 15. On *Torrent*'s place in the mature tail-rhyme tradition, see Derek Pearsall, 'The Development of Middle English Romance', *Medieval Studies* 27 (1965), pp. 91–116; repr. in *Studies in Medieval English Romances*, ed. Derek Brewer (Cambridge, 1988), pp. 1–33 (p. 31).

[3] The Chetham MS is described by N. R. Ker, *Medieval Manuscripts in British Libraries*, vol. 3 (Oxford, 1983), pp. 361–4; Gisela Guddat-Figge, *A Catalogue of Manuscripts Containing Middle English Romances* (Munich, 1976), pp. 238–40. Guddat-Figge notes the predominantly 'moralizing or devotional' character of the items comprising the collection (p. 238).

[4] All quotations are drawn from the edition of the poem by E. Adam, *Torrent of Portyngale*, EETS 51 (1887). A metrically confused earlier edition was produced by J. O. Halliwell, *Torrent of Portugal* (London, 1842).

[5] A McI. Trounce remarks that 'the heroic adventures of Torrent are the real theme': 'The English Tail-Rhyme Romances', *Medium Ævum* 3 (1934), pp. 30–50 (p. 34).

Sir Eglamour (c.1350), a text that *Torrent* closely shadows.[6] Indeed, as if seeking to surpass these forebears, *Torrent* duplicates and amplifies inherited motifs. In a romance replete with magical swords and steeds, tame and noble lions, love tokens and treasures, there are two exiles in rudderless boats, two child-abductions by exotic beasts, three battles with dragons, and no less than five battles with giants.[7]

Picaresque, crowded with diverse episodes, the extant text of the poem accordingly shows little cohesion: the already complex narrative threads of *Eglamour* become further entangled by the muddle of episodes in *Torrent*.[8] Though the narrator at an early stage gamely keeps tally of Torrent's feats (696–7), by the time the hero comes to recount his deeds late in the poem he can be sure only that he has dispatched 'dragons two other thre/ And giauntes meny one' (2230–1). It is through these 'giauntes meny one' that the poem appears to have exerted influence on later romance tradition. Source study of Malory's *Morte Darthur* has uncovered a link between Sir Marhalt's fight with the giant in 'The Tale of King Arthur' and Sir Torrent's combat with his fourth ogre, named Cate.[9] The giants may likewise have played their part in securing the poem's popularity among an early Tudor readership: fragments survive of two early printed editions by Richard Pynson in c.1505 and Wynkyn de Worde in c.1510 (the former preserving a markedly more coherent text than Chetham).[10] And for modern readers, it is this protracted series of giant-killings that promises greatest interest – a succession of defining cultural encounters where notions of the civilized and the bestial, the innocent and the guilty, the monstrous and the manly are brought face to face. Muddled as the extant Chetham text may be, the sequence of giant-killings shows a coherence and design that suggest a problematic is in hand in this romance, one that resolves only in the poem's ultimate embrace of different kinds of cultural encounter – between just and treacherous rulers, Christian and Saracen knights, chivalric and ascetic males.

---

6   Eglamour is edited by Frances E. Richardson, *Sir Eglamour of Artois* EETS OS 256 (1965). On the difficulty of fixing the precise relation between *Torrent* and *Eglamour*, see Richardson's introduction to *Eglamour*, pp. xlv–l and pp. 141–5 and Maldwyn Mills's review of the edition, *Medium Ævum* 35 (1966), pp. 269–73.
7   Dieter Mehl has noted 'the adapter's ambition to outdo *Sir Eglamour* and to make his hero even more perfect and exemplary': *The Middle English Romances of the Thirteenth and Fourteenth Centuries* (London, 1969), p. 84. See also Laura A. Hibbard, *Mediæval Romance in England* (New York, 1924), p. 281.
8   Consequently, some criticism has classified the poem as mere hack-work. For contrasting views, see Lillian Herlands Hornstein, 'Eustace-Constance-Florence-Griselda Legend', *A Manual of the Writings in Middle English*, pp. 125–7; and Dieter Mehl, *The Middle English Romances of the Thirteenth and Fourteenth Centuries*, pp. 83–5.
9   On the influence of the poem's giant-fights and other motifs on Malory, see Edward D. Kennedy, 'Malory and his English Sources', *Aspects of Malory*, Arthurian Studies I, ed. Toshiyuki Takamiya and Derek Brewer (Cambridge, 1981), pp. 27–55 (pp. 35–9).
10 The fragmentary prints are collected in Bodleian Library, Douce Fragm. e.20 (1); STC 24133; 24133.5.

A brief summary of the romance as preserved in Chetham reveals the prevalence of three central motifs: giant-killing, the exiled heroine, the separated family. Italicised sections of the summary represent the surviving sections of the poem in Pynson's print.

Torrent the giant-killer

On the death of his father, Torrent is granted an earldom by Colomond, King of Portugal. Besotted with Princess Desonell, the young earl performs chivalrous deeds for her love. King Colomond promises Torrent his daughter's hand if he will undertake a 'poynt of armys' (68). He must face Begonmese (giant number one) in single combat, a quest from which the treacherous king does not expect Torrent to return.

The dragon-slayer; the Knight of the Lions

Torrent defeats and beheads Begonmese. He liberates five young captives of the giant and acquires two initially hostile lions as companions. The King of Provyns, grateful at the liberation of his son, gives Torrent a sword forged by Weland, the swordsmith of Germanic legend. In Portugal, King Colomond informs Desonell of Torrent's love, which the princess reciprocates. *Secretly opposed to the match, the King forges a letter in Desonell's hand, requesting that Torrent secure for her a rare falcon from the forest of Maudlen – a trap that will involve his facing Rochense (giant number two).*

Torrent the giant-killer

In the forest of Maudlen, Torrent's squire is slain by Rochense. Torrent kills both the giant and a dragon. He returns to court bearing the giant's head as trophy. *King Colomond sets a third and apparently final suitor's test to preoccupy Torrent: combat with Slongus (giant number three).* In the hero's absence, and against the counsel of the queen, Colomond betrothes Desonell to the prince of Aragon. Torrent prevails over Slongus and returns to Portugal where he learns of Desonell's impending wedding to Aragon. To reclaim Desonell, Torrent defeats Aragon's champion, Cate (giant number four). Desonell is divorced; she and Torrent secretly pledge and consummate their love. The resentful king enjoins a politic delay of six months before a public wedding. The interim brings a plea from the King of Norway for defence from Weraunt (giant number five). Torrent accepts the quest not for glory but 'for Iesu is sake' (1382). With God's aid, he triumphs over two more dragons and over Weraunt. *He refuses the hand of Princess Gendres offered by a grateful King of Norway.*

Family separation

When Desonell gives birth to twin sons, Colomond sets the young family adrift in a rudderless boat, each child retaining one of the gold rings Torrent left behind as love tokens. Reaching the holy land, the children are abducted, one by a griffin and one by a leopard. The hermit St Anthony rescues one child, names him Anthony Fitzgriffin, and entrusts him to his father, the King of Greece. The King of Jerusalem rescues Torrent's other son, naming him Leobertus. Desonell is rescued by the King of Nazareth, a sometime suitor. Returning to Portugal, Torrent learns of King Colomond's treachery and, with baronial assent, sets him adrift in a leaking boat. Torrent is crowned King of Portugal.

Torrent the Crusader

Torrent departs for the Holy Land and, after fifteen years fighting Saracens, inadvertently fights Leobertus (his unrecognised son), and falls prisoner to him and the King of Jerusalem. Leobertus is moved by Torrent's laments and negotiates his release. In jousts at Jerusalem Torrent distinguishes himself. Report of the victor and his distinctive heraldic crest – 'A Gyaunt with an hoke in hond' (2408) – reaches Desonell. At her request the King of Nazareth holds a further tournament, attended by the kings of Greece and Jerusalem and their wards (Torrent's sons). Torrent goes on to defeat both his sons in jousts and family recognition and reunion ensue.

The political giant

Desonell and Torrent are at last formally married and celebrations held in Portugal. The kings of Greece and Jerusalem retain custody of their adoptive sons who are nominated their sole heirs. Torrent is appointed Emperor of Rome.

As the summary reveals, the story's premise conforms to the 'giant's daughter' story-type in which a suitor embarks upon a series of daunting tasks set by the obstructive father of his desired bride.[11] While in *Eglamour* three distinct tasks are required of the hero, in *Torrent* the tasks are focused upon repeated acts of giant-killing. The combats are not without variety: the giant Slongus is one-eyed; the giant Weraunt is protected by dragons whom he shepherds with a sinister crook; the ogres meet their deaths by a range of means: crushing, stabbing, spearing, stoning, drowning. Indeed, the differentiation between the combats includes allusion to other celebrated giant-killings. As King Arthur

---

11 On 'giant's daughter' narratives, see Stephen Knight, 'The Social Function of the Middle English Romances', *Medieval Literature: Criticism, Ideology and History*, ed. David Aers (Brighton, 1986), pp. 99–122 (p. 111).

struggled with the giant of Mont St Michel so Sir Torrent must face a hill-top ogre as his first adversary;[12] as the young David felled the giant Goliath with his sling and five smooth stones (1 Samuel 17), so Torrent prevails against Cate with the 'cobled stonys' (1298) he scoops from the seashore: 'He threw stonys on hym so faste, / That he was sad and sare' (1302–3).

Most significantly, these varied renditions of the giant-killing motif are set within a structural frame. The first and final killings are patterned upon closely parallel lines: their few divergences are intriguing. In the first episode, Torrent defeats Begonmese and seeks refuge in the giant's castle. Here he meets Eleanor, princess of Gales and captive of the giant. Unaware that her captor is dead, Eleanor warns Torrent of the giant's fearsome strength:

> Be my trowthe, and he the see,
> Were ther XX lyvys in the,
> Thy dethe than wyll he dyght.   (271–3)

The dramatic irony magnifies the hero's achievement but it also pre-empts the unsettling endurance of monstrous foes in this poem. Though Eleanor's pronounced fear of the giant signals how admirable is the feat Torrent has achieved, she voices an anxiety not dispelled but simply deferred. The unease is deepened by Torrent's ironic description of the giant as slumbering: 'On soche a slepe he ys browght,/ All men of lyve wakythe hym nowght' (298–9). Though Begonmese lies dead, the threat he poses does indeed only sleep. Torrent will be called upon to face four more ogres before his adventures are concluded. Accordingly, when the hero returns to court bearing the giant's head as trophy, the castle porter runs in fear, implying the continued threat posed by the monstrous: ' "Syr kyng," he seyd, "be goddes dede,/ Torrant bryngythe a devyll ys hed" ' (379–80).

The aftermath of the final giant-killing echoes this pattern, cementing the frame around the series of killings. Having defeated Weraunt, Torrent again discovers the giant's castle and once more he meets a young woman. Echoing Eleanor, it is now the turn of the Norwegian Princess Gendres to voice dread that the giant lives still:

> Me for-thinkith, that thou com here,
> Thy deth now is dight;
> For here dwellith a geaunt.   (1647–9)

Again the dramatic irony is sustained as Torrent objectively reports the scene and describes how he has just witnessed pitched battle between Weraunt and

---

12 As related in Geoffrey of Monmouth, *The History of the Kings of Britain*, trans. Lewis Thorpe (Harmondsworth, 1966), pp. 238–40. See Jeffrey Jerome Cohen, *Of Giants: Sex, Monsters and the Middle Ages* (Minneapolis, 1999), ch. 2. On the adaptation of the episode in the fourteenth-century Alliterative *Morte Arthure*, see John Finlayson, 'Arthur and the Giant of St Michael's Mount', *Medium Ævum* 33 (1964), pp. 112–20; Robert Warm, 'Arthur and the Giant of Mont St Michel: The politics of Empire Building in the Later Middle Ages', *Nottingham Medieval Studies* 41 (1997), pp. 57–71.

'a yong knyght' (1661). Gendres, he says, must credit her own senses as to whether the giant lives still:

> Dame, yf thou leve not me,
> Com nere, and thou shalt se,
> Which of hem abade.   (1667–9)

Torrent's refusal to name himself as victor shows deference to God who has aided his victory, and security in his identity as chivalric-adventurer: honourable indeed is the knight who disclaims credit for his virtuous deeds.[13] Accordingly, Gendres counts the anonymous giant-killer among the pre-eminent Christian knights:[14]

> Other he was of god all-myght
> Or seynt George, oure lady kny3t,
> That there his bane hath be.
> Yf eny cryston man smyte hym down,
> He is worthy to haue renown
> Thorough oute all crystiaunte.   (1676–81)

As in the first episode, acclamation is followed by victorious return. This time, the Norwegian herald marks Torrent's return, mirroring the porter of the Portuguese court. The porter had been terrified by the sight of the giant's head carried as trophy, but this time the fear is provoked by Torrent himself. The knight now presents his own awesome and gargantuan aspect, the herald exclaiming:

> Yon I se an armed knyght,
> And no squier, but hym one:
> He is so big of bone & blood,
> *He is the Geaunt, be the Rode!*   (1712–15, emphasis mine)

It is no longer simply Torrent's battle-trophies that inspire fear but his own stature as knight: the hero's rite of passage is concluded in his assimilation of the giant.[15]

This framing of the ogre-killing sequence implies that the five giants of *Sir Torrent of Portyngale* may owe their place in the work to something more than a hack romancer's heedlessness of the law of diminishing returns. What

---

[13] The virtuous knightly quality of forgoing or deferring the claim of credit for a feat achieved is highlighted by John Burrow in relation to *Ipomadon A*: 'The Uses of Incognito: *Ipomadon A*', *Readings in Medieval English Romance*, ed. Carol M. Meale (Cambridge, 1994), pp. 25–34.

[14] The adoption of George as England's patron saint was formalised only in 1415 though popular devotion to the saint was long-standing and further fostered by Edward III's establishment of the Order of the Garter under his patronage, c.1348.

[15] On the centrality of the *rite de passage* and its anticipated invariable success in romance, see Derek Brewer, 'Escape from the Mimetic Fallacy', *Studies in Medieval English Romances*, ed. Derek Brewer (Cambridge, 1988), pp. 1–9 (p. 8).

symbolic function might the series of giant-killings supply? What has enabled Torrent to escape endless iteration of the pattern, to take on, as the porter sees it, the attributes of the giant?

In line with recent scholarship on constructions of medieval masculinity, the series might plausibly be viewed as staging anxieties implicit in the *enfance* narrative. The challenges stipulated for the hero bring supervenient obstacles; the poem's five ogres bring a discomfiting deferral of the hero's progress towards bride and suzerainty. Jeffrey Jerome Cohen has described how 'the fight against the giant in romance images a masculinity that is complete, self-sufficient', the scene turning upon a contrast between the stable, socialised figure of the knight and the monstrous aggression of the giant.[16] Such a view of the giant-battle posits a conception of masculinity as *performance*, where, in Judith Butler's formulation, 'gender ought not to be conceived as a noun, or a substantial thing or a static cultural marker, but rather as an incessant or repeated action of some sort'.[17] Whereas often in romance the giant-battle represents an exceptional or definitive form of adventure, relieving the chivalric male subject of the need for such demonstrative and repeated gender performance, in *Torrent* the encounter is denied this conclusive function. Like the invincible menace of the modern slasher-film, Torrent's nemesis will not stay dead.[18] From such a perspective, the repeated giant-killings might be read as dramatising both the anxieties and the aspirations invested in the 'quest for identity' romances.

Alternatively, if granted a symbolic resonance, the giant-killing series might be viewed as embodying a family drama, where the giant-fights substitute for a displaced struggle between suitor and obstructive patriarch and where that patriarch's relentless resistance is given monstrous embodiment.[19] After all, King Colomond's resourcefulness in frustrating Torrent's fortunes extends to forging letters in his daughter's hand sending Torrent to his ostensible doom, reneging on his sworn oaths, and exiling his daughter and grandchildren.[20] In his most pointed exertion of patriarchal suzerainty, and of textual control, the King glosses the exile with a clear *moralitas*:

---

[16] Cohen, *Of Giants*, p. xix. See also Nicola McDonald, '*The Seege of Troye*: "ffor wham was wakened al this wo?"', *The Spirit of Medieval English Popular Romance*, ed. Ad Putter and Jane Gilbert (Harlow, 2000), pp. 181–99 (p. 185).

[17] Judith Butler, *Gender Trouble: Feminism and the Subversion of Identity* (London, 1990), p. 112. On constructions of masculinity in medieval texts and culture, see further *Medieval Masculinities: Regarding Men in the Middle Ages*, ed. Clare A. Lees (Minneapolis, 1994); *Becoming Male in the Middle Ages*, ed. Jeffrey Jerome Cohen and Bonnie Wheeler (New York, 1997).

[18] The teenager's confrontation of the near-invincible serial killer is markedly analogous to (and likely derivative of) this romance motif. See Vera Dika, *Games of Terror: Halloween, Friday 13th and the Films of the Stalker Cycle* (Rutherford, NJ, 1990), pp. 30–63 and Carol J. Clover, *Men, Women and Chainsaws: Gender in the Modern Horror Film* (London, 1992), pp. 30, 36–7, 41.

[19] The recurrence of this paradigm in medieval romances is explored by Derek Brewer: *Symbolic Stories: Traditional Narratives of the Family Drama in English Literature* (New York, 1988), pp. 54–71.

[20] The couple's exchange of vows and consummation may well have been held to constitute a

Euery kyngis doughter ffer and nere,
At the shall they lere,
Ayen the law to do.   (1816–18)

In a family-drama reading of the romance, true defeat of the ogre would depend upon Torrent's displacement of this moralitas. This he does when the barons depose Colomond in his favour and, with their assent, he subjects the king to the same fate suffered by Desonell and the twins, setting him adrift in a leaking boat, 'Among the wawes to gone' (2130). The correspondence of the fates of father and daughter is flagged when Torrent denies him the sacrament: 'Seth thou gaue my lady none,/ No more men shall do the!' (2141–2). That such a fate, traditionally reserved for female characters, is meted out to Colomond serves to feminise the impotent king.[21] One critic has viewed the scene as 'acting out the suitor's fantasy of killing his bride's father', a move completed by Torrent's immediate appropriation of the crown, and by the subsequent retextualisation of the exile of Desonell.[22] Not disobedient daughters but tyrannical patriarchs are the intended audience for any cautionary elements in this tale:

Loo, lordys of euery lond:
Falshode wyll haue a foule end,
And wyll haue euermore.   (2152–4)

This family-drama reading of the giant killings might also open on to social concerns. It is noteworthy that the king's hostility to the match rests solely upon the objection of rank, the poem having suppressed any implication of the incest theme so often germane to the 'Constance' narrative of the exiled heroine.[23] Though the nobility and the queen acknowledge Torrent's fitness as suitor –'Riche man I-nough is he' (1803) – Colomond remains resolved against the match: 'Madame, were that feyer,/ To make an erlles sone myn Eyer?' (786–7). Hudson has observed how *Torrent*, like other romances of its kind, raises a range of questions concerning social status and patriarchal power, including: 'whether social status should be determined by lineage or self-assertion; whether wealth should circulate through primogeniture or enterprise, whether worthiness derives from ancestry or individual virtue'.[24]

binding 'clandestine marriage'. See James A. Brundage, *Law, Sex, and Christian Society in Medieval Europe* (Chicago, 1987), pp. 189–90; Henry A. Kelly, 'Clandestine Marriage in Chaucer's *Troilus and Criseyde*', *Viator* 4 (1973), pp. 435–57; Neil Cartlidge, *Medieval Marriage: Literary Approaches 1100–1300* (Woodbridge, 1997).

21   In *Eglamour* the King meets his death by falling from a high tower.
22   Harriet E. Hudson, 'Constructions of Class, Family, and Gender in some Middle English Popular Romances', *Class and Gender in Early English Literature*, ed. Britton J. Harwood (Bloomington, 1994), pp. 76–94 (p. 83).
23   On which see Margaret Schlauch, *Constance and Accused Queens* (New York, 1927). In the tournament scene at the poem's conclusion the poet also omits any counterpart to the incestuous marriage of Christabelle and her son in *Eglamour*.
24   Hudson, 'Constructions of Class, Family, and Gender', p. 77.

Such considerations formed pressing concerns for the gentry and mercantile element among the audiences of late Middle English romance and clearly, the spirited and persistent self-assertion of Torrent invites identification from just such quarters.[25] The presence of this constituency among the audience or readership for the poem is implied by *Torrent*'s manuscript context. MS Chetham 8009, a codex containing not just the three romances of *Beues*, *Torrent* and *Ipomadon* but also four saints' lives and seven short devotional and moral texts, has been associated with mercantile reading circles in London.[26] A list of wardens and bailiffs of that city forms the thirteenth item in the manuscript, and the dialect and main hand of the codex accord with late medieval London provenance.[27] The esteeming but sceptical treatment of chivalric themes in *Sir Torrent of Portyngale* might well engage an audience situated in such a milieu. Though the hero's climb is within a feudal structure – earl seeks to marry princess – Torrent is clearly congruent with the image of the mythical knight described by Felicity Riddy as 'an adventure seeker and risk-taker, a uniquely accessible and adaptable locus of fantasy and desire', who proved congenial to what she styles the 'bourgeois-gentry' audiences of late Middle English romance.[28]

While both of these symbolic functions might realistically be claimed for the five renditions of giant-slaying in *Torrent of Portyngale*, perhaps the most persuasive rationale for the series is found in the poem's penitential concern with themes of self-regulation and the curtailment of excess, themes that emerge in the poem's movement away from giant-killing to other kinds of cultural encounter between just ruler and tyrant, East and West, chivalry and ascesis in the poem's devotional climax.

The strong religious cast of *Torrent* prompted several early commentators to posit clerical authorship for the text.[29] In addition to wide use of Passion-formulae invoking Christ – 'god, that Dyed appon a Rode' (112); 'God that sofryd wonddes sare' (335) – the text charts divine intervention in the fortunes of the hero, sedulously noting the solidarity of God in the hero's victories: 'Thus helpt hym god thar' (372); 'Thus helpe hym god of myght'

---

25 It remains notoriously difficult to delimit the audiences of the Middle English romances though a broadening and increasingly self-conscious readership in the fifteenth century is well attested. See Derek Pearsall, 'The Audiences of the Middle English Romances', *Historical and Editorial Studies in Medieval and Early Modern English for Johan Gerritsen*, Mary-Jo Arn and Hanneke Wirtjes (Groningen, 1985), pp. 37–47.

26 For recent work on the manuscript and a catalogue of its contents, see Rhiannon Purdie, ed., *Ipomadon*, EETS 316 (2001), pp. xviii–xxiii.

27 See Rhiannon Purdie, 'Sexing the Manuscript: The Case for Female Ownership of MS Chetham 8009', *Neophilologus* 82 (1998), pp. 139–48 and Carol M. Meale, '*The Libelle of Englyshe Polycye* and Mercantile Literary Culture in Late-Medieval London', *London and Europe in the Later Middle Ages*, ed. Julia Boffey and Pamela King (London, 1995), pp. 181–227 (p. 224).

28 Felicity Riddy, 'Middle English Romance: Family, Marriage, Intimacy', *The Cambridge Companion to Medieval Romance*, ed. Roberta L. Krueger (Cambridge, 2000), pp. 235–52 (p. 239).

29 See Adam, *Torrent of Portyngale*, p. 20 and Richardson, *Sir Eglamour*, p. xlvii. Mehl considers the suggestion unnecessary: *The Middle English Romances*, p. 84.

(1046); 'Iesu wold not, he were slayne' (675).[30] It is striking that deadlock is broken and the chain of giant-killings finally ruptured when the hero slays a giant not at stipulation but at request; not for gain but for God.[31] The request is voiced by the King of Norway, pleading for defence against the giant Weraunt. When Torrent takes up the cause in service of Christ, 'That hath helpid me be-ffore' (1384), the quest again brings supervenient challenges: the hero's companions take fright upon arrival in the giant's forest and flee; the lone Torrent must defeat not merely the giant but the two dragons who defend him.[32] Yet the wearied hero is reassured by a divine voice:

> A voys was fro hevyn sent
> And said: 'Be blith, sir Torent,
> And yeve the no thing yll,
> To ffyght with my lordys enemy:
> Whether that thou lyve or dye,
> Thy mede the quyte he wyll!'   (1568–73)

After so much tangible reward in the treasures accruing from the giant-killings, this spiritual dimension of 'mede' will be unfolded to the hero throughout the second half of the romance as tribulation divorces him from his worldly comforts and achievements. Though he triumphs over Weraunt, his fortunes suffer reversal with the exile of his family and his own trials in the holy land. It is at the conclusion of this fifth killing, we recall, that the Norwegian herald will mistake Torrent himself for the giant. Though the misrecognition is in part comic, it also sounds a darker note, perhaps implying that the hero – who adopts at this stage the image of the giant Weraunt as his heraldic crest – must curb any potential of his own for monstrous excess. Certainly, restraint and self-abnegation are the prerequisites for Torrent's survival in the Holy Land when he responds to the fragmentation of his family by embracing the ethic of crusade. He moves from killing giants to killing Saracens, excelling in fifteen years of sieges and combats and fighting 'euery good ffryday,/ Vppon the Sarȝins bryght' (2231–2). Here, the hero whose prior feats had led to accumulation of goods – half Norway for one deed, half Aragon for another – now finds himself participating in a new matrix of need and reward where goods and commodities are disposed across a wider community. Accordingly, Torrent's success in besieging two Saracen cities is attributed to his having granted adequate provisions to the besieging force:

> All the good, that sir Torent wan,
> He partid it among his man,
> Syluer, gold and fee.   (2196–8)

---

[30] For a summary of the pious formulae employed in the poem, see Roger Dalrymple, *Language and Piety in Middle English Romance* (Cambridge, 2000), p. 188.

[31] On the Christian strand of the chivalric identity, see Maurice Keen, *Chivalry* (New Haven, 1984), pp. 44–63.

[32] This kinship is a further detail shared with *Eglamour*.

This crusading spirit carries the hero to a moment of complete abjection when his campaigns lead him to fight his now grown, now knighted and still unrecognised son, Leobertus. This father–son combat is given unusual elaboration – the more striking since the motifs of *Torrent* are, for the most part, all too familiar. Father–son recognition is long delayed as Leobertus defeats and humbles Torrent. Imprisoning him and proclaiming 'lower is thy pryde' (2280), the son takes his place literally above his father, dwelling in a chamber over Torrent's prison cell: 'His son above his hede lay,/ To kepe hym both nyȝt and day' (2284–5). It is at this point that Torrent catalogues his secular achievements as he upbraids God for his apparent desertion:

> 'God, hast thou forsakyn me?
> All my truste was in the,
> In lond where I haue gone!
> Thou gave me myȝt ffor to slee
> Dragons two other thre
> And giauntes meny one,
> And now a man in wekid lond
> Hath myn armour and stede in hond:
> I wold, my liffe were done!'   (2296–2304)

The complaint might almost represent a moment of sanctification, Torrent's 'God, hast thou forsakyn me' echoing that most dutiful of sons appealing to his Father in extremis.[33] Indeed, it is immediately after this moment of abasement that the hero's fortunes are restored. The lament prompts Leobertus to negotiate Torrent's release, and when both join in jousts, Torrent bearing his distinctive heraldic crest – 'A Gyaunt with an hoke in hond' (2408) – family recognition and reconciliation ensue. Legitimised as patriarch, Torrent is reinstated as head of his family and when the long-delayed wedding ensues, Torrent is proclaimed not simply King of Portugal but Emperor of Rome, the unsought reward recalling the angel's promise of unanticipated 'mede' for God's servant. The sometime Portuguese earl ends the poem himself a political and spiritual giant. Just as the poem's pious opening entreats guidance from God 'In thy seruyse to Ende' (6), so the obstruction to Torrent's progress has given way precisely at the moment when the hero makes explicit his own commitment to God's service, an orientation that paradoxically rewards him with his earthly goals of bride and property. Only when chastened and obedient to God the Father can Torrent displace the obstructive secular father of his bride and reclaim his dispersed family.

But if the hero's capacity for restraint has enabled family reconciliation, wholehearted ascesis is the condition of the assimilation of that family back into society. In a move that quietly safeguards against father–son strife in the reunited family, the twin sons Leobertus and Anthony are appointed sole heirs

---

[33] Matthew 27: 46: 'My God, my God, why hast thou forsaken me?'

of the kings of Jerusalem and Greece. It is a safeguard achieved by one final cultural encounter. For while the King of Jerusalem's lack of a male heir enables the adoption of the first twin, the worldly good fortune of the second is entwined with the unworldly commitment of Greece's rightful heir – the desert hermit St Anthony.[34] Tellingly, the hermit is the subject of an admiring vignette in the poem. First portrayed at prayer and described as 'well with god all-my3t' (1948), Anthony, saviour of Torrent's second twin whom he christens Anthony Fitzgriffin, surrenders the chivalric and feudal roles that are his birthright. When he entrusts Torrent's son to the king his father it is as surrogate male heir who may replenish his place in the succession:

> Thou hast none heyre, thy lond to take,
> For Iesu love thy sonne hym make,
> As in the stede of me!   (1984–86)

Only by this sacrifice is the long shadow of patriarchal struggle dispelled. For all his spirited self-assertion, the ultimate good fortune of Sir Torrent and his kin rests upon a penitential spirit that is not his alone.

To sift though the varied episodes of *Sir Torrent of Portyngale* is thus to be confronted with two competing scenarios. In the first, the poem's proliferation of the popular motifs of the genre suggests a spirit of competition, of seeking to outdo the source text *Sir Eglamour* and the literary giants of the romance tradition that lie behind it. In the second, the poem's five, framed renditions of the giant-killing motif suggest symbolic treatment of a penitential theme of self-abnegation and the curtailment of excess – a theme ultimately realised not in encounters with giants but in encounters between just and unjust ruler, Crusader and Saracen, father and unrecognised son, hermit and foundling. Either way, in *Torrent of Portyngale* we encounter a romance hero who, in his fictional exploits and literary pedigree alike, stands very firmly on the shoulders of giants.

---

[34] The portrait appears to conflate the desert father St Antony, a foundational eremitic figure, with Antony of Padua, the latter often depicted as carrying the child Jesus, just as the poem's Anthony carefully cradles his foundling. See *The Penguin Dictionary of Saints*, ed. Donald Attwater (Harmondsworth, 1965), pp. 49–51.

13

Thomas of Erceldoune: Romance as Prophecy

HELEN COOPER

If Thomas of Erceldoune is now known to the world at large, it is probably under one of his alternative names, Thomas the Rhymer.[1] That is the name he is given as the protagonist of a traditional ballad, which tells how he was carried off by an elf-queen and spent seven years in her country before she returned him to Middle-earth. He himself seems to have been a real person, living in the late thirteenth century. Records of him survive from the Erceldoune area of the Scottish borders (modern Earlston). He is in addition the subject of a whole complex of texts, central among them being a work first recorded in the Lincoln Thornton Manuscript, of c.1440. This starts by telling the same story as the ballad, but then follows it up by recounting how the elf-queen, asked by Thomas for a token to remember her by, left him with the gift of always telling the truth, and a generous store of prophecies. Yet other texts record these or other prophecies and ascribe them to Thomas, some being given a different introduction, some no introduction at all.

This whole array of records, texts and traditions was first brought to the notice of the scholarly world in 1875 by James Murray, a few years before he began full-time work on the *Oxford English Dictionary*, in a collection for the Early English Text Society that he entitled *The Romance and Prophecies of Thomas of Erceldoune*.[2] It contains as its central item the 'Romance' of the title, the fifteenth-century account of the abduction and prophecies, printed from Thornton in parallel with three later manuscripts of the fifteenth and early sixteenth centuries. The volume prefaces that core story with a summary of the records and traditions relating to Thomas, and with two versions of the ballad of *Thomas the Rhymer*, with its narrative of the abduction but no predictions; and it concludes with various other texts that eliminate the elf-queen and put much the greatest weight on the prophecies. It is in many ways a remarkable edition, and the few scholars who have worked on Thomas since then are still dependent on it for the depth and breadth of its coverage. That quality and richness is no accident. Murray had grown up in Hawick, a

---

[1] I would like to express my thanks to the British Academy for the award of a Research Readership, in the course of which I developed the material recorded in this article.
[2] *The Romance and Prophecies of Thomas of Erceldoune*, ed. James A. H. Murray, EETS OS 61 (1875).

few miles south of the Eildon Hills, where the abduction supposedly took place – the precise spot is indeed marked by an inscribed stone named Rhymer's Stone, a couple of miles east of Melrose.[3] As the introduction to his edition makes clear, Thomas was not an abstruse scholarly recovery so far as Murray was concerned: he was simply putting into print a series of stories and rhymes that he had grown up with, and adding what further texts he could uncover. Although the scholarly credentials of the volume therefore go far beyond its editor's familiarity with oral traditions, its remarkable display of erudition bespeaks an insider's comfortableness with material that for later editors has been distinguished more by its strangeness. The point is worth making, not only for its inherent interest – *Thomas of Erceldoune* was, so far as I know, the first medieval text to be recovered on the strength of continuing oral traditions – but because it serves as a reminder of how rich the oral dissemination of Thomas material was even as late as the nineteenth century, and so as a salutary caution against assuming that his modern obscurity was matched in early- or pre-modern times.

The first recovery of the ballad of *Thomas the Rhymer* had also been the product of local researches, as part of a living oral tradition. A few decades before Murray, Sir Walter Scott, whose estate at Abbotsford lay still closer to the Eildon Hills, had first printed the ballad by which the story of Thomas is now best known. It had been recounted both to him and to Robert Jamieson, in slightly different versions, by that arch-repository of traditional ballads, Mrs Brown; Murray incorporates these too into his own edition, though he was rather suspicious of it, thinking it a bit too good to be true – and it certainly is very good, as for instance the description of the journey to elfland, when Thomas believes that it may be the devil who is carrying him off:

> For forty days and forty nights
> He wade thro red blood to the knee;
> And he saw neither sun nor moon,
> But heard the roaring of the sea.[4]

In fact, the general authenticity of the ballad and its closeness to the Thornton text seem to be above suspicion, since later research has turned up a closely similar text whose origins can be traced back to before 1700.[5] Of all the traditional ballads, this therefore has one of the strongest claims to medieval origins. One scholar has even suggested that the ballad version, or something

---

3 The present stone is a modern replacement for an older, uninscribed boulder, which has curiously gone missing; grid ref. NT 5654 3355.
4 *The English and Scottish Popular Ballads*, ed. Francis James Child, 5 vols (1884–98; rpt New York, 1965), no. 37, I.317–26, A.69–72 (Jamieson's text).
5 This oldest version appears as a supplement in Child, IV.454–5. For Murray's suspicions, see p. liii of his edition; they seem odd, since they focus on the closeness of the ballad to the medieval romance, and that had not yet been printed at the time of Mrs Brown's performance (the narrative section was first published by Scott as illustrative material accompanying his printing of the ballad).

very close to it, may be the original form of the narrative, and the romance a development from that.[6] If this supposition is correct, the ballad would be fourteenth-century in origin, in order for the romance version to have been developed in time for the longer text to be available to Robert Thornton for copying in the 1440s. The suggestion is supported by one distinctive feature about the romance text, and that is that it is written, not in the tetrameter couplets or tail-rhyme characteristic of other Middle English romances, but in the quatrains of the conventional ballad stanza, rhyming abab (often doubled).[7]

The narrative part of the 'romance' of Thomas tells a closely similar story to the ballad, though it is fuller in its detail. Thomas is lying on Huntley Banks when he sees riding down by Eildon Tree a lady so beautiful and richly dressed that he believes she must be the Queen of Heaven. When he accosts her, she declares herself rather to be 'of ane oþer countree',[8] defined in the ballad as 'fair Elf-land'. Thomas requests her love, though she warns him of danger to follow if she grants him her favours. In the ballad, he merely kisses her, but in the romance he makes love to her, seven times, whereupon she loses all her beauty and turns hideous.

> Hir hare it hange all ouer hir hede,
> Hir eghne semede owte, þat are were graye.
> And all þe riche clothynge was a-waye,
> Þat he by-fore sawe in þat stede;
> Hir a schanke blake, hir oþer graye,
> And all hir body lyke the lede.   (131–6)

He believes her now to be the fiend, but she demands that he 'take leue at sonne & Mone' (157) and go with her. They enter the Eildon Hills, and after several days of travelling they come out into a land rich in fruit. Thomas is faint with hunger, but she warns him not to eat since the fruit is cursed and will put him into the power of the fiend. Telling him to lay his head in her lap, she shows him the crossroads that lead to heaven, hell, purgatory and her own country. She gives him yet another warning, that he must not speak once he is there: she will tell everyone that she has taken away his power of speech. On entering elfland, she recovers her beauty; he sojourns for what seems to be a mere three days before she tells him that he has in fact been there three years (seven in the ballad), and now she must return him to Middle-earth before the fiend comes to take his tithe from among her people, since she fears that he will choose Thomas. She leaves him at Eildon Tree with the gift of truth-telling and, in response to repeated requests from him for her to continue predicting, a long series of prophecies.

---

6   E. B. Lyle, 'The Relationship between *Thomas the Rhymer* and *Thomas of Erceldoune*', *Leeds Studies in English* NS 4 (1970), pp. 23–30.

7   The ballad as it currently survives rhymes only the even lines, xaxa.

8   Ed. Murray, line 93; the Thornton text is the one quoted, as being the earliest, but the other three manuscripts that preserve this part of the story are closely similar.

Even if this story, in its Thornton or in some earlier ballad version, does go back to the fourteenth century, it would still not be the earliest text associated with Thomas. He enters literary history decisively in the 1330s, in various forms. Most notably, he is described as the author of a set of prophecies unrelated to those appended to the romance. This comprises eighteen lines of what we would now call free verse recorded in British Library MS Harley 2253 – the manuscript of the Harley Lyrics. The Harley manuscript adds a heading that describes the circumstances under which he made the prophecy: 'La countesse de Donbar demanda a Thomas de Essedoune quant la guere descoce prendreit fyn. e yl la repoundy e dyt', and there follows a cheerfully contradictory mixture of the inevitable and the impossible, as he second-guesses when the Anglo-Scottish wars will end:

> When mon is mad a kyng of a capped man
> When mon is leuere oþermones þyng þen is owne
> When london ys forest and forest ys felde
> When hares kendles oþe herþston
> When Wyt & Wille werres togedere . . .
>
> Whenne shal þis be? Nouþer in þine tyme ne in myne
> ah comen and gon wiþinne twenty wynter and on.[9]

If this is a genuine report, then Thomas was playing safe: some of this is always true, some never, and his reputation for truth-telling could be saved either way. That seems indeed to have happened, for it is on this basis that his reputation as a prophet was assured.

At just about the same time, in 1338, Robert Manning of Brunne alludes to him in the Preface to his *English Chronicle*, in an obscure passage that associates him in some way with romance. The lines in question come in the course of Manning's condemnation of the inadequacy of those who attempt to rhyme in English:

> I see in song, in sedgeyng tale
> of Erceldoun & of Kendale:
> Non þam says as þai þam wroght,
> & in þer sayng it semes noght.
> þat may þou here in sir Tristrem,
> ouer gestes it has þe steem

---

[9] Murray prints the Harley text, pp. xviii–xix; for the layout, see *Facsimile of British Museum MS Harley 2253*, intro. N. R. Ker, EETS OS 255 (1965), fol. 127r. The date now generally accepted for the manuscript is c. 1340. A partially overlapping prophecy referring to events of Edward II's reign, represented as prose, is recorded in British Library MS Arundel 57: see Richard Morris's introduction to *Dan Michel's Ayenbite of Inwit*, EETS OS 23 (1866), p.[5]. It is not included in Pamela Gradon's 1965 revised reprint or her commentary volume (EETS 278 (1979)), though she notes there that the prophecies were probably copied some twenty to forty years after the main text (itself dated 1340), and so half a century or so after the likely composition date of this particular Thomas prophecy.

> ouer alle þat is or was,
> if men it sayd as made Thomas.[10]

The passage is part of Robert's complaint about the lack of clarity in much English verse, so its own obscurity is especially frustrating. The opening four lines could refer to stories already in existence about Thomas of Erceldoune and the unknown 'Kendal', which are spoiled in the retelling in the same way that the story of Tristrem is spoiled. Alternatively, the whole passage may be saying that rhymed narratives, including some versions of the English *Sir Tristrem*, are being recited in northern England and lowland Scotland, around Kendal and Earlston; and if only the English poem were as good as Thomas of Britain's original Anglo-Norman, then it would indeed deserve the reputation attaching to the Tristan story. It *could* mean that Thomas of Erceldoune wrote a particularly fine version of *Sir Tristrem* that is being mangled in the retelling, but that would not be the obvious way to read the passage – or it would not be, were it not for the opening of the surviving Middle English *Sir Tristrem* itself, which makes some kind of attribution to Thomas of Erceldoune explicit. The unique copy of the poem survives in yet another manuscript of the 1330s, the Auchinleck Manuscript, produced well outside Thomas's home territory, in London, though the dialect shows a few northern characteristics.

> I was at Erþeldoun
> Wiþ tomas spak y þare
> þer herd y rede in roune
> Who tristrem gat & bare
> Who was king wiþ croun
> & who him fosterd 3are
> & who was bold baroun
> As þeir elders ware
>   bi 3ere
> tomas telles in toun
> þis auentours as þai ware.[11]

So we have a version of the *Tristrem* composed before 1331 (the *terminus post quem* of the Aunchinleck MS), and which claims to have been heard in Erceldoune from the mouth of the same or some other Thomas; and a text from 1338 that tells us that a version of the *Tristrem* by one Thomas is being mangled in the retelling, especially around Erceldoune. The very process of making the claim that links the poem with Thomas, however, imposes an

---

[10] Quoted by Murray, p. xx; for the full context (and for the punctuation here), see *Robert Manning of Brunne: The Chronicle*, ed. Idelle Sullens (Binghamton, 1996), Prologue 93–100.

[11] Murray, p. xxi; and see also Alan Lupack's edition, *Lancelot of the Laik and Sir Tristrem* (Kalamazoo, 1994), ll. 1–11. What were once assumed to be the Scottish origins of the poem have been called into question by recent linguistic scholarship without decisively settling the matter of dialect origin: see Lupack's summary, p. 145.

intermediary between the *Tristrem* that we have, the text that 'I' heard, and whatever poem Thomas may be presumed to have recounted.

What is going on here? There is clearly some association assumed between Thomas of Erceldoune and romance, perhaps even to the point where the Thomas of Britain who wrote the Anglo-Norman *Tristan* was identified with him. As the ballad attests, one of the many names by which the Erceldoune man was known was 'Thomas the Rhymer', or Thomas Rymer. 'Rymer' was familiar as a surname in the Berwickshire–Roxburghshire area, and the name might carry no import beyond that. Thirteenth-century records, on the other hand, refer to a 'Thomas Rymour de Ercildune' whose son is described simply as 'Thomas de Ercildoun', suggesting that the 'rhymer' might indeed be person-specific.[12] Even if 'Rymer' were originally just a surname, it rapidly seems to have acquired the quality of an epithet, bringing an assumption that the Thomas who bore it was a rhymester as well. The earliest recorded text specifically ascribed to him, the Harley prophecy, is notable for its absence of literal rhyme, though it does have a sufficiently distinct rhythm and anaphoric syntactic structure for the Harley scribe to write it out in lines; the earliest rhyming prophecies associated with his name are spoken not by him but by his elf-queen before she departs back to her own country. *Sir Tristrem* provides a rhymed text such as Thomas *might* have written, especially if one were looking for a poem to associate with him, and especially if the story already carried with it an association with one Thomas or another. Thomas of Erceldoune was clearly a name to conjure with, a name that would be taken as a good advertisement for the poem that follows. The *Tristrem* narrator seems furthermore to have had another association in mind with this Thomas, for yet another of the names by which he was known was True Thomas. That epithet records the elf-queen's gift to him of always speaking the truth; and it is echoed in the last line of the verse quoted above, which insists not only that Thomas tells the story of Tristrem, but that he gets his facts right – who was who, who fathered whom, all the things that happened 'as þai ware'.

Sir Walter Scott was convinced that Thomas of Erceldoune was indeed the author of *Sir Tristrem*; the dates would be appropriate, and Scott assumed that the poem was indeed northern English or Scottish.[13] The grounds of his certainty, however, look suspiciously like those that caused the ascription to be made in the poem itself, that is, the natural human desire to identify as the author of any anonymous text the nearest famous person who looks remotely plausible. That may not be a sufficient reason for such attributions never to be true, but the chances are against it. Moreover, the framing of the poem as a retold rather than an authored text would militate against Thomas's being its actual author. What is clear, however, both from the opening of the *Tristrem* and the allusions in Manning's *Chronicle*, is that by the very earliest decades

---

12 Murray, pp. ix–x; for discussion of the surname, pp. xii–xiii.
13 The work was first printed by Scott in 1804 under the title *Sir Tristrem: A Metrical Romance of the Thirteenth Century: by Thomas of Erceldoune, called Thomas the Rhymer*.

of the fourteenth century, the name of Thomas of Erceldoune meant not only prophecy, but romance.

The point is worth emphasising, since in other respects the work that Murray called the 'romance' of Thomas of Erceldoune is not obviously a romance at all. He never quite defines even whether he takes the 'romance and prophecies' of his ambiguous title to refer to the composite Thornton text, with its abduction to elf-land followed by its fairy prophecies, or whether he thinks of that whole work as being the 'romance', and the other, more exclusively prophetic, texts that he edits alongside as being the 'prophecies'. The Thornton *Thomas* is not admitted into Severs' Romances volume of the *Manual of Writings in Middle English*, and the little attention it has received since Murray's edition has tended to concentrate on its relationship to later Thomas prophecies more than on the fairy narrative. Robert Thornton headed some other works in the Lincoln manuscript as romances – 'The Romance of Sir Ysambrace', 'The Romance off Sir Percyvelle of Gales' – but this text is headed simply 'Thomas off Ersseldoune'.[14] It does, however, appear embedded in the section of the manuscript largely devoted to romances; and the story of a man who has an affair with an elf-queen, even if she is a reluctant mistress, has obvious connections with romance, and would tend to raise expectations of that kind. Among the analogues to the story are the various versions of the tale of the loathly lady, the hag who turns beautiful, and whom Chaucer casts in the *Wife of Bath's Tale* as an elf-queen. Although the ultimate function of the narrative section in *Thomas* turns out to be as an introduction to the prophecies, the story always had the potential to be a tale in its own right, as is proved by its existence in the ballad independently of the predictions. Furthermore, the association of Thomas of Erceldoune with romance is not confined to the early fourteenth century. It was still alive and well in the late sixteenth – indeed, the sixteenth century was in many ways Thomas's heyday.

Defining romance is one of the more time-wasting exercises; there is, notoriously, no medieval definition. Equally clearly, however, there was a set of generic expectations of the form that authors often set out to trigger with the very first lines of their narratives. Another Thornton text, *Sir Eglamour*, offers a prime example of initial cueing for romance once the convention of a blessing on the audience has been invoked:

> I will ȝow telle of a knyghte
> þat was bothe hardy & wyght.   (fol. 138v)

Such expectations, once aroused, are fulfilled by a selection from a range of characteristic generic features: what follows will be a story of love or chivalry, or both; set far away or long ago, or both; concerning high-born

---

14 *The Thornton Manuscript (Lincoln Cathedral MS 91)*, facsimile intro. D. S. Brewer and A. E. B. Owen (London, 1978), fols 109r, 161r, 149v.

characters, and, often, aristocratic ideals; frequently including some element of the marvellous or the supernatural; deferring its ending through complications of questing or adventures; but when it does conclude, ending happily. So it is worth asking what Robert Thornton saw when he copied *Thomas of Ersseldoune* into his manuscript, and what cues the text offered to its early auditors or readers.

They are not immediately those of romance, whatever Robert Manning or the *Sir Tristrem* author may have thought about Thomas. The Thornton text, alone of the four surviving manuscripts, is prefaced by twenty-four lines promising a listening audience

> als trewe a tale
> Als euer was herde by nyghte or daye:
> And the maste maruelle ffor owttyne naye,
> That euer was herde by-fore or syene.   (3–7)

'Truth' and 'marvels' contradict each other only superficially: a marvel would not be particularly marvellous if it were admitted to be fictional. This will be both marvellous *and* true. So far, the cues are correct enough both for romance in general and for the narrative that follows, even if they are somewhat unspecific. When the narrative gets under way, however, it turns out to be anomalous in all sorts of ways (and consistently so in all the manuscripts). It starts with a first-person narrator, cast not as the storyteller, as in *Sir Tristrem*, but as the protagonist:

> As I me wente this endres day,
> ffull faste in mynd makand my mone,
> In a mery mornynge of Maye,
> By huntle bankkes my selfe allone . . .   (25–8)

This is the form to which the descriptive term '*chanson d'aventure*' has been given.[15] It is typical in particular of the French *pastourelle*, and of English poems that recount a similar open-air encounter between a male narrator and an accessible woman: the Harley 'In a fryht as y con fare fremede' is a well-known example, and the form has continued generously through into modern folksong in both French and English.[16] Such an opening is entirely appropriate for what happens next, the sighting of the beautiful lady and the predatory tracking of her down, in a process at the opposite extreme from the typical romance structure of deferral: the sex here happens with minimal preliminaries, and close to the start of the text. Not typical of such poems, however, is the fact that between the first sighting of the lady and the decision to proposition her, the first-person 'I' turns without either warning or explanation into the third-person Thomas.

---

[15] By Helen Estabrook Sandison, *The 'Chanson d'Aventure' in Middle English* (Bryn Mawr, 1913).
[16] *The Harley Lyrics*, ed. G. L. Brook, 3rd edn (Manchester, 1964), no. 8. The modern English folksong equivalents typically begin 'As I was going to . . .'.

Swylke one ne saghe j neuer none . . .

Thomas laye & sawe þat syghte . . .   (46, 73)

There is no narrative separation between the first- and third-person protagonists, and from the evidence of all the manuscripts, no one bothered to regularize the story – though the ballad is told throughout in the third person, and later versions of the prophecies (discussed below) sorted out the anomaly in a different way. The *chanson d'aventure* expectations are further encouraged by the specificity of the location. Such poems often cite a familiar place (Huntley Banks is still identifiable), and their first-person narration insists that the incident has happened in the very recent past – typically 'l'autr'ier' in French, 'this endres day' in English. This is the very opposite of the settings distant in time and space that romance most often evokes.

In keeping with that sense of the here and now is the status of the protagonist. Thomas Rhymer of Erceldoune was a real person, as well attested as anyone else who makes an appearance in thirteenth-century records; we are not solely reliant on the reputation that attached to him for evidence of his existence, whether that reputation has to do with his obscure prophetic remarks to great men and women as recorded by later chronicles, or with the less verisimilar business of the abduction to the Otherworld. Erceldoune was a more important place than the modern Earlston, but even by medieval standards it did not confer much status on its local lord. Thomas was important enough to witness a deed alongside the abbot of Dryburgh, but he was very far from being the heir to an earldom that elsewhere tends to constitute the minimum requirement for romance heroism. The handful of squires or stewards' sons who make the grade of heroism do so by taking the chivalric world by storm through their prowess, and Thomas is far from doing that either. He is singularly lacking in any of the qualities and emotions that normally confer entitlement to heroism: he never so much as carries a sword, and his affair with the fairy is entirely opportunistic. There is no pretence of any emotion for her, though his readiness to go ahead despite her warnings might be thought to show a certain derring-do. Other romance heroes win the hand of an heiress to raise themselves to rank and power, but after his affair with the elf-queen Thomas is returned to the Eildon Hills with no more wealth or title than his store of prophecies and the promise of a reputation for truth-telling.

Those prophecies, which extend to four hundred lines beyond the three hundred of the initial story, take the work still further away from romance. By the early sixteenth century they were taking over the text almost entirely, with the appearance of a new version, *The Prophisies of Rymour, Beid, and Marlyng*, which scraps the elf-queen altogether – though its earliest readers might not immediately have realized that. In this text, the first-person narrator is rationalized into a narrator who meets another man and asks him for news, specifically news of the future:

Whan shall all these warres be gone
Or trewe men lyve in love & lee?[17]

These are the kinds of questions that Thomas had specialized in answering ever since the Harley prophecy, but the first reaction of the prophet figure here is not to speak but to show:

He said, 'man, set thy fote on myne,
And ouer my Shulder loke thyn lie
The fairest sight I shall shewe the syne
That euer saw man in thy countre.'   (13–16)

The incident seems to be based on the elf-queen's instruction to Thomas to lay his head in her lap in order for her to show him the divergent roads to the different worlds; but what the narrator sees in this text is a beautiful and gorgeously apparelled woman, closely modelled on the elf-queen. Early readers might indeed have at first taken her as such (one manuscript, British Library Lansdowne 762, contains both texts, and its readers must have had something of a sense of *déjà vu*). Each rides on a dapple grey steed, and wears clothes adorned with pearls; even the *a* rhymes of the eight-line stanza describing her are the same in both versions. Where Thomas had believed his woman so beautiful that she must be the Queen of Heaven, however, this lady really is the Blessed Virgin. She is accompanied by angels, and by two armed knights, also on horseback, who are identified by their coats of arms as St George and St Andrew. In keeping with the long tradition of Thomas prophecies as specializing in Anglo-Scottish relations, they are inclined to come to blows, and have to be kept apart by a sharp reminder from the Virgin that they are 'saints in heaven' and ought to behave in keeping. Only after that, when this vision has disappeared, does the man who has shown the sight to the narrator give his own series of prophecies, citing as his sources, as the conventional title indicates, 'Arseldoune', Bede, and Merlin.

This work was both popular and dangerous – the two to a large extent going together. As with all political prophecies, it can be dated by its transition from correct 'prophecy' of the past to a future that never happened. It can be securely dated after the arrival of the Tudors, since Henry VII's arrival at Milford Haven to challenge for the throne is described with only the barest enigmatic disguise:

Then shal entre at Mylford haven
vpon a horse of tree

---

[17] Murray, pp. 52–61, ll. 9–10, from BL Lansdowne MS 762. The other, later, major manuscript version, in Bodleian Library MS Rawlinson C.813, is edited by Sharon L. Jansen in her *Political Protest and Prophecy under Henry VIII* (Woodbridge, 1991), pp. 69–90, with useful annotation. In an adapted text recorded still later, 'The Prophecie of Thomas Rymour' printed in 1603, this bearer of tidings identifies himself as Thomas, though here he remains anonymous (see n. 21 below).

A banyshed barone that is borne
of brutes blode shalbe. (143–6)

The 'horse of tree' is of course a ship, and the reference to Brutus' blood picks up Henry's claim of British origins through his Welsh ancestry. The return of the lost heir from over the sea, as Rosalind Field notes elsewhere in this volume, carried particular symbolic weight in England, and the lines are clearly designed to pick up that weight. After 1530, however, the prophecies outline a history that never happened. They speak of a good king who is to rule in England, who will have a triumphant entry into Rome and win back the Holy Cross. He will reign for 55 years, die in the vale of Jehoshaphat, and be buried in Cologne alongside the Three Kings. His reign will institute a state like the New Jerusalem, when wars will end, everyone will live in charity, and falsehood will be exiled. The prophecy was probably inspired by resistance to Henry VIII, and it seems to have enjoyed a popularity well beyond the evidence of the surviving manuscripts; Sharon Jansen suggests that it was the most popular prophecy of the decade.[18] The Privy Council attempted to stamp it out, even to the point of executing one man for disseminating it; when that policy was evidently not succeeding, they seem to have considered promulgating an alternative interpretation, by which the king's entry into Rome would represent Henry's triumph over the Pope.[19] It was, however, generally regarded as deeply subversive: indeed the whole genre of political prophecy was typically a way of expressing political discontent, and with that of encouraging the belief that things must of necessity change – prophecy, in Keith Thomas's phrase, provided a 'validating charter' for revolution.[20] The dissemination of prophecies was therefore forbidden by statute, a prohibition repeated under Elizabeth. That did not stop their circulation, but it did prevent their being printed: hence the delay in printing any form of the Thomas prophecies until 1603, after Elizabeth's death.[21]

The 1603 'Prophecie of Thomas Rymour' has one major advantage over the 1520s *Prophisies*: it manages to get its prophecy of the future right. It cuts the *post facto* prediction of the arrival of the Tudors, but it does contain a genuine prediction of the Stuart takeover of the whole of Britain. Thomas himself is now back to being the key figure, who shows the first-person narrator the vision of the Virgin and who himself speaks the prophecies. The text ends as follows:

---

[18] Jansen, *Political Protest*, p. 63; and see also pp. 1–6.

[19] Ibid., pp. 57–8.

[20] Keith Thomas, *Religion and the Decline of Magic* (1971; Harmondsworth, 1973), p. 503; the term is adopted from anthropology.

[21] It appeared as an item in *The Whole Prophesie of Scotland*, published in 1603 under an Edinburgh imprint that may, however, be false – see *A Short-Title Catalogue of Books printed in England, Scotland, and Ireland 1475–1640*, compiled by A. W. Pollard and G. R. Redgrave, 2nd edn, rev. and enlarged by W. A. Jackson, F. S. Ferguson and Katharine F. Pantzer, 3 vols (London, 1976–91), no. 17841.7, where it is described as 'possibly a London piracy'.

'Who shal rule the Ile of Bretaine
From the North to the South sey?'
'A French wife shal beare the Son,
Shall rule all Bretaine to the sey,
that of the Bruces blood shall come
As neere as the nint degree.'
I franed fast what was his name,
Where that he came from what countrie?
'In Erslingtoun, I dwelle at hame,
Thomas Rymour men calles me.'[22]

The Tudor descent from Brutus of the 1520s text has now turned into the Stuart descent from Robert the Bruce – though the sharp-eyed might have noticed that it was a generation out: James I and VI was of the tenth generation, not the ninth. The prophecy was presumably composed shortly before the birth of a child in 1542 to Mary of Guise, the French wife of James V – a child who turned out to be a daughter, Mary Queen of Scots. The text was still widely enough known at the end of the century for commentators after Elizabeth's death to note that James's occupation of both thrones had indeed been predicted by Thomas of Erceldoune; its familiarity was clearly not reliant on its publication.

Once the ban on printing prophecies was lifted, they appeared by the dozen, most often collected into anthologies; prophecies ascribed to Thomas of Erceldoune feature in these regularly, often without any opening frame. One such anthology, of 1652, is exceptionally interesting, since the text it prints is not one of these Blessed Virgin texts, but the original fairy narrative itself.[23] Its appearance at this date was occasioned by the sense of imminent apocalypse and the accompanying craze for prophecy that characterized the early years of the Commonwealth (and which were encouraged by an eclipse of the sun early that year), but it also places it interestingly close to that mid-seventeenth-century collection of medieval texts that had likewise continued an underground existence in popular form, the Percy Folio Manuscript. Attempts to modernize spelling apart, the 1652 text is closely faithful to the medieval original represented by Thornton.[24] It is almost the only

---

[22] Murray, pp. 48–51, ll. 239–48.

[23] 'The Prophecie of Sir Thomas of Astledowne', *Sundry Strange Prophesies of Merlin, Bede and Others* (London, 1652), pp. 19–24. It was given its first modern printing in an appendix to William P. Albrecht's *The Loathly Lady in 'Thomas of Erceldoune'* (Albuquerque, 1954), and is reprinted by Ingeborg Nixon in her edition of *Thomas of Erceldoune*, Publications of the Department of English, University of Copenhagen 9, 2 parts (Copenhagen, 1980–3); neither, however, prints the extension to the medieval text that carries the prophecies forward to 1600 (pp. 25–8), discussed below.

[24] The Percy texts are, however, in most cases known to possess printed intermediaries, as the *Thomas* text had not. Although the 1652 text contains the opening 24 lines found elsewhere only in Thornton, its variant readings demonstrate that it was not based on any of the surviving manuscripts. Its date would in theory make it possible as a source for the traditional ballad, but the chances of a text buried so deeply within a London anthology being picked up in its home area in

prophecy in the whole collection to be in verse rather than prose, and it is printed in double columns, finishing the medieval part of its text at the foot of a page. The prophecies, however, continue on the next page in the same format without a break, and they take events forward to around 1600. To any reader, they would have seemed an integral part of the original, and there is no evidence that the compiler of the volume did not receive them in that form. And if the 1520s prophecies were dangerous, these would, at the time when they were compiled, have been dynamite. They are accurate up to the reign of Mary and her marriage to Philip of Spain; but they describe a history for England in the later sixteenth century, the 1590s in particular, that is indeed heading for apocalypse. There will be civil war, father shall kill son and brother brother, 'ladies shal waile that ever they were born'. The prophecy is general enough to continue to be taken as true even after its accurate 'predictions' were past. It could have been this text, or something like it, that helped to inspire governmental scares over prophecy in the 1580s.[25] By that date, its apocalyptic tone would have appeared to voice the fears current over the inevitable end of Elizabeth's reign, with no heir born to her and no successor named.

That account of the sixteenth-century history of the Thomas texts may seem to have moved a long way away from romance, but one thing that remains constant is that there is, in some sense or form, a continuing association between the romance part of the narrative (the affair and the abduction) with political prediction: an association that testifies to a wider association between romance and prophecy, even though there is nothing else quite like this. Merlin would be the nearest analogue, just as his prophecies often appear in conjunction with Thomas's. His prophecies were originally composed by Geoffrey of Monmouth, but although Merlin himself becomes a figure within Arthurian romance, romance narrative and prophecy never usually display this kind of detailed intermingling, where the two genres exist in symbiosis with each other. The conjunction at first sight seems odd – as odd as those associations of Thomas with romance in the 1330s. Yet romance and prophecy are not in practice so far adrift from each other. One of the most familiar forms of romance is the ancestral or genealogical variety: the association indeed goes back to before romance was invented as a formal genre at all, to the *Aeneid* as a founding legend for Rome. All the romances deriving from

---

the Scottish borders is inherently unlikely; and the ballad in any case preserves local forms (such as Eildon Tree for the print's Elden Tree) that confirm its independence.

25 Thomas, *Religion*, pp. 480–3. This section is in fact in part related to a prophecy more often connected with Merlin, which predicted the return of E, Edward VI, here also described as 'the joyful sice' (the throw of a six at dice); but it was easy to take E as Elizabeth and the sice as James, giving the prophecy the illusion of greater accuracy than it in fact possessed. The 1652 text indeed seems to have incorporated the identification in its line noting, 'Then shal sice and ace be of one device' (p. 28). See also Thomas, pp. 498–501, who notes the existence of a different prophecy about Edward in the 1652 volume.

Geoffrey of Monmouth's *History of the Kings of Britain* have something of that foundational quality about them, not least the legends of Brutus and Arthur. Outside Geoffrey's sphere, the romance of Guy of Warwick served to create an ancestry for the earls of Warwick, and *Bevis of Hamtoun* offered a genealogical connection with the Arundel dynasty whether or not it was specifically written with such a purpose. Not all of these romances contain explicit prophecies (though the *Aeneid* offers a model for such a process), but even when they do not, they tell stories set in an imaginary past to justify and explain the present of their writer and readers, just as prophecy sets itself in the past to demonstrate that the present is shaped and authorized by what has gone before. Ancestral romance and prophecy both invent a past that contains the seeds of the present.

The primary function of prophecy is rarely in fact to predict the future. It is most often written retrospectively, set in the past in order to make a claim about the present. Prophecy requires a past to be written from, just as ancestral romance requires a past to bring the present about. Both are located backwards in time in order to look forwards, to the here and now. Such a process is given emblematic expression in that moment in the 1520s *Prophisies* in which the narrator is invited to set his foot on the prophet's and look backwards over his shoulder: only by looking backwards is it possible to see forwards. Ancestral romances themselves increasingly made that forward-looking explicit. *Melusine*, the late fourteenth-century French romance that describes the legendary foundations of the house of Lusignan, masterminded by another fairy mistress, includes a series of prophecies of doom to come, so explaining, not just the rise to power of the Lusignan dynasty, but the troubles it was undergoing at the time.[26] Ariosto brings Merlin himself into the *Orlando Furioso* to give a long prophecy of the future of the house of Este, a future that brings history forwards as far as the patrons of the poem. And Spenser gives a whole series of prophecies of the future of Britain down to the Tudors in the *Faerie Queene*.[27]

Both Ariosto and Spenser have their major sets of prophecies made to their heroines: to Bradamante, and to Britomart. Both are virgins, but each has as her own personal destiny to become the sexually active foundress of a house, the mother of a dynasty. The fairy narrative of *Thomas of Erceldoune* offers a sexually active woman as its heroine, but she bears no offspring: instead, it is as if the encounter begets the prophecies, a verbal continuation into the future – a pattern of future history rather than the people of future history. Much of that pattern is devoted to disaster, perhaps in a way that links with the elf-queen's capacity to turn hideous, just as the fairy Melusine's offspring are all marked or marred in some way. The potential of romance for expansion

---

[26] See the account in Laurence Harf-Lancner's introduction to her modernization of the rhymed version of the original prose text, *Coudrette: Le Roman de Melusine* (Paris, 1993).

[27] Ludovico Ariosto, *Orlando Furioso*, ed. Lanfranco Caretti, 2nd edn (Turin, 1992), III.9–20; Edmund Spenser, *The Faerie Queene*, ed. A. C. Hamilton, 2nd edn (London, 2000), III.iii.25–49.

has often been noted, and that expansion, as with the adventures of the later generations of Melusine's descendants, or the series of sixteenth-century sequels to *Amadis de Gaule*, may not just encompass additional adventures along the way but also carry the story forwards into a future unimagined in the original narrative. Similarly with the Thomas texts, and as is demonstrated by the mid-sixteenth-century coda to the version printed in 1652, the prophecies are capable of indefinite expansion forwards, as history moves on.

The prophecies made by Thomas's elf-queen, however, are not like those in the *Orlando Furioso* or the *Faerie Queene*, which describe what for the author and readers is already the past, and which can therefore afford to be explicit. Most of the early Thomas prophecies are heavily enigmatic, so that, like those of Nostradamus, they can be applied to almost any moment given sufficiently free interpretation and wishful thinking. Even explicit error is overlooked if the fit of the rest is enticing enough: the fact that the 1603 prophecy of James's accession to the throne of England was a generation out never seems to have given anyone the slightest pause once Elizabeth was dead. If one wants to predict the real future, however, enigmatic predictions are much the safest variety, because they are not falsifiable – you can't be proved wrong if no one can be quite sure what you meant in the first place. There may also have been some element of self-protection involved, since anyone caught circulating them could deny having any idea as to what they might be about. It is true that the Thomas prophecies acquire increasing precision as they move away in time from the original texts; but their supposed origins may again have been thought to offer some degree of protection, since the predictions are overtly not those of the person passing them on, but were made long ago by someone else. This particular set, furthermore, does not have a merely human authority, for the fairy narrative takes Thomas himself out of the role of predictor, and makes him instead the medium for passing on the 'ferlies' told him by the elf-queen. The substitution of the Virgin for the elf-queen found in the variants produced in the sixteenth century offers an even firmer supernatural endorsement for the predictions. Both versions locate the origins of dangerous speech outside the rational or the human, or even the prosecutable – though it was never enough in practice to prevent prosecution. *As* prophecy, however, it is important that they do not lose touch with the here and now; so even though the story isn't, and can't be, quite *now* (because the present needs a past to be predicted from), it can and must be *here* – hence, perhaps, the insistence on Huntley Banks, the known place within this world.

Thomas of Erceldoune presents a fairyland that co-exists with the human world, and that can address its interests, in particular its military and political interests. The figure who mediates between the two is not so much Thomas as the elf queen, the fairy queen. Given the evidence for the broad dissemination of the Thomas prophecies in the sixteenth century, the confluence in Spenser's work of fairyland, prophecy and the sexually available fairy queen who appears to Arthur in what may or may not be a vision begins to acquire a less random look. It looks still less random in the light of the *Prophisies of Rymour* texts, where the Virgin appears accompanied by two armed knights, St George is introduced first:

> I se come ouer a bent rydaunde
> A goodly man as armyde knyght.
> he shoke his spere ferselye in hand,
> Right cruelly and kene;
> Styfly & stowre as he wolde stonde,
> he bare a shylde of syluer shene.
> A crosse of gowles therin did be.   (*Prophisies* 47–53)

He is identified first just by his appearance; only a couple of stanzas later does the Virgin name him, and describe him as 'my knight' – 'Our Lady's knight' being his traditional epithet. Did Spenser have these lines in his mind when he wrote the opening lines of Book I of his own *Faerie Queene* – lines as specifically about Gloriana's knight as St George is 'our lady's' – and if he did, could he assume that his readers would recognize them? Although the coat of arms is inevitably the same, it is still a very small step from the St George of the *Prophisies* 'ouer a bent rydaunde', riding over a plain, to

> A gentle knight was pricking on the plaine,
> Yclad in mightie armes and siluer shield,
> Wherein old dints of deepe wounds did remaine,
> The cruell markes of many a bloudy fielde . . .
> As one for knightly giusts and fierce encounters fit.
> But on his brest a bloudie Crosse he bore . . .
> Vpon his shield the like was also scor'd.[28]

If Spenser did have such a knowledge, and if he could assume the same knowledge in his readers, then the *Faerie Queene* is coded as political prophecy from the very opening lines of its narrative just as surely as it is coded as romance. Political prophecy was too febrile, too dangerous, to write overtly, but in a very real sense, it is what the poem is all about. It is set in the past, but in order to explicate the present; just as the primary function of prophecy is not to foretell the future but to authorize the present, to insist that it *has been foretold*.

It has always been something of a puzzle as to why Spenser should have set his work in Faeryland, with a Fairy Queen as its protagonist. *Thomas of Erceldoune* may perhaps provide the answer. Spenser's Prince Arthur, like Thomas, has his first amorous, open-air encounter with the Faerie Queene comparatively early in the poem.[29] The detail of the episode suggests a connection with *Sir Thopas*, though it is hard to see how Spenser could have

---

[28] *Faerie Queene*, I.i.1–2.
[29] Ibid., I.ix.13–14.

thought of that as generating the national epic he is composing. If he has the Thomas elf-queen in mind too, however, then many things fall into place. The incident does not, as in *Thomas*, provide an instant satisfaction of desire; the ending of the poem is still far deferred, and indeed Spenser never reaches it. That deferral, however, allows space for a whole series of political prophecies – prophecies of what for the protagonists is the future, but for the readers of the poem is the past or the present. The Faerie Queene can thus become, as in *Thomas of Erceldoune*, a mediating figure for the whole of English history: a figure who contains that history within herself. Yet Spenser is also writing himself into an aporia: for the Faerie Queene is also Elizabeth, and by the 1590s it was clear that she could not live much longer. One text of the Thomas prophecies, the fairy narrative printed in 1652 but already current at the time Spenser was writing, was predicting total social and political breakdown for the end of the century. Spenser's method commits him to writing a better future for Britain, but, as with all political prophecy, textual certainty cannot take him forward. The accession of James was already predicted in the Thomas prophecies, and with it an end of the Anglo-Scottish conflicts in which those prophecies specialized. But it had not yet happened, and Spenser could neither be sure that it would, nor write any such ending as speculation. His fairy queen, Arthur's fairy mistress, and the prophecies of his poem, are caught in that moment between initiation and completion, present and future. It was left to other writers to take up the prophecies after her death, and to read into them something like an end of history.[30]

---

[30] See Thomas Dekker's *The Magnificent Entertainment given to King James*, *The Dramatic Works of Thomas Dekker*, ed. Fredson Bowers, 3 vols (Cambridge, 1953–8), vol. 2, and the discussion in Helen Cooper, *The English Romance in Time: Transforming Motifs from Geoffrey of Monmouth to the Death of Shakespeare* (Oxford, 2004), pp. 195–7.

Index